Praise for *A Bollywood State of Mind*

'Bright, brilliant and beautifully researched, this glorious book is my biggest recommendation of the year. Sunny Singh's honouring of story and history shine through powerfully – an exquisitely enjoyable read!' – **Nikita Gill**

'A fascinating and enjoyable account of the many journeys and multiple lives of one of the world's most popular and enduring cultural institutions.'
– Prof. Priyamvada Gopal

'Totally engaging. It felt like Singh was writing just for me and I was transported back to the cinema with my family or indeed pushing the video cassette into the VHS and settling into a Sunday afternoon viewing. In the world she deftly creates, I can hear violins cascading as the all-dancing Bollywood heroines, heroes and villains lip sync to delicious lyrical songs. Singh's book is an unrivalled celebration of Bollywood films, there is so much mirch in this masala of drama. For me, the nostalgia unfurled the sepia vignettes of memory from a distant, almost forgotten past into the glittering joy of the present day.' – **Shobna Gulati**

'Part history, part personal reminiscence, *A Bollywood State of Mind* is a thoughtful, magical journey through the annals of the world's largest, most spectacular and most vivacious film industry. A gem of a book and a must for film lovers everywhere.' – **Abir Mukherjee**

'A masterful memoir, Singh's love story with Bollywood is one told with precision, authority and panache, capturing the all-singing, all-dancing joy and wonder of Indian cinema.' – **Monisha Rajesh**

'This is a gorgeous, perfect, mini-blockbuster of a book that tells story upon story within story of India's beloved Hindi cinema and all those who make and love it, in India and wherever they – we! because I count myself among its lovers – have travelled all over the world. Part personal and family memoir, part social history of modern India and its neighbours and diasporas, part expert (but never, ever stuffy) analysis of how India's classic dramatic storytelling aesthetics have morphed into modern cinema, part close explanation of the cinematic techniques makers use to entrance and enfold their audiences – Sunny Singh's genre-defying book gets to the essential emotional heart – the rasa – of Bollywood cinema. I loved this joyful, wonderful book with my whole heart.'
– Dr. Katherine Schofield

'A deeply personal, deeply political dive into one of the most popular forms of entertainment today. Part memoir, part film criticism, part cultural excavation, Singh writes with passion, clarity and introspection.'
– Nikesh Shukla

A Bollywood State of Mind

Dear Jmi Much love

A BOLLYWOOD STATE OF MIND

A journey into the world's biggest cinema

Sunny Singh

x x

Sunny Singh

FOOTNOTE

First published in 2023 by
Footnote Press

www.footnotepress.com

Footnote Press Limited
4th Floor, Victoria House, Bloomsbury Square, London WC1B 4DA

Distributed by Bonnier Books UK, a division of Bonnier Books
Sveavägen 56, Stockholm, Sweden

First printing
1 3 5 7 9 10 8 6 4 2

A CIP catalogue record for this book is available from the British Library.

ISBN (trade paperback): 978-1-804-440766
ISBN (hardback): 978-1-804-440421
ISBN (ebook): 978-1-804-440452

Printed and bound in Great Britain
by Clays Ltd, Elcograf S.p.A.

MIX
Paper from
responsible sources
FSC
www.fsc.org   FSC® C018072

For my mother who told us '*baaz ke bachhche munder pe nahin udte*' (Falcons' hatchlings don't fly near the nest). And then gave us the sky.

Contents

This Is a Strange Story, Who Knows Where It Begins or Ends[1]

I WAS EIGHT WHEN I realised that stories were not simply magic; that they didn't arrive into the world already formed. Like puppies or babies or films.

Two months before that birthday, the very first non-Congress government had swept to power in India, and with it, the end of the Emergency which had suspended civil rights for nearly two years. The new government struggled to balance the many domestic and international demands, but I remember that our home seemed oddly lighter that spring. I remember that Coca Cola was 'thrown out', a term I did not understand except that the beverage disappeared as the occasional treat. By the summer holidays – and my birthday – debates around our dinner table had grown more heated. I remember only a few of these but they all featured the 'Shah Commission'. Justice Shah was a hero or a villain depending on who was arguing. That was when I first learned that a point of view can change the appearance of the world, that reality shifts with the one telling it.

I turned eight in 1977.

It was also a bumper year for Hindi cinema! Manmohan Desai – one of the greatest commercial filmmakers ever – released

---

[1] *'Ajeeb dastaan hai yeh, kahaan shuru kahaan khatam . . .'* from *Dil Apna Aur Preet Parai* (Heart is Ours, Love is Another's, 1960).

not one or two but four of his biggest hits: *Amar Akbar Anthony*, *Chacha Bhatija* (Uncle, Nephew), *Dharam-Veer* and *Parvarish* (Upbringing). From veteran directors like Nasir Hussain to auteurs like Hrishikesh Mukherjee, from the brave *Doosra Aadmi* (The Other Man) to the Akira Kurosawa knock-off *Inkaar* (The Refusal), from a formulaic *Darling, Darling* starring a fading Dev Anand, to Shyam Benegal's challenging *Bhumika* (The Role), 1977 produced many of the films that are now touchstones of Indian, and world, cinema. Even the poet-director Gulzar, known for his careful, deliberate filmmaking despite the pressures of the commercially driven movie-churning machine, released not one but two feature-length films, *Kinara* (Shore) about a grieving dancer and *Kitaab* (The Book) about a young boy who runs away from home.

Most of my uncles and aunts were at university that year, and many of them were keen film fans. They'd tune in to Radio Ceylon every week for the *Binaca Geetmala* count down. The glamorous *Stardust* was delivered to our home every month by a fascinated khaki-clad postman and received with excited chortles by my aunts and with eyerolls by my grandmother. I later learned that our *Stardust* subscription – a glossy film magazine often deemed outré even in India's big cities – raised more than a few eyebrows in our small town. It marked us as . . . modern, although that is not a term I apply even today to my feudal, mostly agrarian, extended family!

I saw most of these films much later than 1977. My family practised a strict curating system based on the 'grapevine', or word passed down by trusted colleagues, acquaintances, family friends, most of whom were likely to be young men and 'first day, first show' types who would apply their own idiosyncratic classifications to the new releases: family watch, ok-for-kids, take-the-wife, fun watch for mixed gender friends, and *do not watch with anyone but male* friends. Growing up, I was permitted the ok-for-kids movies, although Gulzar's *Kitaab* slipped through this quixotic rating system and promptly traumatised me for many years afterwards. Very occasionally, I was also allowed films deemed appropriate for the full family, which were mostly blockbusters and our own version of PG-13.

Parvarish sat in this second category. In retrospect, it seems a poor choice as it features a terrifying sequence of two young children watching their parents being violently murdered, shot entirely from the points of view of the children hidden inside a barrel. Given that my extended family had deemed me sensitive – I was prone to stress-induced asthma attacks – the choice of this film has always seemed surprisingly careless.

I remember that we occupied almost an entire a row in the balcony of the cinema hall. I sat in the centre and my aunt and cousins cocooned me from both sides. My uncles sat in the seats closer to the aisles. Friends and acquaintances sat in the rows behind and before us. Even in the darkened cavernous hall, I felt coddled, comforted and safe. One of the adults brought us super salty popcorn and odd-tasting Thums-Up, the indigenous replacement of Coca Cola that had recently hit the market. Afterwards, as we made our way home on a cycle rickshaw, my cheeks were chilled by the winter breeze coming off the Ganga and I snuggled into the warmth of my aunt's arms. My uncle raced ahead on his motorcycle and then back again to check on us, like a one-man guard of honour. And I remember the comfort of my grandmother's breathing next to me when my nightmares woke me late that night, and on many nights after.

For a film that I now know comprehensively, I have no actual memory of watching it that evening.

But I know that's when the itch was born. And it has lingered. In nightmares. In daydreams. In the retellings. I knew there was something important that I was missing. There was a mystery that I could sense but not access. For weeks afterwards, I badgered my family with questions that began 'When in *Parvarish* . . . .' And I grew increasingly dissatisfied with their bafflement, their growing annoyance with what my aunt called 'my obsession'.

For weeks afterwards, I drew and wrote and rewrote the storyline of the film in a *play copy*, a leftover school notebook from the year before that I was allowed to use as I pleased. I tested out different plotlines, rearranged the events, worried over why and how the film had made me happy and sad, made me laugh or jump in fright. Why had it mattered? Why did it continue to matter even after the screen had gone dead, after we had come home, after many, many days had passed?

Most of all, I remember the sick feeling in my stomach that told me that something was being kept from me. Like so much else – terrible or glorious – that the adults withheld from me, there was something special about films, about those stories on the vast white screen. I was sure that once I learned the secret, and only then, I would be a master, a magician, a secret bearer. And then I would be grown up.

* * *

Twenty-five years and several hundred films later, many of which I watched on repeat, I began working on my second novel, *With Krishna's Eyes*. My central character was an aspiring filmmaker and made the perfect vehicle for an exploration of an India that was simultaneously attempting to free itself from its colonial past, dreaming of a postcolonial future, and attempting to narrate itself as a nation and culture on its own – even if messy – terms. And at the heart of this popularly produced and consumed national narrative was cinema. Of the exuberant, wildly popular, highly commercial kind often classified (or dismissed) as Bollywood!

By this point, I had lived in half a dozen countries, watched and studied international cinemas, even dabbled behind the scenes of film production.

Yet the old mystery of my favourite cinema had remained: why do some films, ostensibly with similar tropes, not only become box-office successes but also fan favourites while others disappear without a trace? Why do some films seduce the viewer into repeat viewings? Why do so many fans of this kind of cinema – including myself – re-watch parts of a favourite movie rather than the whole, just for a quick mood fix? And most of all, why did it comfort, inspire, move me more than any other cinema?

I began to isolate and examine the elements that went into a perfect popular Indian film: the internally coherent narrative structure, the technically unique cinematic aspects including *mis-en-scène*, sound and editing, the roller-coaster ride through emotional states, and finally that ineffable quality that turned some films into feeling as complete and satisfying as a well-prepared meal while others – despite technical finesse, star power, high production values – felt . . . incomplete.

This parsing made me examine my location as a viewer of not only Indian but all cinemas. As a child, when I was allowed to watch 'foreign' films (mostly British or American comedies), it was for 'educational' purposes, as a way to improve my ability to understand and speak the English language. To me, those films had seemed exotic, not only for their language, but also for their narrative structure, aesthetics and content. They hadn't satisfied me as child although at that point, I could not have explained the reasons for the sense of dissatisfaction and alienation I felt from viewing them.

Cut to my thirties: living in Barcelona meant I had easy access to a vast repertoire of cinemas, and I spent my afternoons watching Spanish, Italian, French and German films, both classic and current. Afterwards, I would make my way up the Passeig de Gràcia back to my flat, crossing from the wide boulevards of the Eixample into the narrow lanes of my neighbourhood. There, over a hastily thrown-together meal and a glass of local – affordable – Priorat, I would watch an Indian film on DVD, in part to tease out its differences from the European counterparts, but mostly to reset my emotional and aesthetic states.

Slowly I began to articulate the racial, cultural and aesthetic distancing I had experienced instinctively as a child watching English language productions. Those films – like the European cinema I was rapidly consuming – were not 'our' films. They did not tell 'our' stories, and nor did they feature 'us' as anything more than minor actors with walk-on parts. Still later and after much reading, I realised that my discomfort – even alienation – was also a postcolonial condition.

This sense of alienation regarding Western cinema – both Hollywood and the 'auteur' European brand – grew more acute as I realised that cinema could be and was an intellectual pursuit. My non-Indian colleagues often knew little of my cinema, at least little beyond the usual name-check of Satyajit Ray. Often this was compounded by a general disregard of all commercial cinemas as somehow 'lesser'.

In the early 2000s, commercial Indian cinema, under the general description of Bollywood, was making initial inroads into European distribution channels. But discussions of such cinema remained mired in colonial, Orientalising discourses, often describing it as an inferior and pedestrian product, a poor imitation at best of the grand Hollywood productions. In part, this vein of criticism may be attributed to ignorance of the extensive Indian film canon, which often leads to comparing mediocre or poor-quality films with an idealised Western 'canon' of quality. More insidiously, Bollywood has long been considered as a sort of mindless entertainment package created for an impoverished, mostly illiterate audience. It is, to this day, often dismissed as escapist fare for an uneducated poor population unable to understand 'good cinema'. The toxic combination of intellectual snobbery and more than a whiff of imperial condescension means this century-old cinematic tradition receives relatively little critical thought. Perhaps the kindest, most honest response was of scholarly bafflement and avoidance, on the grounds that the evaluation of such cinema is enormously difficult as there is no accepted critical methodology with which these films can be analysed.

As my novel progressed, so did my interest in making sense of the cinema I had grown up loving. I began seeking out film critics and scholars from India and abroad. I had long been a closet 'popular Indian movie' fan, finding aesthetic and emotional sustenance in my movies. Yet for years, I had avoided even casual discussions or viewings of my favourite films with

Western – especially white – friends and colleagues. In large part, this evasion was because I did not have the words to explain why this cinema was essential to millions, billions, of people like me – educated, not impoverished, capable of reason and thought – across multiple continents.

As I read and watched and thought about cinemas from across the world, about the histories and politics of their producers and their consumers, about styles and fashions and aesthetics, I found myself wanting to share this love with an audience. A British-Asian friend helped me set up an old-fashioned film club in the back of her dance school in Barcelona. I came up with a list of the 'classics': *Mother India* (1957), *Sholay* (Embers, 1975), *Bandini* (Prisoner, 1963) and *Kaagaz Ke Phool* (Paper Flowers, 1959). Then added to the list a sprinkling of newer works: *Devdas* (2002), *Maachis* (Matchstick, 1996) and *Mission Kashmir* (1998). I made trips down to Pakistani shops in the Raval to acquire DVDs. Meanwhile, my friend designed an invitation flyer that we handed out to those we considered 'simpáticos': those who loved India – or at least were curious about the country – and loved cinema.

For the first viewing, daringly hosted on a Sunday afternoon, we rigged up a projector and a speaker system, bought bottles of the most affordable yet drinkable Catalan wine to go with packets of Haldiram's namkeen mix – also acquired in the Raval. I introduced the session with a hastily cobbled-together history of filmmaking in India (starting, of course, with the arrival of the technology in Bombay in 1896). And we were off!

We had chosen *Asoka* (2001) as a gentle introduction, although privately I anticipated that the Buddhist angle would be an additional draw for the largely European audience. As the film unfolded on a makeshift screen, I sat at the back and chewed on my nails, trying to intuit reactions from the dozen or so people who had shown up. I wasn't sure which reaction I dreaded most: boredom or dislike or condescension. The first I could rationalise. The second I could dismiss. But the third? Could I grow used to it?

7

Thankfully, the film ended to unanimous applause. More importantly, everyone stayed for an impromptu discussion: questions about everything from the star system, cinema history, narrative forms to those regarding technical and stylistic choices all came flying at me. We talked movies and politics and aesthetics until the wine ran out and someone popped into the shop next door to get some more. That evening, and for the first time outside India, I felt like an equal participant in a cultural conversation.

It was dinnertime when everyone left. While my friend locked up the space, I sat on a bench outside, in the Plaza de la Revolución, staring at the night sky. As was usual for this time of the evening, the plaza was full of people grabbing drinks and tapas before heading up the street to the historic Verdi cinema. I remembered the curiosity and joy of my fellow cinephiles as we had sat in the darkened back room. I thought of all the questions I had been asked and had been unable to answer because I just did not know enough. I savoured the joy of the most wide-ranging, equitable conversation I had had on the continent that was, at that moment, my home.

I knew what I wanted to do after finishing my novel. A PhD in film studies with a focus on my cinema would be my next project. I would study and learn, and develop the language I needed to share the films I have loved all my life. And I would find ways to share that love with my colleagues, friends, and even strangers, in words they already knew. Gradually, I was sure, they'd learn my words as well as I had I learned theirs so we could sit together before a screen to watch, and to love, the same films.

Why Do People Fall
in Love? Why?[1]

ONE OF MY EARLIEST memories is of standing on the raised
veranda of an old Himalayan bungalow, waiting, while my father
helped my mother settle onto a gentle chestnut mare. The pleats
of my mother's sari gleamed, the slivers of gold brocade catching
the final rays of the sun sinking beyond the western peaks. Dad
checked if her feet were secure in the stirrups, humming as he
packed her high-heeled, strappy shoes in his saddlebag. Only
then did he turn to pick me up, jumped onto an enormous black
horse, holding me securely before him. We wound through the
narrow deodar-lined paths, around the mountain, and up to the
officers' mess for another dinner, perhaps even a party, the evening's festivities tinged with an unspoken anxiety because
generally this meant that Dad and his men would be heading
out to danger soon. Parties have since been inextricably linked
in my mind with anxiety, sadness and, most of all, a sense of
impending danger.

The narrow trail we took ribboned up the mountain. I
remember my parents rode slowly that day, speaking of everyday
nothings, breaking every so often to point out distinct geological

---

[1] *'Jaane kyun log pyaar karte hai . . .'* from *Dil Chahta Hai* (The Heart Desires,
2001).

features or a damaged tree or spots for potential future landslides. The path had long stretches where we rode in single file and Dad repeatedly turned to check on my mother. He sang as we rode: the romantic '*Phoolon ke rang se . . .*' (I wrote to you with ink from flowers . . .) for my mother; the jaunty '*Hum hain raahi pyaar ke . . .*' (We travel the paths of love . . .), which remains one of my favourites because I remember how Dad had let the horse canter; and the melancholic '*Main zindagi ka saath nibhaata chala gaya . . .*' (I followed the paths on which life led me . . .). I learned much later that these are songs from my parents' favourite films. And, even later still, that Dad's song choices were not, are still not, incidental.

Even in our cantonment town in the hills, films were inter-twined with our lives. Late in the evening, after dinner in the rambling, draughty old officers' mess, I would gather with the other children to peer over the banisters as the adults danced; we watched them do the twist made popular by Shammi Kapoor and Mumtaz, and listened to the psychedelic, hippie pop that had begun sweeping the country with Zeenat Aman's debut film *Hare Rama Hare Krishna* (1971). As the night deepened, the hills beyond the line of parafin lamps disappeared into the dark, and people began to leave. I remember watching my parents dance slowly to '*Yeh raat yeh chandni . . .*' (This night, this moonlight . . .) with Dad occasionally surprising my mother with a sudden twirl that made her giggle. On such evenings, I would often fall asleep watching them, knowing that they would be the last to leave the dance floor, that Dad would carry me home, that I would wake up warmly tucked under our big down quilt to the sound of my father humming yet another familiar song. Even before I would fully awaken, I'd know from his choice of tunes whether that morning my mother's eyes would be bright with laughter or strained with anxiety despite her smiles.

Over the years I have managed to unpick the many elements of this memory: imperial history persisted not only in the rambling English architecture of that old cantonment town but also in the traditions – the army mess, the glamorous parties, my mother

10

riding side-saddle in formal wear – that blended colonial manners with post-Independence living; the confusing and violent geopolitics that swirled around us at national, regional, global levels; and the impossible task that my parents and the other adults – the first postcolonial generation – faced in trying to make sense of a world that was changing too much, too fast and for which they had not, could not, have been prepared. Only recently, I have begun to recognise all that Hindi films and their related materials – songs, dialogues, fashion, attitudes, mannerisms – offered us: plausible expressions of our realities, situations to make sense of our world and, most of all, narratives to hold us together, individually and collectively.

I had intuited some of this as a child: our – not only mine or my family's but the wider collective's – lives were saturated with cinema even when we were not watching it. Stars dominated our shared visual field: the romantic Rajesh Khanna in the early 1970s, followed almost instantly by Amitabh Bachchan's 'angry young man' figure raging against injustice. The cosmopolitan Zeenat Aman stared sultrily from movie posters that lined city walls along with the more traditional beauty of India's 'dream girl' Hema Malini. My uncle's friends at university dressed like the movies too: exaggerated flares and pop prints inspired by *Hare Rama Hare Krishna* were a mark of modernity as much as the handwoven kurtas paired with jeans from *Mere Apne* (My Own, 1971) indicated an interest in progressive politics. In nursery school, even I was dressed in psychedelic prints popularised by Aman. And as a teenager, I learned to save up fabric from old school ties to tuck into the lapel pocket of my school blazer, just like Bachchan.

I knew the songs from radio and recognised every film star from posters and newspapers. Radio was our primary medium of live entertainment and was often used on cricket match days in our home to tune in to its commentary on shortwave channels. Yet once a week, we would gather in the dining room, led by my excited aunts who'd start rapidly turning the dials of the beloved Phillips device to search for Radio Ceylon. My grandmother would

11

grumble good-naturedly from the kitchen as she prepared the evening's meal. Channel identified and set, the volume raised to the loudest, we'd all wait around the little cream box for *Binaca Geetmala* to begin. With less than a minute to spare, my uncle would breeze in, often with a book clutched in his hand, and take a seat just as presenter Ameen Sayani's instantly recognisable voice began his weekly countdown of recent film songs.

I had known films before I had ever watched one. Down in the plains, on cold summer evenings and baking long summer nights, adults would take turns telling stories, mixing fairy tales, folk narratives, history with their familial and personal memories. From my grandmother came stories of the great epics, recent regional and family anecdotes, and personal memories of the British Raj from which I was already well removed. An uncle who voraciously and eclectically devoured global literatures wove tales that I later recognised as retellings of Miguel de Cervantes, Maxim Gorky, Somerset Maugham. Someone would take up *Dharmayuga*, the Hindi cultural magazine that arrived weekly at our home, and read out a poem or a story. Alongside these would be stories from films: the English classics and sometimes French ones from my uncle, recent popular Hindi ones from my aunts, and my favourites, the old ones from the 1940s and 1950s from my grandmother. She'd weave in her memories of going to the cinema, often with my grandfather (who had died before my birth), and even act out bits of dialogue and her own reactions as a viewer. Every time the veteran actor Ashok Kumar came up in her stories, she would not fail to mention his well-tailored suits that were 'worn properly' just like my grandfather.

In those days before re-releases, repeat television broadcasts – there was not widespread television broadcasting networks in India and my family did not own a television until the 1980s – or personal video libraries, these retellings became my only mode of learning about the Indian film canon dating back decades before my birth.

Because of the idiosyncratic distribution system of films in India in the 1970s, we watched films in an eclectic, non-chronological, even chaotic fashion. My grandmother's home was in Varanasi, a relatively significant town, and the newest releases would arrive at select cinema halls where tickets would be difficult to procure until the excitement died down a little. Some of the smaller, slightly shabbier cinema halls in the city simultaneously played older beloved films that had been released years or even decades before. Sometimes, even in the 1970s, a theatre would acquire a floating copy of an old favourite like *Mother India* (1957), about an impoverished single mother's struggle to raise children in rural India, or *Chaudvin Ka Chand* (Full Moon, 1960), about two friends who end up in an accidental love triangle. The original fans would turn up to watch their favourites and bring younger relatives who would then be drawn into the ongoing transgenerational cinephilia. Smaller towns near the border posts where Dad was frequently assigned received new releases much later than the bigger cities and cinema halls there would play whichever films they could procure. This meant that films as far apart from each other as *Upkar* (Favour, 1967), about a farmer who joins the army during the 1965 Indo-Pakistan war, and *Dharam-Veer* (1977), director Manmohan Desai's big-budget historical fantasy about twin brothers separated at birth, could be found playing at different theatres at the same time. Dad was also often stationed at or near army cantonments and this added to my anachronous exposure to films, especially during school holidays. Indian armed forces regularly procure and screen films for the troops and at the officers' mess, often on patriotic themes. This meant that the screening choices at the army mess even in the late 1970s could include *Himalay Ki God Mein* (In the Lap of the Himalayas, 1965), about a young doctor who moves to the mountains, and *Hum Dono* (Both of Us, 1961), about two army officers who have an eerie physical resemblance to each other. With the expansion of television broadcasting in the 1980s, the national television broadcaster, Doordarshan, found a treasure trove of ready content in the archives. This meant that classic films like the romantic comedy *Chalti Ka Naam Gaadi* (That Which Moves Is Called a Car, 1958), about brothers who own a car repair business, and dramas like *Khamoshi* (Silence, 1973), about a psychiatric nurse who had worked with injured soldiers and who struggles with her own mental health, suddenly became easily available to new audiences. Most of the films were frequently chosen with little consideration of their cinematic quality or the commercial and critical success they may have had during their release. Instead, availability was often the most important criteria for selection. Fortunately, this also meant that our exposure to cinema through television programming became wildly varied.

My classmates and I learned about India and the world, determined our enemies and friends, and chose our moralities thanks to films. *Amar Akbar Anthony* taught us the value of religious tolerance. *Prem Pujari* (Worshipper of Love, 1970) taught us the necessity of violence for the sake of the nation, even as we professed non-violence. *Deewar* (Wall, 1975) taught us to make the right choice: that even when crime seemed more glamorous, it would exact a high price. We learned the ways of romance and falling in love: *Kabhi Kabhi* (Sometimes, 1976) and *Love Story* (1980); to be dutiful and responsible despite the personal price: *Yaadon Ki Baaraat* (Procession of Memories, 1973) and *Sholay* (Embers 1975); and to be brave and rebellious: *Kaala Patthar* (Black Stone, 1979) and *Lawaaris* (Illegitimate, 1981). In short, films were a shared experience that extended far beyond the hours of their viewing times. They formed the content for our memory games, built our narrative skills, and created our moral and social universe.

It was during this same time that I, along with some of my school friends, acquired vague American accents by watching Hollywood comedies that were screened locally. However, despite this exposure, none of the English language films we saw meant more than an exercise in learning English. They didn't satisfy me at some intrinsic emotional level or provide a sense of *'paisa vasool'* ('money's worth' – a key concept for the commercial film audience). In addition, both children and adults reacted intuitively to imperial memories – direct and transferred – that often girded these films. My very first memory of an English language film is of *The Bushbaby* (1969) set in Kenya at the cusp of independence where a young English girl must return a galago/bushbaby to its natural habitat before leaving with her father for London. I know it was around 1972 and we watched it in Varanasi, although I have only vague memories of the film itself. I found it traumatic and cried until my frazzled father decided to take us home midway through the screening. *Chitty Chitty Bang Bang* (1968) fared no better but it provided great amusement to my family as I was terrified by the very idea of dinner plates on wheels. American films went down better, although the adults would have to explain the plot afterwards as the narrative structure left us children utterly confused. Sometimes, as in case of *Ben Hur* (1959), a film that reached us nearly two decades after its release, the explanation would take weeks to unravel until my uncle finally found a copy of the novel to remind him of all the details.

Curiously, this sense of alienation did not extend to Soviet cinema, which would come to us dubbed into Hindi, perhaps because the stories were already known to us from children's books translated from Russian into English and Hindi. So *Ivan's Childhood* (1962), about an orphan who befriends Soviet officers while working as a scout during the Second World War, or fairy story adaptations such as *The Snow Queen* (1957) or *Through Fire, Water and . . . Brass Pipes* (1968) seemed more 'ours'. Not only were the narratives familiar, but the dilemmas that their characters faced seemed closer to the ones we knew and could relate to, like overcoming poverty, showing courage in times of war, or plots centred around friendships and love. This familiarity was embedded in our imagination in part due to Raj Kapoor's lavish *Mera Naam Joker* (My Name is Joker, 1970), about a circus clown's life, which featured Soviet actors and was partly shot in Moscow. The same applied to martial arts cinema from Hong Kong, which seemed to follow familiar narrative patterns and themes, with a focus on familial and community ties, characters in economically straitened circumstances, often rural settings, and unjust rulers.

Many years would pass before I would be able to articulate the racial, cultural and aesthetic distancing we experienced instinctively as children watching Hollywood productions. Not only were 'we' never the protagonists, but also if any film did feature us, it would usually be in the depiction of savage tribes that needed to be civilised and saved, or as outright barbaric villains. From old prints of *Gunga Din* (1939) that showed up every so often for a morning show at cinema halls in the 1970s to the awful *Indian Jones and the Temple of Doom* (1984), it was clear that this was not my – our – cinema. Unsurprisingly, when Persis Khambatta was cast as Lieutenant Ilia in *Star Trek: The Motion Picture* (1979), she became my instant favourite, although never quite as much as Zeenat Aman whose many screen avatars I adored to the point of imitating their hairstyles, outfits and mannerisms, especially after her role as a vengeful martial arts specialist in *Don* (1978).[2]

This sense of alienation regarding Western cinema grew more acute when, in the mid-1980s, as a teenager I moved with my family to New York City. In college, and in film clubs, talking of Fellini and Bergman, admiring Capra and Polanski, cinema became an intellectual pursuit. The only form of Indian cinema acceptable or known amongst my non-Indian colleagues was of Satyajit Ray. In many scholarly circles the general attitudes towards commercial Indian cinema were dismissive or condescending. Not surprisingly then, over time, I learned to intellectually 'talk' Western films but formed no personal connection with them.

Fortunately, as a latecomer to Western cinema, I never managed to rid myself of my first love of commercial 'Bombay' cinema, although I did not have the ability to explain it. How could I when even its name shifted constantly? Scholars spoke of Indian commercial or popular cinema and the 'all-India' film. Others spoke of the Hindi film, which specified the language

---

[2] Aman still informs my clothing sense, although only the keenest of her fans are able to spot this. This instant recognition has long helped me open conversations and form deep connections with strangers across the world.

used for a movie and not their filmmakers who spoke multiple and various languages. Film reviews in local papers spoke of 'masala movies', a spicy balanced feast that could be savoured on repeat viewings: as boisterous entertainment with friends, a hopeful date with a romantic partner, a celebration with multiple generations of the family, and with each viewing the film would deliver! English language film journalists derisively named it Bollywood, a chaotic, poor man's version of the big-budget, glitzy American cinema, and that term has grown increasingly popular in the global north as a shorthand for a vast range of Indian films produced in Hindi, and even in other languages. The word is loathed by many in the film industry, including its biggest star of the past half century, Amitabh Bachchan, and it is not a term I use in India – or indeed in places like Jordan, Egypt, Senegal or Malaysia – because everyone already knows and loves the movies. Yet in London, Barcelona, New York, Bollywood is a convenient shorthand for my cinema as well as a conversation starter that at least gives me an opportunity to counter some of the misconceptions about it.

A part of me loves that my cinema had, and continues to have, many names just like many Indians (and me) who often have separate names that our family and friends, romantic partners, professional colleagues call us by! One of my aunt's university tutors laughingly described this cinema as 'romantic thrillers replete with song and dance, action and fights, and laughter and tears' (*naach gaana, maar dhaad, rona-dhona, hansi majaak se bharpur rahasyamaya romanchak chalchitra*). It wasn't exactly a name, but it did clarify that, like all of us, our films contain multitudes!

I did not then, as a young student in the United States, have the words or the concepts to explain that my cinema was not one of meaningless digressions. Nor was it juvenile or unformed. That its many parts that seem disjointed or inconsistent to the uninitiated viewer made perfect sense if only one knew how they all fitted together. Still, like many of my generation, living in the global north, as a student in New York and Boston, I learned to become a closet Hindi movie fanatic, even as I publicly professed my faith in the Italian neo-realists and expressed my undying admiration for Satyajit Ray. It was the easiest option when names like Manmohan Desai, Prakash Mehra, even Gulzar, drew either blank looks or, worse, pitying sneers followed by kind-hearted attempts to teach me about 'real cinema'.

Sadly, there is still little knowledge or understanding of this cinema in many parts of the global north. Even many fellow cinephiles know little of this brand of popular, dizzying films that we call 'masala movies', although increasingly, more people are familiar with films that are grouped under the shorthand 'Bollywood'. It is also due to a lingering colonial gaze that often understands the Hindi film as something designed for large, impoverished, often uneducated and thus culturally unsophist-icated audiences, and as the exact opposite to Hollywood's view of itself, its cinematic conventions and its audience.

As late as 1988, the British film magazine *Screen International* announced that overseas appeal of Bollywood cinema was considered 'essentially limited', restricted to markets with a tradi-tionally anti-American stance such as the Soviet Union. Of course, such declarations ignored this cinema's large mass markets around the globe, especially in postcolonial societies of West and East Asia, and large parts of Africa where commercial cinema from India – mostly in Hindi but also in other languages – had long consolidated its position as a viable commercial and ideological alternative to Hollywood. The former Soviet bloc was a long-standing export market for Indian cinema, so when a Hindi song casually popped up in *Little Vera* (1989), I wasn't surprised although I did do a little jig in that theatre in Boston. Then I took great pleasure in explaining both the provenance and my cinema's influence to my American friends.

In the global south, Bollywood has long opened doors for me in places as disparate as Marrakesh, Kuala Lumpur and Lima, where the question 'are you Indian?' is instantly followed by an enthusiastic discussion of favourite films and film stars. Some years ago, a Greek acquaintance in London recognised '*Pyar hua, ikrar hua*' (I fell in love, I confessed my love) from the 1950s

18

because her grandmother had been a Nargis fan and begged for a classics playlist to remember her. I later discovered that Greece has an entire musical genre that translated and rerecorded popular tunes from Indian films with local instruments. More recently, these old numbers are often remixed with techno and contemporary pop and find their way into nightclubs and bars. A Romanian colleague in Barcelona broke into tears when '*Yaadon ki baaraat*' (A procession of memories) from the 1970s came up on my speakers in our shared office because it reminded her of her family that she hadn't seen in years. After weeks of exchanging the most basic pleasantries in a mix of English and Spanish, we suddenly bonded over singing the entire plaintive number. After that, Hindi, which she had learned from the movies, became our secret language.

The understanding of this cinema began slowly changing in the 1990s, primarily due to processes of globalisation, India's embrace of economic liberalisation and consequent sociopolitical changes. Recognising movie markets beyond the global north, *National Geographic* acknowledged in 2005 that Indian cinema reached 3.6 billion spectators around the world, a billion more than Hollywood! However, the change in popular understanding or discussion of this cinema's content and form has been slower. On moving to London in that same year, I remember my delight at seeing Hindi cinema being reviewed in the *Guardian* and discussed on the BBC. However, the excitement quickly faded when I realised that those considerations hadn't moved past the same old colonial view of the industry (and country). Scholarly circles have been still slower to change, even as an increasing number of scholars from India, the diaspora and elsewhere are producing exciting research.

In Western academic circles, Hindi – indeed all Indian – cinema is generally referred to only in passing even by academics purporting to write a 'history' of global cinema. As such, the unique cinematic codes, multiplicities of languages, styles and contents, along with the vast range of influences and reflections generally flummox not only the average Western viewer but also many critics. Unsurprisingly the long-standing critical success of Satyajit Ray's films in the West is not unrelated to their formal similarity to the realist styles of European cinema. Ray had sought out the French auteur Jean Renoir before making his classic *Pather Panchali* (1955), which follows the challenges faced by an impoverished young boy Apu and his sister Durga who live in rural Bengal.[3] Nearly two decades later, at a screening of *The River* (1951) in Los Angeles, Renoir confidently if a little mistakenly described Ray as the 'Father of Indian Cinema'. For decades since, Ray has often been the only Indian filmmaker known to many non-Indian cinephiles. In contrast, even when commercial Indian films find success with wider Western audiences, they remain seen merely as exotic novelties. Even the 2022 success of the anti-colonial Telugu action film *RRR* – despite its Golden Globe and Oscar wins – remains in this vein.

* * *

Like many Indians, I did not – and still do not – distinguish between popular films made in languages other than Hindi. In part this is because this cinema does not require language fluency in order to watch or enjoy, which meant that in days before subtitles I could still watch movies in Tamil, Marathi or Bengali. In most popular Indian cinema, narrative structures and formal elements often cut across linguistic constraints. Moreover, these are often familiar to the spectator from other forms of narrative performance such as classical dance forms like Kathakali or Odissi, or popular theatre productions like the Ramlila, the annual theatrical re-enactment of the epic *Ramayana*.

---

[3] Ray continued Apu's story in *Aparajito* (The Unvanquished, 1956) and *Apur Sansar* (The World of Apu, 1959). The three films won numerous awards in India and abroad.

Increasingly, however, given specific and fascinating traject-ories of the many film industries in the country, I feel it is a shame that all too often popular Indian cinema is equated to 'Hindi film', regardless of the actual language of production. This is in part because since the 1960s, Indian cinema has been largely seen as one of two things: either the popular 'Hindi movie', a category that has encompassed films in a dozen or more languages, or 'Satyajit Ray', which is a general category of art-house cinema made by a range of different directors creating 'serious' cinema that explicitly focusses on social issues and attempts realist depictions in terms of form and style.

Fortunately, the past decade has seen changes in this popular understanding of the Hindi film, which has increasingly and often inaccurately been described as Bollywood, while film industries in other languages ranging from Tamil, Telegu, Malayalam to Bengali and even Bhojpuri assert their distinctiveness. The national and global success of movies in Tamil, Telegu and others over the past decade has also begun – at least within India – shifting the popular discourse on cinema. At the international level, the generic label 'Bollywood' still threatens to subsume all commer-cial cinemas from India into a single megalithic category. Perhaps this is inevitable given the commonalities in form, style and narrative structures, although it often, and rightly, infuriates both practitioners and audiences for whom the distinctions are important and necessary.

Regardless of language and region, it is clear that there is an overarching framework that can, and does, hold an Indian film together and forms the basis of understanding and appreciation by its primary audience which in turn decides the commercial and critical success or failure of the film. Of an average of 700 commercial feature films produced annually in India, only a few dozen are accepted by the audiences as 'good' films, even fewer are 'hits' at the box office, and the rate of failure is very high. Given that a wildly diverse group of commercial filmmakers has chosen to make similar narrative, formal and structural choices over various decades, it indicates that there is a clear and coherent set of filmmaking principles at work. At the same time, the longevity and popularity of this cinema means that not only is the audience discerning about the filmic elements but that there is more than simply a 'loosely structured' sequence of 'attractions' or self-contained 'episodes' that they seek in a film. The habitual audience of this cinema seeks, identifies and judges not only narrative structures and formal and aesthetic criteria but also a philosophical underpinning to the movies.

Perhaps learning these peculiarities will help us understand the power of this cinema. Would this understanding not open up a century of fascinating, dazzling, brilliant cinema to new audiences? And most importantly, if learning stories is a way of understanding those we do not know, won't learning the codes of Indian cinema open up ways of understanding the country itself? Not only in the ways it has been narrated by outsiders but by Indians to themselves?

Come! Let's Return. The
Country Awaits[1]

I DON'T REMEMBER THE exact moment that the 'stereo system'
entered our home, but I know very clearly that its arrival marked
a before and an after. The before involved family members
huddling around the portable cream Bakelite Philips shortwave
radio. The after involved a prized turntable flanked by an amplifier and two speakers that were nearly as high as me. Only adults
could work the turntable with its ultra-fragile needle that would
jump and slide at the slightest disturbance. And only they could
handle the precious, shiny black discs that mysteriously produced
'hi-fi' sound loud enough to rattle my teeth and set my heart
racing. The amplifier, however, was both special and accessible
to the rest of us, with buttons and knobs and four sliding switches
that could alter not just the volume but the very quality of sound
that emerged from the speakers. I quickly learned to slide the
bass slowly, secretly, all the way to the top. The thump of drums
would set windowpanes rattling, and an adult would soon race
in to reset the controls. But by then I would be nestled with a
book in the corner furthest from the stereo.

---

[1] 'Aa ab laut chalein . . .' from *Jis Desh Mein Ganga Behti Hai* (The Land
Where the Ganga Flows, 1960).

With the stereo came the LPs, huge black discs in brightly coloured jackets, that reflected the varied tastes of the extended clan: the Beatles, Boney M. and Police rubbed shoulders with soundtracks of *Kaala Patthar*, *Don* and *Hare Rama Hare Krishna*. A single track from this last album – a heavy-bassed pop number in Usha Uthup's husky voice, starting at the fifth groove on the shiny black disc – had long been my favourite on the radio. But the stereo transformed that song – and after it, all others – forever. Sliding up the bass to the very top meant my heart could be set thumping in time with the rhythm. My ears would fill up, almost to the point of pain, and my breath would run short. On particularly fortunate days, my aunt would wink cheekily and slide the volume right to the top too. We'd count the minutes until my grandmother stormed in, scolding us for playing music 'loud enough to make the dead walk right off their pyres'. I would watch as the music was lowered to a respectable volume and my grandmother sternly told off any adult in the room. But I'd catch her grin as she left the room and know that she wasn't truly angry.

The most prized – and monumental – album in the family collection was a three-disc edition of the full soundtrack of *Mughal-E-Azam*, K. Asif's 1960 magnum opus purportedly about the emperor Akbar and his son Salim whose love for the courtesan Anarkali shook the Mughal empire. On the front of the LP jacket was an image of the stars rendered in oranges and red, much like the hand-painted hoardings we were used to seeing at the front of movie theatres. The jacket cover folded out in multiple ways, with the discs secured in numbered sleeves. The inside was dotted with black and white publicity stills placed on the same red-orange background. The album stayed at the very back of the record shelf, too heavy for me to pull out on my own, too precious for regular handling.

Every few weeks, the entire clan would gather for a meal. Early in the morning, my uncle would head to the butcher's to acquire the best cuts of a freshly slaughtered goat. My aunts would be in the kitchen, chopping up hills of onions, kneading mountains of dough, and washing high heaps of rice in the gleaming bell metal troughs. My grandmother would supervise, measuring out the spices, her sharp eye magically keeping track of a dozen hands busy with a dozen different tasks. I would huddle against the large rice tin, its metal cool against my back, a book held in front of my face, listening to the chatter and stories and giggles.

Each stage of cooking lingers in my mind: the tickle in my nostril from chopped ginger, the sting in my eyes from sliced onions; a deep breath for the fragrant rice as it hit boiling water; the heavy and almost unpleasant smell of roasting meat cut by cardamom, clove and black pepper; and finally the earthy, rich smell of the bubbling do-pyaaza – meat cooked in twice as many onions – that would bring the clan trooping in to eat.

Oddly I have few memories of the meals themselves and none at all of what we finally ate or the taste of the food so painstakingly prepared. Instead, my memories are of the over-whelming, loud sound of many simultaneous conversations, petty arguments, and laughter that filled our home during such mealtimes. In any case, for me, the main attraction of these gatherings was what my uncle termed 'post-prandial activity': replete from the feast, the adults would move away from the table to lounge on sofas, low divans and rugs. Pillows would be passed around along with soft cotton wraps and light velvet quilts. My uncle would pull out the heavy *Mughal-E-Azam* album and set it to play. As the opening dialogue, in the sonorous, portentous voice of Prithviraj Kapoor, filled the room, the chatter would die away and we'd settle into the movie. Most of us had never seen the film so our minds filled in the images. I would examine the album jacket, imagining the costumes, the sets, the acting based on the photographs. My aunt had watched the film – or perhaps she just claimed she had – and filled in details: the arch of Madhubala's eyebrows, how her heart skipped a beat when the actress first appeared on screen, the magnificence of the elephants in the battle sequences, the swoon-worthy romance – we didn't use the word sexy – of the 'feather scene'. And most of all, the absolute wonder of the enormous glass palace created for the final song, one of the earliest uses of colour film in Indian cinema.

I did not know then that this way of 'watching' cinema was popular and of longstanding habit in South Asia, dating back to the advent of movies in the region. Nor did I realise that it would baffle many overseas.

* * *

Cinema arrived in India within six months of the Lumiere brothers presenting their new technology in Paris, portentously in a venue named Salon d'Inde, in 1896. Within a year, local enthusiasts had embarked on producing films, although these were mostly limited to documenting notable sites like the Varanasi ghats or newly popularised inventions such as steam trains. Even in its early years, however, cinema's political, pedagogical, cultural significance was clear, but it was nearly two decades before the first Indian feature film hit the screens.

Dadasaheb Phalke, often called the grandfather of Indian cinema, was an established photographer who recognised the potential of this new form. Having viewed *The Life of Christ* (La Vie du Christ, 1906), he decided that India needed to put its own stories on screen. He was encouraged by the views of the poet and Nobel laureate Rabindranath Tagore, who understood the political potential of cinema in a country where an over-whelming percentage of the population was illiterate (imperial census data placed literacy levels across colonised India at the start of the twentieth century in low single digits).

The story of Phalke's quest to make the country's first feature film, *Raja Harishchandra* (1913), would not only make a great film in itself, but also features some of the tropes now familiar from a century of Indian cinema: an almost impossible dream, a group of friends committed to aiding the hero's cause, a supportive wife who pawns her jewellery to help fund the venture. Few of us watching the 1957 epic *Mother India* would ever link

Radha's (played by Nargis) pawned jewellery that her son Birju (Sunil Dutt) steals from the cruel moneylender to Indian cinema's origin story. Yet the practice of women pawning jewellery and its cinematic representations are deeply etched into the modern Indian psyche: innumerable films right into the 1990s relied on it as a shorthand for representing impoverishment, injustice and sacrifice. In a case of life echoing art which echoes life, the biography of India's chief nuclear scientist and president, APJ Abdul Kalam, includes a description of his sister pawning her gold jewellery to finance his university studies.

The raised funds helped Phalke travel to Britain to learn filmmaking and import film production and exhibition equipment from Europe. He even shot a short film to attract investors for his venture. The stock had to be sent to Britain for processing and then shipped back. Despite these obstacles, *Raja Harishchandra* was released less than two years after Phalke began the project. Aimed at a multilingual audience, the silent film had intertitles in English, Marathi and Hindi.

For his protagonist, Phalke chose the popular mythical figure of King Harishchandra, held up as an exemplar of justice, generosity and sacrifice, who undergoes Job-like trials. As punishment for interrupting an ascetic's meditations, the king gives up his kingdom and goes into exile. His miseries add up: his young son dies and Harishchandra is unable to afford wood for cremation (another trope signalling desperate poverty that has long remained popular in cinema). On her way to beg for help, his wife is arrested and falsely accused of murder. She is tried, declared guilty and Harishchandra is ordered to execute her by beheading. At the last moment, Shiva, the deity, intervenes and the king's realm and son are restored to him. Although only two reels of the film survive, there is ample documentary evidence of its contents, not least because Phalke remade the film and played on its themes repeatedly over the subsequent years. The surviving reels are fascinating examples of early special effects, with an emphasis on creating 'wonder' in the spectator not only with the images on screen but also the technology itself.

Premiered at Olympia Theatre and released at Coronation Cinema in Bombay (now Mumbai), *Raja Harishchandra* was an instant commercial success. Initially, Phalke had made a single print of his film, but he quickly made more copies for screenings that would take place beyond the city. For many in the audience, the movie was their introduction to film technology and it was greeted with enthusiastic wonder. However, the film's success was not unpredictable as it drew heavily on a Parsi[2] theatre production of the same name. Produced initially in 1875 in Gujarati with the title *Hariścandra*, the play as well as its subject matter were familiar to audiences across the country. Between 1892 and 1922, *Hariścandra* along with *Nal Damayanti*, another play based on a story about the travails of a loyal wife, were performed for over four thousand shows by the Victoria Drama Company.

Phalke's success triggered a movie 'gold rush' that brought a wildly varied range of people to filmmaking, ensuring that the incipient industry diversified beyond the confines set by the urban classes or the colonial elite. The countrywide success of cinema lured capital and adventurers to the industry. Liquor importers, cosmetics and textile merchants, and household goods manufacturers all rushed in to try their hand at making films. At the same time, theatre actors, courtesans, poets and writers also began to flood to Mumbai, the coastal metropolis, seeking opportunities offered by this new medium. Although this diversity continues to impact the heterogeneous styles, themes and concerns of Indian cinema, especially the films in Hindi made in Mumbai today, it was not new. It was rooted in the successful conventions and forms of the earlier Parsi theatre.

In the mid-nineteenth century, students of Elphinstone College in Bombay had begun staging their own performances which

---

[2] Parsi literally means Persian and in India is applied to Zoroastrians, who form one of the country's smallest religious minorities. The community is centred primarily around Mumbai, Bangalore and the state of Gujarat in India and Karachi in Pakistan.

drew inspiration from English plays staged by the British community in the city. This new form of theatre used Western elements such as the proscenium stage to perform English plays not only translated into vernacular languages but entirely transformed for the local audiences. Characters would be renamed, assigned caste and community identities and given more culturally familiar motivations; the settings were transferred to more familiar parts of Asia; and storylines were changed to fit the social and moral conventions of the local populace. In 1853, Parsi Natak Mandali (Parsi Drama Company) performed its first play, *Roostum Zabuli*, based on the tragic story of Rostam and Sohrab, a tale of a father and son with echoes of the Greek tragedy *Oedipus Rex* by Sophocles.[3] The play's success marks the beginning of India's most popular modern theatre form that combined entertainment and spectacle with a social message and used Western influences like the proscenium stage with its elaborate backdrop and curtains. This theatre depicted popular stories from Persian literature and Sanskrit epics along with adaptations of English plays – Shakespeare was an early favourite – that were 'Indianised' with the insertion of songs, music-and-dance and narrative structures familiar to audiences from folk theatre. Persian fantasy plays, adaptations of the Hindu epics, depictions of 'reformist' social issues like child marriage, and contemporary political events such as the Franco-Prussian War were all turned into performance pieces for an eager and growing audience.

Parsi theatre drew freely from and influenced other forms of drama that were already familiar to the audience including Marathi tamasha, the serious and structurally formal natyasangit, the Bengali jatra, which deploys song and dance to address complex social and political themes, as well as nautanki from Uttar Pradesh, khyal from Rajashtan, manch (literally, 'stage') of Madhya Pradesh and the Gujarati bhavai. The plays therefore

---

[3] The tragedy of Rostam who mistakenly kills his son Sohrab forms part of the epic tenth-century Persian epic *Shahnameh* by Ferdowsi.

incorporated elements that audiences expected and would usually start with an on-stage prayer and end with a ritual expression of gratitude and a farewell song. The scenes would move swiftly between moods as well as feature songs and dance in a range of styles. Even when theatre companies used Western instruments, the music was drawn from popular and folk styles. The plays themselves were often performed in Hindustani, a colloquial mix of Hindi and Urdu, Gujarati and Marathi. Parsi theatre quickly became one of the most important forms of popular entertainment in South Asia and companies proliferated rapidly, with many touring through not only South Asia but travelling as far as Myanmar, Singapore and even London.

Financed by the Parsi entrepreneurs, primarily written by Muslims and Zoroastrians, acted by performers from all religious, linguistic and ethnic backgrounds, and presented for a predom-inantly Hindu audience, Parsi theatre in many ways was emblematic of a particularly Indian modernity. This brand of modernity was also uniquely well suited for a cinema that could address audiences across ethnic and religious lines in the colonial period. After Independence, and in the aftermath of Partition and massive communal violence, it could be deployed for constructing an idea of India as a modern, democratic and secular state. The diversity of the people involved in creating this drama form ensured that – in addition to the popular Hindu theatre traditions – Islamic *sufi* poetry, Persian romantic conventions as well as European drama were freely combined into this modern form of narrative performance. This new theatre not only reflected but drew heavily on the composite culture made up by the country's diverse popu-lations and extensive historical links across Asia, Africa and parts of Europe. Medieval Sufi and Bhakti traditions – the former rooted in Islam, the latter in Hindu beliefs – had been developed and transmitted over the past millennium through works of poets such as Amir Khusrau, Mirabai, Kabir and Tulsidas, and continue to inform popular culture and imaginations. For example, while stories of star-crossed lovers are not particular to South Asia, the trope of representing lovers as a deity and their devotee is drawn

30

from Sufi and Bhakti traditions. Similarly, lyrics and dialogue often included imagery – that of the veil or of a moth drawn to flames – that were familiar to audiences as expressions of human erotic love as well as metaphors for spiritual love. Parsi theatre not only drew on popular tropes, narratives and metaphors of these traditions but gave them a contemporary and urban form and language.

When cinema arrived in India at the start of the twentieth century, filmmakers found a readily available bank of popular – and commercially viable – narratives that the audiences already knew and loved from Parsi theatre. In addition, during these early decades, financiers, managers, directors, writers and actors often cut across the stage and the screen, either moving entirely to the more lucrative form of cinema or working across both forms. Many of the country's early films were versions of plays produced by Parsi theatre companies and well known across the region. Examples include not only Phalke's debut, but also *Raja Gopichandra* (1921), about a king who renounces his throne, *Nal Damayanti* (1920) and the many versions of the tale of Rustom and Sohrab, including an adaptation in 1963. One of the country's first talkies, *Indrasabha* (Court of the Gods, 1932) was not only based on a play by Agha Hasan Amanat that had been first staged in 1853, but most of its songs were already popular with the audiences due to its many theatre performances.

When the arrival of sound split the film industries and its audiences on linguistic lines, adapting Parsi theatre's convention of freely mixing languages led to the emergence of a 'filmi' Hindustani. This became a cinematic *lingua franca* that could be understood across the region as it was not only a combination of Hindi and Urdu but also developed a rich vocabulary by borrowing from Marathi, Gujarati and Bengali. In the decades since Independence, the 'Hindi' film industry, centred around Mumbai, has also incorporated into its linguistic fabric Bhojpuri and *purabiya*' from Uttar Pradesh and Bihar, Goan-Christian lingo, *tapori* or Mumbai-street slang, and Punjabi. More recently, films have been using Indian English and 'Hinglish' (a combination of

31

Hindi and English). This flexibility has been particularly helpful for expanding the reach of Hindi films to audiences not only in India but also its neighbouring countries, especially when compared to the more linguistically particular cinemas.

There are clips of Phalke's first film, *Raja Harishchandra*, on YouTube although the originality of those are contested. Some believe that the surviving reels, the source of these recent online uploads, are from his 1917 remake of his debut. Although I cannot claim to have seen the first Indian film, I have known of Phalke and *Raja Harishchandra* since childhood because detailed descriptions were passed on not only by those who had seen it but also by the many who would never experience cinema except by hearsay. These narrations were passed down the generations as accounts that not only included the on-screen narrative but also contextual details: how the trip to cinema came about (generally thanks to work in the city), the beauty of the venue itself (movie theatres or 'picture halls' as we called them exemplified the most extravagant twentieth-century architecture in South Asia), the reactions of the viewer and their fellow audience members. Even the food consumed would be lovingly detailed, passed on not as mere secondary information around the film but rather as an essential sensory component of that crucial life experience.

Within a decade, Phalke's mythologicals had been joined by social 'realist' drama such as Baburao Painter's *Savkari Pash* (The Moneylender, 1925), about an unscrupulous moneylender who cheats peasants and forces them to give up farming and work in mills,[4] and contemporary satire such as N.C. Laharry's *Bilet Pherat* (England Returned, 1921), about a young Bengali man who returns from England with a colonial education that places him at odds with local culture, and which experimented with a range of *mise-en-scènes*, narratives styles, aesthetics and themes. These two streams consistently chosen by early filmmakers can be

---

[4] The first screen outing of the figure of a greedy moneylender or a pawnbroker that remained a popular on-screen figure for decades afterwards.

described as Janus-faced since they looked to combine perform-ance narratives, styles and traditions from the past with influences from Hollywood, French, German and other European cinema. Over time, and even to this day, Indian cinema draws liberally from literature, films, music, fashion and other arts from across the globe while remaining rooted in the country's political, social and cultural realities as filmmakers continue to try to make sense of a rapidly changing world.

*　　*　　*

The British rulers of India were not unaware of the political potential of the nascent cinema industry and the Imperial Legislative Council decided to regulate films as early as 1917. The Cinematograph Act introduced the next year not only set age restrictions but also granted the ruling authority the right to suspend films that were deemed 'likely to cause a breach of peace'.

The British built on their earlier measures such as the Press Act of 1910 that limited the use of literature (including poetry and songs) as a means of disseminating anti-colonial ideas. The regulation of theatre had long been a concern of the colonial authorities because of its ability to incite a live audience. No wonder then that the movie gold rush almost instantly triggered coloniser anxieties about the new medium's reach to impact political discourse even though in those decades, the over-whelming number of films screened in India were American and European productions.

Even before the Cinematograph Act, British authorities – under the guise of audience safety and concerns about law and order – regulated screenings or 'cinematographic shows' which had grown popular in many cities. There was some historical truth to this concern as the first attempts to regulate film screenings dated back to the Bazar de Charite fire in Paris that killed 126 people in 1897, just a year after the birth of cinema. (The fire was an accident involving nitrocellulose, a compound used in explosives, which was also what film stock was made of in those early days. When mixed with camphor, this compound became nitrate film, which was highly flammable.)

The 1918 Act was introduced just as the anti-colonial movement was gaining momentum in India. Throughout the First World War, the Raj had struggled with violent and non-violent opposition in India: most notably, Bal Gangadhar Tilak had launched and led the Home Rule Movement, which pushed for greater local autonomy, and the Ghadar (Revolution) movement made up of Indian expatriates was active overseas, in British colonies, Germany and the USA. The end of the war added greater impetus to the anti-colonial struggles, which were given a boost by the Anarchichal and Revolutionary Crimes Act, popularly known as Rowlatt Act after the president of the committee led by Sidney Rowlatt. The law, passed in March 1919, indefinitely extended preventative emergency measures of indefinite detention and imprisonment without trial or judicial review. Less than a month later, this new imperial measure kicked off the first major non-violent protests led by M.K. Gandhi and culminated in the brutal Jallianwala Bagh Massacre. On 13 April, Colonel Reginald Dyer ordered his troops to open fire on men, women and children who had gathered to celebrate the spring Baisakhi festival in a walled park in Amritsar. Dyer's troops had blocked off the park and the people had been given no warning. Although the number of casualties remains contested, the government's own records show that the firing continued for ten minutes and that the soldiers used up most of the 1,650 rounds of ammunition they had been issued. The incident marked a point of no return for colonial rule in India and, although various political agitations were suspended in the immediate aftermath of the massacre, violent and non-violent anti-colonial movements gained force in the months and years that followed.

Simultaneously, cinema became crucial to the dissemination of anti-colonial messages in the country. Filmmakers and colonial authorities embarked on a cat-and-mouse game of sneaking political content past the censors: films about unjust rulers who cared little for their people, lost princes who organised peasant revolts, and stories featuring masked avengers proliferated, often set in mythical lands and fantastical milieus. Filmmakers also readily drew from the *Ramayana* and the *Mahabharata*, although the latter seems to have been the more popular choice, perhaps because its episodes of war could be more easily marshalled for political purposes. Stories from the other classical texts including the Puranas provided additional stories: *Narsinha Avtar* (1920) centred on the half-lion, half-man incarnation of the Hindu deity Vishnu who appears to save a devotee from a cruel king, while *Kansa Vadha* (Slaying of the Tyrant, 1920) depicts the popular story of Krishna slaying Kansa, another unjust ruler. 1921 saw the release of *Bhakta Vidur*, superficially inspired by the stories of the *Mahabharata* and told from the point of view of one of its minor characters, but which turned out to be the first explicit critique of the British rule in general and the Rowlatt Act in particular. At the same time, filmmakers also created films focussing on social issues such as child marriage with *Balika Badhu* (Child Bride, 1920) and about women's role in marriage with *Pati Bhakti* (Wife's Devotion, 1923). The latter also became the first film to be censored when a song was excised for 'obscenity'. Another group of filmmakers embarked on lavish, extravagant productions: Himanshu Rai and Franz Osten made *Prem Sanyas* (Light of Asia/Die Leuchte Asiens, 1925), loosely based on the life of Buddha, and then *Shiraz* (1928), depicting the story of the Taj Mahal. Unsurprisingly, narratives derived from historical, historical-fantasy, and mythological sources also offered the lushest of visuals and set designs. Sadly, many of these films are now lost, although their traces remain in printed and oral descriptions.

However, colonial censorship of the period was not only limited to Indian films. Given the slump in post-war European cinema, over ninety per cent of films screened in India in this period were from Hollywood. These too were often seen as dangerous for two reasons: politically, their focus on freedom aligned them with local anti-colonial messaging; socially, Hollywood depicted white characters behaving in immoral ways and thus undermined the image of British imperial superiority. As a result, Hollywood films bore the greater brunt – at least in numerical terms – of the Raj's attempt to censor cinema.

As the decade drew to a close, technological developments led to the most important change in India filmmaking: the advent of sound. *Alam Ara* (Light of the World, 1931) was India's first 'talkie' and sadly also one of the most important 'lost films' as no print or gramophone recordings survive. Pieced together from descriptions of the time, it appears that the film was an audio-visual extravaganza consisting of tropes deeply familiar to audiences of Indian cinema: a prince whose life is under threat; a scheming stepmother who will stop at nothing to be queen; the daughter of a falsely imprisoned army commander who fights to free her father.

The need for sound made casting for *Alam Ara* complicated. Prefiguring the dilemma featured in *Singing in the Rain* (1952), the leading star of silent cinema and the filmmaker Ardeshir Irani's first choice Ruby Myers, better known by her screen name Sulochona, could no longer be cast in the role as she did not speak Hindustani at the time (however, she was quick to remedy this and continued acting well into the 1950s). This opened the space for Zubeida Begum, one of the few stars to transition successfully to talkies. The male lead Master Vithal, another major silent era star, broke contract with his original studio – with the help of Mohammad Ali Jinnah, the anti-colonial leader and founder of Pakistan – to be part of the movie.

Alam Ara featured seven songs and although no recordings survive, the album was immensely popular. Nearly fifty years after the film's release – and loss – I remember hearing a particularly melodious, old beggar on the banks of the Ganga in Varanasi whose plaintive voice would soar in the dawn air. He often sang '*De de khuda ke naam pe pyaare*' (Give in the name of God . . .), a song I have never heard in a recorded version although it is listed in the film's soundtrack. It also features heavily in contemporaneous accounts of *Alam Ara*. I now wonder if the beggar's song was the lost one from the movie. Was the accidental soundtrack of my childhood forays to the river possibly the first recorded film song in the country?

The arrival of sound transformed Indian cinema forever as films could now be made in multiple languages and targeted specifically to regions, with Calcutta and Madras taking early leads. While *Alam Ara* was the first talkie released in 1931, it was followed in the same year by *Jamai Shashthi,* a short film in Bengali, *Bhakta Prahlad* (yet another film adaptation of the story of a devotee saved by Vishnu who appears as half-lion, half-man) in Telegu and *Kalidas* (about the fifth-century poet and play-wright) in Tamil. The first film in Gujarati, incidentally also about the life of a poet, *Narsinh Mehta* was released in 1932. In the same year, *Alam Ara*'s director, Irani directed and produced the world's first Persian language film, *Dokhtar-e Lor* (Lor Girl), about a young girl kidnapped by bandits who falls in love with the man charged with dealing with them.

Bombay remained the filmmaking hub where directors began experimenting with technology, filmmaking techniques and distribution. In 1933, V. Shantaram's *Sairandhri* (titled for the name adopted by Draupadi in the *Mahabharata* while in hiding), a bilingual film in Hindi and Marathi depicting an episode from the epic, was processed and printed in Germany and became the very first colour film in the country. This period between the two World Wars is marked by a wide ongoing exchange with German cinema which included directors like Franz Osten living and working in India, the legendary filmmaking couple Himanshu Rai and Devika Rani[5] training in Berlin, and technicians like Wolf

---

[5] Perhaps the first film power couple in India, the two produced, directed and acted in some of the most successful films of the period. While not much of their work survives in the public domain, their steamy kiss from *Karma* (1933) remains available online and is a touchstone for movie buffs and historians alike.

M. Henius heading the country's first cinecolour process labor-atory for Irani.[6]

The ability to reach specific audiences via different languages also helped the anti-colonial cause as films and their soundtracks now reached far into the rural hinterlands: the travelling gramo-phone-wallah, a man who traversed the countryside with a handful of records and a single gramophone often packed on the back of a bicycle or a bullock cart, became a popular figure. Songs also quickly became an effective strategy for promotion and a secondary income stream for films. They also offered endless opportunities for musical innovation and cinematic spec-tacles, creating a rise in demand for lyricists, composers and musicians, all leading to a dizzyingly rapid growth of the industry. For all the enthusiasm, filmmakers quickly realised that there can be too much of a good thing: 1932's *Indrasabha* (Court of the Gods) was 211 minutes long and featured seventy-one songs! The film, the first to be made entirely in Urdu, is set in the court of Indra, the king of gods, and focusses on a love story between a fairy and a prince. The film drew on multiple classical song traditions from north India and was commercially successful. However, its 1936 Tamil adaptation chose to feature fewer songs.

Meanwhile, the anti-colonial struggle had been gathering steady force. Gandhi's strategy of peaceful non-cooperation allowed for mass dissent in ways that left colonial authorities increasingly unable to control the populace. While protest marches and demonstrations were the most public aspects of this, many more could participate privately too by boycotting British-produced consumer products: the rejection of textiles made in Manchester was a keystone of Gandhi's political tactics. Films continued to play their part by presenting anti-colonial

---

[6] The Second World War ended this collaboration as the British government declared German citizens in the colonies as 'enemies', and detained, expelled or interred them. Post-war conditions in Germany and India were so vastly different that nothing of the scale ever redeveloped.

content overtly or covertly through mythological narratives and stories that addressed social ills. The latter often focussed on gender and caste issues which were inseparable from the anti-colonial struggle: *Achyut Kanya* (Untouchable Girl, 1936) examined caste discrimination through a love story between an upper caste man and a lower caste girl, while *Kisan Kanya* (Peasant Girl, 1937), India's first indigenously made colour film, based on a script by Saadat Hasan Manto, explored the plight of poor farmers; *Duniya Na Mane* (The World Does Not Accept, 1937) denounced forced marriages and advocated widow remarriage. This last film also daringly included documentary footage of anti-colonial leader Vallabhai Patel which was ordered to be removed by the censors. Recognising the growing anti-imperial sentiment, filmmakers began seeking out public endorsements from anti-colonial leaders like Gandhi and Patel for their films.

The 1930s also saw the rise of the hugely popular action/stunt film. These often packaged a fast-paced series of action sequences – sword or fist fights, horse- and car- chases – with a general message against the injustices meted out by a cruel elite, which meant they were likelier to make it past the censors than the overtly political cinema. Often these action films featured a lost prince or princess organising a ragtag group of supporters or a masked vigilante figure fighting for the people. Many stunt films featured major women stars of the era including Pramila, Gohar Karnataki, and Sulochana, the highest paid star of her time and often considered Indian cinema's first sex symbol. Focussing on female stars offered additional possibilities in such visually extravagant films to add glamorous costumes including high boots, tiny shorts and swathes of satin.

One of the most successful of these stars was Mary Ann Evans, better known as Fearless Nadia, an Australian-born, Bombay-raised daughter of a Scottish army volunteer. Nadia had worked in theatre and the circus before trying her hand at films. Although her blonde hair and blue eyes limited the roles she could play, stunt film directors Jamshed 'J.B.H.' Wadia and Homi Wadia found her a perfect fit for their work. Starting with *Hunterwali* (Woman with a Whip, 1935), the trio would create a series of wildly successful films throughout the next decade where Nadia rode horses and trains, fired guns, fought hand-to-hand, and performed breathtaking stunts all in the service of protecting the innocent and the vulnerable. Although the storylines for these films were often rudimentary and forgettable, the action sequences and Nadia's glamorous performances mesmerised filmgoers.

Despite the British censors' attempts to restrict and control what they deemed dangerous cinematic content, filmmakers found ways to go around them. In 1930, the colonial administration of the Madras Presidency banned the Tamil film *Thyagabhoomi* (Land of Sacrifice) by K. Subramanyam after a wildly successful twenty weeks in theatres. Focussed on a family's political awakening, the film explicitly glorified the freedom struggle as well as Gandhi and his ideals. Worried by the film's success and undisguised political content, the administration decided to ban its screenings. In retaliation, the filmmakers began free and continuous screenings at Madras's (now known as Chennai) Gaity theatre. As word of the ban spread, local people gathered around the theatre, creating cordons against the police and taking turns to watch the film. By the time police entered the theatre to seize the print, the message of the film, if not the film itself, had reached more people than if it had been allowed to run its course.

The banning of *Thyagabhoomi* also demonstrated what filmmakers had known since the advent of the talkies: recorded film soundtracks including songs and dialogues were harder to censor than the films themselves. Colonial authorities could shut down cinemas, seize prints, and otherwise ban dissent on celluloid. However, once gramophone records with the film's soundtrack were released into the market, it would be nearly an impossible to track down and confiscate each item. These records were often packaged with printed pamphlets or 'songbooks' containing the song lyrics, and soon these pamphlets began to be sold separately and extremely cheaply. They were often reprinted or copied, which added another layer of dissemination that was impossible to curtail or control. In addition, the availability of songbooks and gramophone records meant that film songs took on a life of their own outside of the film itself, circulating far beyond those who could access movie halls. Filmmakers quickly seized the growing phenomenon to include political songs in their works. Even if the censors demanded their removal from the film prints itself, they would reach the people through the records and the songbooks.

The arrival of sound also completely transformed film consumption in India. Till then, Hollywood and European cinema made up over ninety percent of all films screened in the country. This changed almost overnight, and by the country's independence in 1947, foreign films made up a small proportion of cinema consumed in the country. Despite political changes and technological innovations, the public consumption of foreign films remains extraordinarily low even today.

* * *

From its early days, the two streams of the mythological and the social remain the clearest classifications of popular Indian cinematic genres. These also reflect the influence the classical dramatic tradition had on filmmaking. Classical Sanskrit drama was characterised by two distinct forms of narrative performance: nataka or the 'heroic', which often featured mythological and semi-mythological representations, and prakarana or the 'social' that focussed on trials and tribulations of humans with a focus on stories of love (shringar) or courage (vira). These in turn are rooted in the concept of rasa, which literally means 'juice' but has been deployed for centuries to signify the essence of a work of literature, theatre, music, dance, and in the past hundred years, cinema. Rasa is the very essence of a work of art, created by the careful balancing of elements by the artist and experienced as a feast of pleasures by the reader, listener or viewer.

Although many early 'gold rush' filmmakers – like many in the industry today – had little knowledge of classical texts or classical aesthetic theory, they gravitated towards these genre distinctions, indicating that they not only drew liberally from traditions that were deeply familiar to them and their audiences but also recognised the intent of their work: to create a visual and narrative feast that the viewers could savour much like a satisfying meal. Through the past decades and even today, Indian filmmakers and spectators often talk about cinema in particular ways, emphasising the importance of creating emotions on screen and experiencing them fully. The Indian audience's corresponding alacrity in rejecting a bulk of the cinema made every year suggests that they have a finely tuned palate for the cinema they choose to savour.

The adoption of these forms also suggests that 'genres' in Indian cinema are better understood as similar to earlier narratives that would be often differentiated as martial, sacrificial or romantic and were performed in their distinctive styles and contexts. Most, though not all, martial stories turned on male heroism, power, social obligations, group solidarity, and revenge and were represented and resolved through physical or political conflict. At first glance, *Karan Arjun* (1995), focussing on the reincarnation of twin brothers who are reborn to avenge their mother's travails, including their own murders, has little in common with *Zanjeeer* (The Chain, 1973), where a young policeman's quest for justice leads him to his parents' murderers. Yet male heroism, the quest for vengeance, and eventual solidarity amongst the disenfranchised in order to confront the powerful lies at the heart of both movies. These are also not dissimilar to the action/stunt films of the 1930s, not only for their action sequences but also for the righteous protagonist fighting for justice.

In our home, the martial or vira rasa remains the preferred form of cinema. I realised as a teenager that most of my parents' favourite films centred on a soldier protagonist: from *Prem Pujari* (Worshipper of Love, 1965), a love story that wound its way through Indian political anxieties about another Chinese military incursion,[7] to *Achanak* (Suddenly, 1973), about a navy officer who murders his wife's lover (based on the infamous Nanavati murder case).[8] Once we acquired a VCR in the early 1980s and began collecting films, Hollywood and British films joined the list: *First Blood* (1982), *The Eagle Has Landed* (1976), *A Few Good Men* (1992) and *Stalag 17* (1953). They not only occupied the pride of place but made for regular repeat viewing. Curiously, my parents had – and still have – little time for the more glamorised screen depictions of the military and of warfare: the subsequent Rambo films, *Top Gun* (1986), and *American Sniper* (2014) do not seem to hold their attention past a few minutes. Neither do the many recent 'army films' produced by India.

A few years ago, my father and I wandered through the Arc de Triomphe in Paris. It was late at night and the monument was deserted. At one point, we leaned against the cold stone, craning our necks to look at the inscriptions on the ceiling. My father was pensive, ignoring my chatter about the monument's history and the trivia I had to offer about the French Revolution and the Napoleonic Wars until I fell silent. We stayed there for a while until he murmured, 'What a waste of men. And for what?' Soon after, we walked away but his question lingers in my mind. The moment also provided a sudden, strange insight into my parents' love of cinema that represents the messy, painful parts of heroes and heroic lives.

In contrast, films that draw from sacrificial epics foreground social norms which are often presented as righteousness or 'dharma'. The conflicts depicted in these narratives are emotional,

---

[7] China invaded parts of northern India in 1962. Indian forces were unprepared and took heavy casualties. Politically, it marked the end of Nehru's unilateral attempt to remain a 'peaceful' nation-state.

[8] In 1959, Naval commander Nanavati murdered his wife's lover and then drove to the naval base, confessed to the murder and surrendered the weapon. The case was avidly followed by the press and remains a historical legal and social turning point for independent India.

internal and quieter. Often set in domestic spaces, these also tend to centre on female protagonists and are generally resolved through sacrifice or superhuman endurance and perseverance. *Mother India* (1957) follows Radha's struggles as she single-handedly raises two sons. She is abandoned by her husband, impoverished and indebted, reliant only on a barren piece of land for subsistence. Yet she holds to her moral core: refusing to trade sexual favours for debt relief with the moneylender, tirelessly working the barren land and finally killing her wayward younger son Birju to protect the moneylender's daughter. The urban and affluent setting and the well-educated characters in *Damini* (Lightning, 1993) may appear to have little in common with *Mother India*, even more so as its first part depicts a rather frothy romance. However, the film changes track quickly when the protagonist – Damini – witnesses her brother-in-law raping a domestic worker and chooses to support the victim. This brings Damini into conflict with her husband's powerful family who are able to mobilise various elements against her until she forges an alliance with an alcoholic, disillusioned ex-lawyer to help her and the victim get justice.

Finally, while romance is a key element in most classical narratives, a romantic epic or one that emphasises the shringar rasa focusses on personal freedom and the quest for love. It contrasts with sacrificial films by privileging personal happiness over familial obligations and social demands. This category can be further divided into two sub-categories, the failed and the successful, depending on whether the lovers unite at the end. Unsurprisingly, these make up the largest categories of cinema with tropes that are instantly recognisable: a couple meet, fall in love, overcome difficulties to live happily ever after . . . or not. Romance narratives also provide the greatest opportunities for glamorous locales – the Swiss mountains have long been a favourite of Hindi filmmakers, in part as they are quite similar to the geography of Kashmir (frequently described as a 'paradise on earth'); fashionable outfits which then percolate into consumer choices; and of course song sequences that can reflect the many

44

moods of love including anticipation, excitement, curiosity, longing, joy, celebration, pining and sorrow.

As with much other Indian cinema, I learned of romance films before even watching them, primarily through their songs. The songs in turn introduced us to the richness of the metaphors they employed, often drawn from classical and medieval poetry in the region's many languages and even from Persian and Arabic literary traditions. Many of the hits of the 1950s, the 1960s and the 1970s were penned by some of the country's best-loved poets who rendered complex literary devices and philosophical ideas into popular language. As a result, I knew dozens of songs about the 'moth drawn to the flame' as a child, but only recognised their connection to Sufi philosophy and to Persian poetry as a young adult. It was also with belated embarrassment that I realised the sexual innuendos of the many songs about bees and flowers that we gleefully sang in the playground. At the time, none of us understood the full tragedy and violence encapsulated by the popular '*Inhi logo ne chheena dupatta mera*' (These people robbed my veil . . .) sung by a courtesan lamenting her fate. Neither did we grasp why the snappy '*Khullam khulla pyaar karenge hum dono . . .*' (The two of us shall love freely) elicited scandalised gasps from the wimpled nuns who taught us.

Like the other categories, the romantic film also reflects the most pressing anxieties of modern India, with social class – with implicit indications of caste – as the largest challenge posed for lovers. In sharp contrast to popular Hollywood romances where divisions between the rich and the poor are rarely addressed, and if raised are quickly resolved (*Dirty Dancing* (1987) is a brilliant exception!), Indian romantic films are keenly aware of the intractable challenges posed by wealth: *Jab Jab Phool Khile* (When Flowers Bloom, 1965) traces the love story between a rich heiress Rita (Nanda) on holiday in Kashmir who falls in love with a local boatman Raja (Shashi Kapoor). Rita's father objects to Raja, pointing out that he cannot 'fit in culturally' into their family. Reminiscent of a gender-reversed *My Fair Lady* (1964), Rita then teaches Raja urban, Westernised behaviour so he can enter the affluent Bombay society, only to discover that her father has been setting the couple up to fail. The film also gave Indian cinema one of its most popularly repeated sequences: the lovers finally reconcile their differences on a train platform and the film ends with the man pulling the woman up into the moving train and his arms. The sequence has been replicated multiple times over the decades, most popularly by Shah Rukh Khan and Kajol in *Dilwale Dulhaniya Le Jayenge* (The Bravehearted Shall Take the Bride, 1995).

The tragic romance epics end with the lovers defeated by the same challenges and choosing death over separation. Ranging from *Milan* (Union, 1967) to *Qayamat Se Qayamat Tak* (From Doomsday Until Doomsday, 1988), the lovers in these films are either foiled by social norms or by a Romeo-and-Juliet style familial rivalry. In each instance, the audiences are not only familiar with the tropes but anticipate them. The pleasure of the tragic romance is in following the travails that accumulate into the final failure of the lovers, despite knowing they will fail.

Such a classification can also help explain the dominance or resurgence of particular genres at certain periods in time: the tragic hero *Devdas*, based on Bankim Chandra Chatterjee's 1917 Bengali novel of the same name, has had eleven cinematic versions, in multiple languages, although the three most significant ones in Hindi are from 1936 starring K.L. Saigal as Devdas, 1955 with Dilip Kumar in the role and 2002 with Shah Rukh Khan playing the lead. It has also been referenced by dozens of films, most memorably in *Kaagaz Ke Phool* (Paper Flowers, 1959), actor-director Guru Dutt's final movie about a tragic love affair between a failing film maestro and his actress muse. The tale of the eponymous protagonist, a wealthy young man who drinks himself to death after his love for his childhood friend is thwarted by her parents, has exercised an unparalleled hold on the Indian cinematic imagination. While the novel critiqued the ossified customs of the Bengali landowning class, at the time experiencing gentle but inexorable decline, the film adaptations tend to focus more on the challenges posed on the lovers by societal norms, a stance that can be modified to suit each generation and seems to have the greatest resonance at periods of socio-political transition where no clear way forward appears possible. While the novel was written during the First World War, Saigal's 1935 screen adaptation arrived at a time when anti-colonial resistance was increasing in intensity but also splintering along religious lines (eventually leading to the Partition of the region in 1947). The 1955 version with Dilip Kumar, Indian film's 'king of tragedy' reached screens when the independent republic was experiencing enormous economic and social changes – including the implementation of the new Constitution, the first decade of the Five Year Plans for economic development, and the heavily contested right to divorce for Hindu women.[9] Sanjay Leela Bhansali's 2002 big-budget, glamorous adaptation starring Shah Rukh Khan arrived a decade after India implemented economic liberalisation policies and as the rise of the Hindu supremacist polity gained force. In each adaptation, Devdas's despair goes beyond that of a lost love and embodies anxieties that are specific to the era.

Similarly, the 1970s and the 1980s were marked by increasingly violent films, centred on themes of revenge and attainment of power. The early optimism for building a new nation had faded by early 1970s as the first generation born in independent India came of age. The previous decade had seen the passing of the political leadership that had led the country to independence. There had been three major wars in the interim: the 1962 Chinese incursion along the Himalayas, and the 1965 and 1971 wars with Pakistan, the latter leading to the formation of Bangladesh from the erstwhile East Pakistan. Alongside, the country struggled with enormous unemployment, abject poverty and multiple murderous famines. The victory in the 1971 war did not quell growing discontent amongst the youth for long and the country

---

[9] Civil rights in colonised India were determined on religious lines and inherited by the independent nation-state. This has meant that rights such as marriage, divorce and inheritance can vary wildly across religions.

was consistently roiled by student and trade union protest actions. The country's first nuclear tests in 1974 – even though declared as being for peaceful purposes only – provided an opportunity for martial posturing in domestic and international arenas although they did little to help the political dispensation. In 1975, Prime Minister Indira Gandhi declared the Emergency, a twenty-one-month period when democratic rights were suspended. Tens of thousands of political dissidents were jailed, many were tortured. The turmoil continued into the 1980s, with the country's first, albeit short-lived, coalition government in 1977, the rise of various violent opposition movements across the country, the assassination of the re-elected Prime Minister Indira Gandhi in 1984 that was followed by the mass violence against India's Sikh minority. The 1980s concluded with violent protests against caste-based affirmative action by upper caste Hindus[10] and the assassination of another (former) prime minster, Indira Gandhi's son, Rajiv Gandhi.

It is no surprise that this zeitgeist was exemplified by the star persona of Amitabh Bachchan as 'the angry young man', whose films through the period featured a protagonist single-handedly battling a corrupt, unjust economic and political 'system'. Over nearly two decades, Bachchan dominated Indian screens, with his blockbuster movies repeatedly taking on greedy mine owners, construction barons, corrupt politicians and dishonest policemen. In 1980, the country's most important weekly news magazine, *India Today*, declared him 'the one-man industry'. Much of his stardom and long-lasting success may be attributed to the qualities of 'male heroism' demanded by the social and political convulsions of the period, and linked to the martial *Mahabharata* heroes, Arjuna and Karna.

---

[10] The Mandal Commission report had submitted recommendations in 1980 for affirmative action to redress caste discrimination including quotas in government jobs and public universities. Indian government led by Prime Minister V.P. Singh attempted to implement these recommendations. Widespread protests by upper caste students led to Singh's resignation in December 1990.

In contrast, the 1990s saw contradictions of a new kind: India opened its economy to the globe, creating an economic boom that went hand in hand with the destruction of the Babri Masjid, a sixteenth-century mosque in Ayodhya, by the Hindu far right in 1992. The rapid globalisation that created a vast middle class marched shoulder to shoulder with the political enfranchisement of the Hindu supremacist ideology espoused by the Bharatiya Janata Party (BJP). The aspirations of this new middle class were reflected by a shift from the 'heroic' to 'successful romantic' films. An ageing Bachchan ceded his superstar crown to the post-liberalisation superstar Shah Rukh Khan, whose screen persona is also constructed in the heroic mode, although linked intertextually more to the *Ramayana*. Unlike the lone warrior against injustice, Khan's persona on screen and beyond draws clearly on the figure of Rama as the embodiment of 'the good son, father, brother, husband and a just ruler'. More recent films featuring the star have constructed a similar 'heroic' persona for Khan, although centred more on social obligations and group solidarity. Khan's own religious identity as a Muslim exemplifies the contradictions intrinsic not only to his star persona or even the Hindi film industry but perhaps also to the Indian audience.

The unprecedented entrenchment of Hindu far right politics in India in the past decade has thrown up interesting contradictions. There have been few 'blockbuster' Hindi films since 2014 and much of the big film successes seem to have shifted southwards from Mumbai with period fantasies in the 'heroic' mode such as S.S. Rajamouli's two-part *Baahubali* (2015, 2017), set in a mythical kingdom with a lost-and-found prince and a warrior princess resisting a cruel regime to restore power to the true king, and the more recent *RRR* (2022), set in colonial India where two men join forces against a cruel English administrator. The Hindi film industry with its exuberant mix of region and religion has long been a target of the Hindu far right. Its secular ethos is seen as a threat to their exclusionary, Hindu supremacist idea of India. In recent years, key figures in the film industry have been targeted by politically motivated harassment. Various stars have been investigated on allegations of drug use although few charges have been filed. Any hint of political dissent has been met with organised mob violence: sets have been damaged and filmmakers attacked. An organised and well-funded online 'Boycott Bollywood' campaign has targeted new releases and has been boosted by a highly politicised legacy press. Yet after nearly a decade of strategic silences and fumbles, Hindi cinema again appears to be staking a claim to not only the 'all-India film' but also its long-standing idea of an India based in diversity and heterogeneity.

On a chilly autumn evening, as the world emerged fearfully from the Covid-19 pandemic, I found myself in a mostly empty theatre in London watching *Brahmastra: Shiva* (2022). The first of a superhero trilogy that draws inspiration from Hindu mythology, the film features a cast from various Indian film industries, bringing together current favourites Ranbir Kapoor and Alia Bhatt as the lead couple with a host of veteran stars including Amitabh Bachchan, Shah Rukh Khan, Nagarjuna and Dimple Kapadia. Despite the superhero wrapping, the film's plot is familiar: a young man falls in love, discovers he has mysterious superpowers, and must learn how to control them while outrunning a murderous enemy. The film was simultaneously released in Hindi, Telegu and Tamil, and heavily marketed in the south of the country. Like many recent Bollywood films, it too had been targeted by the Hindu far right for 'not respecting' Hindu traditions even before its release. An old video interview of the lead star Kapoor talking about eating beef had been dug up for circulation as evidence of the star's anti-Hindu bias, regardless of his own religious affiliation. Yet I found myself finding familiar comfort in extravagant colours and song sequences, and marvelling at the action sequences and special effects. The film also features a surprisingly explicit political statement, the kind that Bollywood has avoided in recent years. The threat to the film's protagonist, and the world, is from a supernatural being who can raise armies of unquestioning fanatics!

A similar campaign was launched against the high-octane action thriller *Pathaan* (2023), superstar Shah Rukh Khan's first feature release since 2018. The film's title seems a nod to Khan's own heritage and religious affiliation – a defiant choice in times of politically ramped-up Islamophobia in the country – and features the star as an intelligence operative chasing down a fellow rogue officer who plans to target India with nuclear and biological weapons. The film was released simultaneously in Hindi, Telegu and Tamil, and to coincide with India's Republic Day. Pre-release statements from Telugu and Tamil stars and social media chatter amongst filmmakers and stars from various Indian industries suggest that, for the first time since the advent of sound split cinema by language and region, the country's many film industries are attempting to bridge divides by actively and systematically reaching out to audiences and filmmaking colleagues across India.

My Heart is a Vagabond[1]

JULY 1982. MY FAMILY was living in Islamabad when the news arrived that the superstar Amitabh Bachchan had been injured on a film set and was fighting for his life. For millions of Indians, as well as vast numbers of film fans across the world, this was our 'where were you when JFK was shot?' moment.

I had returned from school that afternoon, raced through finishing my homework and, as had become custom, had been repeat watching *Lawaris* (Illegitimate, 1981) for the nth time, making notes in a spare notebook where I jotted down my observations on film. My self-directed study of cinema had advanced to organised analysis by this stage, as had my conviction that films held a mystery I needed to solve.

Though we owned a VCR at that point, my viewing times and choices were still restricted by parental decree. This meant that I rewatched *Lawaris* in bits, sometimes rewinding and repeating the same half hour of the film for days on end. After all, I had already seen the full movie and knew how it unrolled. I knew every song by heart. I could explain every scene in detail with precise descriptions of its setting, costume and dialogue. The near daily repeat viewings were now intended to understand how

---

[1] '*Hai apna dil to awara . . .*' from *Solva Saal* (Sixteenth Year, 1958).

all these pieces fitted together, why they made me feel sad and thrilled and brave in turns. That my obsession drove my mother spare was just a bonus.

That fateful day, however, a part of me noticed that my mother had been growing anxious as the afternoon faded. My father's position at the Indian embassy in Pakistan meant that our family lived in a high-security environment. I also knew – even though the adults would not discuss situations in detail – of the violent shadowplay between India and Pakistan where every few months an embassy staffer would be picked up by security forces, beaten, brutalized and then released. The move would be swiftly countered by retaliatory action on the other side of the border, after which both nations would settle back into uneasy calm for the next few months, the only casualties being the injured and traumatised personnel who would be returned home for medical treatment, rehabilitation and redeployment somewhere else.

That afternoon I kept a discreet eye on my mother even as I reversed-and-forwarded between the two versions of '*Jiska koi nahin uska to khuda hai yaaron . . .*' (Those who have no one have god). The use of two versions of the same song, often with very different pace, rhythm and mood, is a popular device in Indian cinema, and in *Lawaris* the song moved from a peppy tune to a version replete with sombre stoicism. Normally, I hummed it or sang it in my head when confronted by playground bullies, but that afternoon the lyrics felt portentous as I worked through scenarios in my mind: had my father been targeted? Surely some of the embassy personnel would have arrived at our home for support if so? Had another plane been hijacked? The year before, a flight from Delhi to Amritsar had been hijacked and diverted to Lahore. Until the hostages were released, I remember spending tense hours at home with my mother, who diligently recorded every broadcast of the incident on Pakistan's national broadcaster, PTV (for Indian authorities to analyse later), while Dad had left for Lahore to organise, liaise and do the other mysterious things he did for the government. He hadn't returned that night and my mother, as was her habit, had kept vigil. There was a familiar comfort in waiting with my mother. My first memories are from 1971, during the war between India and Pakistan, when the two of us would wait by a single candle as my mother alternated between singing fragments of Dad's favourite songs, telling me long complicated stories – I preferred Dad's as hers were always less boisterous – and listening for the siren signalling the end of a possible air-raid.

There are more memories of being bundled off to bed and waking up to find my mother staring out at the mountain peaks, lost in the night, waiting for Dad to return home from one military operation or another. I would stay silent, hiding in the heavy down-filled quilts and hold my hot-water bottle close, watching my mother unguarded and delicate, by the window, until sleep took me again. Sometimes, my mother would hum a song that I don't remember Dad singing: 'Har taraf ab yehi afsaane hain, hum teri aankhon ke deewane hain' (There is gossip everywhere now that I am crazy about your eyes) from *Hindustan Ki Kasam* (Oath to Hindustan, 1973), a film loosely based on the Indian air force attack on the Sargodha air base during the 1965 Indo–Pakistan war. I learned early to recognise the hummed bars as a sign of my mother's anxiety and sometimes even fear.

The night of the hijacked airplane, for the first time, she had allowed me to stay up and wait with her. After dinner, we had snuggled up to watch films that my parents loved but I had never seen: first *The Eagle Has Landed* (1976), then *Prem Pujari* (Devotee of Love, 1970), about a pacifist in the Indian army who finds himself unable to kill the enemy and instead takes up spying for the country. My mother's smile had been strained as the night advanced and she had forced her voice to be cheery. As I had nodded off, my head on Dad's pillow, I recognised that my mother was sharing something important and intimate with me although I could not completely grasp it.

That July afternoon, aware of my mother's growing anxiety, I stayed before the television, pretending to watch *Lawaris* until Dad walked in, his briefcase in his hand, his tie still immaculate at his neck. The embassy received urgent national news directly.

And that afternoon, the news had been succinct: Amitabh Bachchan had been injured and was near death in a hospital.

I remember turning back to the screen to continue watching the film, my reversing and forwarding forgotten. Stunned, shocked, realising – fully, viscerally realising – that stories on screen were performed by real people. For all the film gossip magazines that my aunts read, the film reviews in newspapers, the radio countdowns, the LPs in their bright sleeves, and the many ways films saturated our lives, it was only on 26 July 1982 that I understood that actors – perha ps even stories themselves – were human, mortal . . . fragile. Just like Dad. Just like us.

The weeks that followed were educational. In India, national radio regularly updated the nation on the star's progress. While the press breathlessly followed every development at the hospital where Bachchan was admitted, fans gathered at temples, mosques, gurudwaras and churches to pray for his recovery. It was no different on the Pakistan side of the border. My classmates at school constantly asked after Bachchan's health. Our neighbours, dissidents under house arrest, checked daily across the shared wall that divided our homes. The embassy phone lines were jammed by callers looking for information and, in the days following the initial report, people would gather at the gates to ask for information. Even the terrifying ISI (Inter-Services Intelligence) men who kept watch on the embassy buildings and its personnel broke cover to check for news. At first, I thought that it was only Bachchan – my favourite star – who transcended borders. But many weeks later, as both nations and fans across the world celebrated his recovery, a senior officer in General Zia's regime noted to my dad: '*Janab*, if you ever want to invade us, have Doordarshan broadcast *Mughal-E-Azam*. Your troops will reach Multan before any of us takes our eyes off our televisions.' I think he was only half-joking.

* * *

If the 1930s were tumultuous for India and its cinema, the years and decades that followed were transformational. The Second World War did not slow the pace of political dissent and while the embattled Empire fought on in Europe, Africa and Asia, the anti-colonial movement gained strength: on 22 March 1940, the Muslim League led by Mohammad Ali Jinnah tabled its demand for a separate homeland for the Muslim population, which would lead to the creation of Pakistan in 1947 and the Partition of India. At the same time, anti-colonial leaders rejected British proposals to support the war efforts. This rejection was amplified by Gandhi's individual Satyagraha, a form of non-violent resistance, which encouraged widespread personal dissent by hundreds of Indians refusing to join the army or working in ammunition factories. Meanwhile, Subhash Chandra Bose, a former political colleague of Gandhi and Nehru, escaped to Germany and eventually turned up in Japan where he raised the anti-British Indian National Army. The gathering protests gained force with the Quit India movement in 1942. In retaliation, colonial authorities imprisoned the key leaders and thousands more. It is possible that the Empire's growing inability to retain control over their favourite colony played a part in the then British Prime Minister Winston Churchill's war-time policies leading to the Bengal Famine of 1943 that killed millions and devastated the region for decades to come.[2] With political repression at a peak and most political leadership in jail, films became a key method of disseminating anti-colonial messages. At the same time, and perhaps distracted by the war at home or a resigned acceptance of the impending loss of colony, British censorship grew lax. The growing shortage of film stock and

---

[2] *Famine in Bengal* (1943) is a fascinating anomaly in some ways. Directed by Bimal Roy, who would grow into a legendary film auteur, the documentary short depicts the devastation. Curiously, Roy chose a narrator who pleads in Punjabi, a language spoken at the other end of India, to plead '*Madad karo, madad karo, madad . . .*' (help, help, help . . .).

56

other war-related restrictions that hampered film production may also have helped lull the censors.

However, despite the political conflict at home and the war abroad, another kind of cinema-related propaganda battle raged on. Intending to convince the audience at home more than in their colony, the imperial propaganda machine churned out films such as *Tools for the Job* (1941), lauding India's contribution to the war effort, *Men of India!* (1941), showcasing Indian soldiers even though Empire had grown distrustful of colonial troops by this time, and the seemingly triumphant *The Trouble in India* (1942) about the Quit India movement that inadvertently reveals British desperation to retain control over the region. Made primarily for a British audience, these short documentaries were screened across India too, but appear to have had little impact on Indian audiences who preferred more rousing emotive tales of fighting injustice over the dry documentation of imperial might.

In contrast, Indian filmmakers pushed ever more explicit anti-colonial messaging through films like *Aaj Ka Hindustan* (Today's Hindustan, 1940) about two brothers one of whom is part of the freedom struggle and which featured the popular song '*Charkha chalao behno*' (Spin the wheel, sisters) in a direct reference to Gandhi's exhortation to boycott British-made cotton; *Apna Ghar* (Our Home, 1942), about a social worker working to unionise people against deforestation and who finally marries a lumber contractor; *Naya Tarana* (New Song, 1943), an explicit political movie about the historical oppression perpetrated by landowners, unscrupulous war profiteering and the Bengal Famine thinly disguised as a love story between two idealistic young people; and *Kismet* (Fate, 1943), which includes tropes that are now recognised as 'typically' Bollywood including a kind-hearted thief, a love story, a lost-and-found son, etc. although the film is best remembered for its defiant '*Door hato ae duniyawalo, Hindustan hamara hai*' (Beware world, Hindustan is ours . . .). Woven into rousing, moving tales of love, courage and justice, anti-imperial messages on screen resonated ever more loudly with the audience who continued flocking to cinema halls despite the growing political unrest. Even the publicity around film grew bolder, with *Chal Chal Re Naujawan* (Keep Going, Young Man, 1944) – a film title drawn from a popular song from *Bandhan* (Ties, 1940) that exhorted young people to keep marching towards a distant dream – bearing the tagline 'Bringing Light to a Vexed Nation'. In the 1970s, my grandmother would sing this song as she hurried her children and grandchildren through preparations for the day. The hopeful lyrics by the poet Kavi Pradeep provided a cheerful soundtrack for our mornings. Soon after the successful publicity around *Chal Chal Re Naujawan*, the posters for another film, *Hum Ek Hain* (We Are One, 1946), demanded 'Turn East – and Hear India Speak!' and in the lead-up to Independence the movie *Ek Kadam* (One Step, 1947) daringly included images of Subhas Chandra Bose on some of its publicity material.

Kismet did attract the attention of colonial censors, who ordered the arrest of its lyricist Pradeep and composer Anil Biswas. The duo went underground until the producers of the film offered a face-saver to the censors by explaining that the song was intended to counter the Axis alliance of Germany, Japan and Italy, and not the British empire as it contained the line: '*Tum na kisi ke aage jhukna, German ho ya Japani*' (Do not bend before anyone, be they German or Japanese). The censors were appeased, and the song became a nationalist anthem.

A generation after Independence, I learned this and other patriotic songs from films of previous decades at school: the peppy '*Ao bachcho tumhe dikhay jhanki Hindustan ki*' (Children, let us show you a glimpse of India) from *Jagriti* (Awakening, 1955) about a rebellious teenager sent as punishment to a residential school; the reverent '*Vande Mataram*' (Mother, I bow to you), the poem by Bankim Chandra Chatterjee set to music for *Anand Math* (1952) that focussed on an eighteenth-century rebellion against the East India Company by ascestics in Bengal; and the disturbingly cheerful '*Nanha munha rahi hoon, desh ka sipahi hoon*' (I am young traveller, and soldier for the nation) from *Son of India* (1962) about a child of an unhappily married couple.

These were joined by the plaintive '*Ae mere watan ke logon*' (O people of my country . . .) written specially (not for a film) by veteran film lyricist and poet Pradeep to honour Indian soldiers killed during the Indo–Chinese war of 1962 and which has since featured in innumerable movies including, most recently, *Pathaan*.

All of these songs are easy to sing, especially by large groups of people, and have memorable tunes and rousing lyrics. At the morning assembly at school, we'd rush through a non-denominational prayer in English or Hindi, switch to the national anthem and end with a patriotic song. I was seven when my father was briefly assigned to a remote town on the Indo–Chinese border that was designated a 'family station'. I attended the local school and struggled to communicate with my classmates, who primarily spoke Galo and Adi along with some Hindi and English. Yet the order of the morning assembly at school and choice of tunes remained the same as those in the towns and cities where we had previously lived. Each morning, as the high peaks of the Himalayas soared above us, we'd all gather before class. We would clap our hands and stamp our feet, belting out the numbers completely out of sync and mostly tunelessly until dust rose high in the playground. It was not until many years later that I began to examine the intent, role and purpose of Hindi film songs deployed for a vast, popular, nationalist exercise.

* * *

At the stroke of midnight on 15 August 1947, India became inde-pendent, although that midnight gave birth to not one but two – and soon to become three – nations. The Partition of the country on religious lines and the haphazard, hasty withdrawal of imperial powers ensured that joy at political liberation was leavened by sorrow and, as violence broke out, with increasing horror. The change of political boundaries and the division of assets between the two new nations – including armed forces, civil services and the treasury – were accompanied by one of the largest transfers of population in history with an estimated fourteen to eighteen million people moving from one side of the newly drawn borders to the other. An estimated million people died in widespread violence that marked the event. Distraught, poet Faiz Ahmad Faiz declared this was not the long-awaited dawn.

Indian cinema saw its own partition, with the Bombay industry losing some of its most eminent Muslim members when they left the city for newly created Pakistan. Filmmakers Shaukat Hussain Rizvi, W.Z. Ahmed and Nazir Ahmed, actors Swarnalata, Ragini, Ghulam Mohammed and Shamim, and composers Feroz Nizami, Ghulam Haider and Khwaja Khurshid Anwar were amongst those who emigrated. The extremely popular singer and actress Noor Jahan, who had delivered a string of hits in the decade preceding Independence, chose to relocate to the country that held her place of birth. Author and scriptwriter Sadaat Hassan Manto had not planned to leave India, but the growing horrors of the communal violence convinced him to migrate. In turn, the film industry in Lahore saw an exodus of Hindu members including actors Om Prakash and Pran who grew into fixtures of the Indian film industry for decades afterwards. For many, the decision was personal and few expected the division of the country to be as longstanding or entrenched. On the eastern flank, the powerful Bengali language film industry suffered less from exodus of personnel in 1947. Instead, the formation of East Pakistan – that split from Pakistan in 1971 to become Bangladesh – meant a catastrophic loss of a vast chunk of its market. In the midst of the upheaval of Partition, a Muslim lawyer from Peshawar, on the north-western side of Pakistan, chose to remain in India. His son, born and raised in New Delhi, is Shah Rukh Khan, one of India's biggest film stars who has retained near invincible status at the box office for the past three decades.

However, just as independent India was facing cataclysmic transformation at political, social and economic levels beyond the challenges of Partition, so too was the Hindi film industry undergoing rapid and dizzying change where pre-Independence film stars faded rapidly to be replaced by an entirely new screen pantheon that was reflective of the new India. This was accompanied by a rise of new narratives that reflected the aspirations and challenges of the fledgling nation-state. While filmmakers continued producing devotional and mythological films, and these remained popular in many parts of India, the ensuing decades were marked by the rise of contemporary narratives that explicitly or metaphorically addressed topical political and social challenges.

Steadily, films set in contemporary milieus attracted bigger budgets and bigger stars. Mythological films were overshadowed by cinema squarely aimed at negotiating modernities: Nehruvian romanticism of Raj Kapoor, grittier, darker *noir* of Dev Anand, and stylish romance with frequent taints of tragedy of Dilip Kumar. Similar in age, all three stars had seen initial success before Independence but would grow to rule the box office for the next two decades, each developing a distinct style of acting, choice of narratives and fan following.

Raj Kapoor, son of Prithviraj Kapoor (a theatre actor and silent era star whose deep voice brought him greater success with the advent of sound), was the quickest to find his feet in the new nation-state. Raised in the film industry, Kapoor had worked as a clapper-boy for the historic Bombay Talkies studio[3] and with his father as stage actor, production manager and art director. His first screen appearance had been in a small role at the age of eleven in *Inquilab* (Uprising, 1935) set during an earthquake in Bihar. The state – along with the neighbouring kingdom of Nepal – had been hit by an 8.0 magnitude earthquake the year

---

[3] Founded by the power couple, Himanshu Rai and Devika Rani in 1934, Bombay Talkies had state-of-the-art technology and facilities, ties with international filmmaking including German technicians, and produced a string of extremely successful films with progressive political content and style in the next decade. Rai died in 1940 and Rani divested from the studio in 1945. The studio finally shut down in 1953.

before and was still reeling from the devastation when the film was released.[4] In the ensuing years, Kapoor had appeared in over half a dozen films including period dramas and mythologicals and worked as an assistant director. With his filmmaking knowledge and on-screen as well as behind-the-scenes experience, he was particularly well positioned to launch his own production company, R.K. Films, in 1948. The company released its first film the same year, *Aag* (Fire), about a young man who refuses the family tradition of studying law to pursue his love for theatre. The film launched one of the most successful on-screen romantic pairings – Kapoor and Nargis – who then not only went on to appear together in a number of critically and commercially successful films in the following decade, but also collaborated closely on production and direction. *Aag* also offered many of the now-familiar tropes in a slick modern package: conflict between family traditions and individual dreams, challenges and eventual victory of true love, and the threat of social, political and economic precarity (in this case, the love interest had been rendered homeless by Partition). The duo followed up this phenomenal success, replicating some of the same themes and tropes in *Awara* (Vagabond, 1951), about a petty criminal who discovers that the judge presiding over his case is his estranged father. The film was a huge success not only in India but in markets like the Soviet Union, west Asia and Africa where its memories linger in cinema and wider culture and turn up in unexpected places. For example, Jia Zhangke's 2000 Chinese film *Platform* explores the impact of the Cultural Revolution on a group of young performers from the end of the 1970s to the 1990s. In its opening sequence, *Awara* plays in a local theatre of the small Chinese town. In 1950s Turkey, young men adopted

---

4 My grandmother had vivid memories of the earthquake that had silted up wells and thrown up deep fissures in the ground. She often recounted escaping from the house – clutching her infant sister and a cage with her parrot – out into the rice fields as the ground around her opened up in deep cracks.

the baggy suits, trousers upturned at the ankles and rakish hats and declared themselves 'Avare', leading the authorities to act against 'vagrant' activity while columnists and politicians fumed about the adverse impact on both morality and national culture. Undeterred, Turkish filmmakers produced multiple adaptations of the film and musicians created local versions of the title song. It is still not uncommon to hear a Turkish version of 'Awara hoon ...' (I am a vagabond) floating out from a shop in the Grand Bazaar in Istanbul or a café in Ankara.

While Kapoor appeared in and made a number of films over the next few years, most with a vague idealism regarding the new nation, a meeting with Frank Capra and the work of Vittorio De Sica changed the course of his filmmaking. He created a recurring screen persona of a good-hearted Chaplinesque tramp to explore the pressing political themes of poverty, unemployment, corruption and acute economic inequalities with a light comedic touch. Kapoor's loveable tramp would turn up as a small-time conman choosing between true love and ill-gained wealth in a string of films including *Shree 420* (Mr 420, 1955; the number referring to the section of Indian Penal Code about property fraud), a terrified peasant who wanders into an affluent block of flats in search of water in *Jagte Raho* (Stay Awake, 1956), an impoverished young man accused of murder in *Anari* (Naive, 1959), a wandering singer who falls in with a group of bandits in *Jis Desh Men Ganga Behti Hai* (The Land Where the Ganga Flows, 1960) and *Chhalia* (Conman, 1960) about a criminal who helps a woman abandoned by her family after Partition.[5]

In the Soviet Union, Kapoor's films not only formed the basis of bilateral politico-cultural exchange between the two countries but also lingered long in popular memory. In the early 1980s,

[5] This final was also the directorial debut of Manmohan Desai, who grew into a master of the masala movie and perfected the many tropes and techniques that are now considered hallmarks of cinema known as Bollywood.

when my family lived in Islamabad, Soviet diplomats would often spontaneously belt out not only 'Awara hoon' but also 'Mera joota hai japani' (My shoes are Japanese) from Shree 420, taking great pleasure in the line 'sar pe lal topi rusi, phir bhi dil hai Hindustani ...' (the red cap on my head is Russian, but my heart is still Indian). The song served as a friendly greeting and declaration of national 'friendship', and had the additional advantage of flummoxing American and European diplomats. Against the backdrop of the Soviet–Afghan war, the overarching threat of mutually assured destruction, and the end game of the Cold War, breaking into a Bollywood song was a petty yet funny public gesture in a setting that was and remains all too stiffly formal and tense. It was also a reminder that many parts of the world shared an entire film and music canon that few in western Europe or North America knew. And that knowledge produced a transnational in-joke and a secret sense of empowerment.

A decade later, the Soviet Union had broken up, the Berlin Wall had fallen, and Germany had again become a single state. The world had become effectively unipolar, and apparently we were witnessing the end of history. I was working as a journalist in Mexico City at the time and one evening had gone to the Goethe Institute for an instantly forgettable event. As I walked out into the warm streets, I heard someone whistling a familiar melancholic tune, 'Cheen aur Arab hamara, Hindustan hamara, rehne ko ghar nahin, saara jahaan hamara ...' (China, Arabia is ours, Hindustan is ours, we have no home, but all of the world is ours) from Phir Subah Hogi (Morning Will Come Again, 1958). Surprised, I turned to find a Russian embassy official who had attended the same event. I countered by singing out the first line of 'Aasman pe hai khuda, aur zamin par hum' (God is in the skies, we on the ground, he doesn't often look our way). We walked together for a few blocks, singing Raj Kapoor songs, two strangers brought together briefly by memories of classic Hindi films of the 1950s until we went our separate ways.

Raj Kapoor was not the only star who rose to fame in the post-Independence era. His contemporary Dilip Kumar[6] charted a very different path. Although he starred in patriotic films like *Shaheed* (Martyr, 1948), about a young freedom fighter, *Naya Daur* (The New Era, 1957), where a horse-cart driver who starts opposing a bus route through remote rural hinterlands ends up building a new road, and swashbuckling action films like *Aan* (Pride/The Savage Princess 1952) and *Azaad* (Free, 1955), about a Robin Hood-like bandit, he more frequently played the suffering romantic lead which became his trademark. He played the jilted lover in love triangle films like *Andaz* (Style, 1949), *Babul* (Father's House, 1950) and *Sangam* (Confluence, 1964), a lover faced with impossible odds in movies like *Daag* (The Stain, 1952), about a young man addicted to alcohol, *Yahudi* (The Jew, 1958), about a Roman prince in love with a Jewish girl, and Emperor Akbar's young son in love with a courtesan in *Mughal-E-Azam* (1960). Kumar's films promised – and delivered – an excess of sorrowful tears both on screen and from the audience. The grim *Deedar* (Love, 1951) starred Kumar as a love-lorn singer who blinds himself and kicked off a string of similarly tragic films including an adaptation of *Devdas* (1955), about a love-lorn aristocrat who drinks himself to death. Kumar was soon dubbed the 'tragedy king'.

Kumar continued acting for the next few decades with regular and spectacular success. He posted another round of blockbuster hits in the 1980s when he reinvented himself as an 'angry old man' (a play on Bachchan's popular title of the 'angry young man'), taking on roles as the dissatisfied ageing patriarch in films like *Kranti* (Revolution, 1981), a period film about the fight against British rule, *Shakti* (Power, 1982), about a dedicated cop whose son – played by Bachchan – takes to crime, and *Mashaal* (Torch, 1984), about an honest journalist who turns to crime

---

[6] Born in Peshawar in north-western Pakistan as Mohammad Yusuf Khan, he was talent-spotted by legendary producer and actress Devika Rani, who also encouraged him to adopt a Hindu-sounding screen name.

after a series of personal tragedies. However, Kumar's 'tragedy king' reputation loomed large over these and a lovingly performed death scene remained a necessity for almost every movie.

This excess of sorrow meant that Kumar's films were unpopular in our home. My aunts described them as 'weepies' and my mother declared that there was nothing to be gained from watching such fatalistic, pessimistic fare. Even when video collections of film songs became popular in the 1980s, my mother would diligently fast-forward tracks featuring Kumar. For years, my only exposure to his films remained the listening sessions of the *Mughal-E-Azam* album with my uncles and aunts. When I finally watched his films at university, I found myself, much to my horror and embarrassment, agreeing with my mother. I too had no stomach for such fatalistic, pessimistic fare.

The third superstar to come up in post-Independence India, Dev Anand was a contrast to both Raj Kapoor and Dilip Kumar. From the start of his career, Anand nurtured a westernised and urbane persona, often adopting fashions from Hollywood. The persona worked perfectly for a stream of films including the crime thiller *Baazi* (Gamble, 1951), about a down-at-heel gambler, *C.I.D.* (1956), about a cop attempting to bring down a criminal mastermind, *Nau Do Gyarah* (Nine and Two Make Eleven, 1957), about a man who finds his inheritance stolen by murderous relatives, and *Jaal* (The Trap, 1952), about a mysterious man from the big city hiding in a remote fishing village. Working with a close team that included his brother, the filmmaker Chetan Anand, and friend, the auteur Guru Dutt, Anand was key to the creation of a brand of Indian noir that aesthetically and thematically explored the underbelly of the new nation. Alongside, Anand starred in romantic comedies like *Solva Saal* (Sixteenth Year, 1958), about a runaway bride, and *Teen Deviyan* (Three Goddesses, 1965), about a playboy trying to decide between proposals from three women. For decades, Anand starred in, directed and produced films that pushed social boundaries with films like *Guide* (1965), an adaptation of the R.K. Narayan novel about a small-town tour guide who helps a dancer escape an unhappy marriage. An English version was simultaneously directed and produced by Tad Danielewski and scripted by Pearl S. Buck for the American market.

Anand and his frequent co-star Waheeda Rehman were favourites of my parents, perhaps because even his noir films retained a fiercely optimistic streak. His cosmopolitan screen persona that freely moved between small Indian towns to diplomatic cocktail parties in Europe also perhaps served as a model for their own increasingly international lives, a reminder that such constant cultural and geographical negotiations were not only possible but could be done with panache. Unsurprisingly, it was mostly songs from Anand's films that Dad sang on those horse rides through the Himalayas and later on, during long drives through the Khyber Pass. As I grew older, my siblings and I joined my mother in humming and singing along with him. Gradually I learned to identify the exact level of stress my parents were under and the severity of threats we all faced, simply by Dad's choice of song.

Anand's career as an actor, director and producer continued well into the 1990s, although with diminishing returns. However, perhaps his legacy was established with the second film he directed, *Hare Rama Hare Krishna* (1971), about a man tracing his sister, a troubled young woman who has run away from home. This is also the film that made me a second-generation Anand fan (although less for him as an actor and more for his casting choice). The film introduced Zeenat Aman as Anand's ultra-modern, hippie young sister and purported to offer an anti-drugs message. However, Aman's stylish clothes, extended and loving depictions of drug use and the thumping soundtrack ensured that few in the audience would think of '*Dum maro dum*' (Take a hit) as anything but an invitation to partake of the drugs on offer. As a toddler, I could not have watched the film but the song, which played regularly on the radio and on our Panasonic tape recorder, became an instant favourite. I grew deeply enamoured of the bright psychedelic prints on Aman's clothing, again familiar to me from posters that lined the streets and photographs in magazines. Fortunately, both were equally loved by the adults in the family, which meant I could wear pop print kurtas to kindergarten, and everyone was happy to endless rewind and play the song on the cassette player for me.

Preferences for different kinds of cinema extended to audiences: rural and semi-rural audiences seemed to prefer films about mythological stories and historical fantasies while urban ones looked to films with modern settings. Unsurprisingly, as the country's first prime minister Jawaharlal Nehru pushed major industrialisation that resulted in the rapid growth of urban centres, this rural-urban division soon acquired a whiff of snobbery. For years, I noticed the streets lined with bright posters of *Jai Santoshi Maa* (1975), a film about a goddess who protects female devotees. My school bus drove past the theatre that screened the film for years on end. Crowds made up mostly of women in their finest saris, often holding plates full of sweets, flowers and other accoutrements of religious offering, would teem at the entrance. Songs from the film were blasted from the speakers at religious festivals. And yet nobody in my family, school or neighbourhood had ever watched the film. Even my grandmother would gently roll her eyes at the idea of blurring the boundaries between devotion and entertainment, grumbling that the women queuing up to offer prayers to the goddess on screen should 'just go to the temple'.

The division was not new and had played out in homes across the country before. My paternal grandfather remained unmoved and even suspicious of films until his demise. He had returned to farming soon after Independence and the nearest cinema hall was a few kilometres away from his village. However, even while he worked in multiple cities across north India in the past, he had remained unimpressed by the silver screen. Occasionally, exasperated by his children's pleas, he'd dispatch them to the nearest cinema with a guard who had been instructed that they only watch something educational or at least something with a moral dimension. This generally meant a mythological or historical film. Dad gleefully recalls the time they were sent off to watch *Aan*, a title that means pride although its release title for UK and USA is more apt for the roller-coaster adventure film that it was, involving kings, murders, and a romance between a poor man and a headstrong princess: *The Savage Princess*. Dad still laughs when he remembers the absolute joy of watching a film that wasn't religious and the excitement with which he and other children returned home to recount the wonders they had seen on screen. Sadly, the suspect morality and lack of educational value of the film became quickly apparent and my grandfather promptly stopped the children from going to the cinema! In contrast, my maternal grandfather was an avid fan of cinema, although of the more contemporary kind, often teasing his children that they did not understand real fandom. He would declare that young people lacked dedication because they claimed to be fans after watching *Devdas* with Dilip Kumar[7] in the eponymous role a mere four or five times. He would proudly note that, in contrast, he had watched K.L. Saigal's 1935 version at least twenty times!

Perhaps my obsessive viewing of *Lawaris*, a film I have watched at least fifty times in its entirety and twice as many times in parts, was merely keeping up family traditions. However, a voice in my head notes that the effort and resources required to watch films on the big screen make for more dedicated fandom than my much easier route to slotting in the VHS cassette and turning on the television.

* * *

The first post-1947 generation came of age not in the utopia imagined by India's freedom fighters but rather in a country

---

[7] Dilip Kumar also stars in *Aan*, as the impoverished young man determined to woo the arrogant princess (played by Nimmi).

battered and bruised by abject poverty, famine and war. The 1960s had been a brutal decade. The euphoria of pushing out the Portuguese from Goa in 1961 was followed just months later by Chinese military incursion into disputed territory along India's mountain regions – at least in part as retaliation for support the country extended to the Dalai Lama and the Tibetan government-in-exile. The month-long military conflict ended when China unilaterally declared ceasefire but not before Indian forces had suffered heavy losses. Nehru's requests to Kennedy for military assistance had been rebuffed and the war nudged the country closer to the Soviet Union, although it maintained its commitment to the Non-Aligned Movement, a grouping of mostly postcolonial nations that were attempting to steer an increasingly narrow path between two superpowers. Nehru died soon after, in 1964, and was succeeded by fellow reformer and freedom fighter Lal Bahadur Shastri. However, there was little respite as a second war with Pakistan broke out in 1965. This one ended in India's favour despite extensive losses on both sides. Meanwhile the country was heavily dependent on monsoons for its agriculture and on US food aid to make up the gaps in food supplies. Through the decade, successive failed monsoons and draughts left the country's leadership reeling and its population on the brink of starvation. Unemployment remained high, national literacy rates could not rise rapidly enough, resources remained limited, and economic uncertainty was not only a condition for individuals but also the country as a whole. The optimism of the previous decade faded as the promises of independence grew dimmer in the face of foreign and domestic challenges.

Indian cinema, curiously, came into its own in the midst of this tumult and the 1960s are often described as the 'golden age of Hindi cinema'.[8] Despite economic constraints, production

---

[8] This is a contestable and perhaps generational distinction as fans and scholars may choose otherwise. My personal 'golden age of Hindi cinema' is the period 1972–1982, which saw the production and release of many films now considered classics, some of which are my personal favourites.

budgets steadily increased and by end of the decade, colour films became the norm.[9] Furthermore, the decade also witnessed a steady growth of an urban middle class as literacy rates steadily rose. The controversial Hindu Marriage Act of 1955 – dealt with in a surprisingly heavy-handed way by auteur Guru Dutt in his romantic comedy *Mr & Mrs '55*, released the same year – had granted Hindu women the right to divorce. Although it had little impact on the divorce rates of the time, the act was a significant step towards expanding women's rights. It also provided greater impetus to other aspects of women's rights, including abortion which was finally legalised in 1971. This was also the first decade where notable numbers of educated women joined the professional ranks ranging from the civil services, posts in the banking sector to medicine and law. In themselves, these can seem small steps but they formed some of the cornerstones of the vast – and irreversible – social, political, economic and cultural transformation of the country with immense collective anxiety as a corollary: what did modernity mean? What would be gained from it and at what cost? What of the traditions that would inevitably be abandoned on the road to change? How could this road to modernity be negotiated when the path and destination were unclear and the dangers unidentified? The clash between the safety of traditions and risks of modernity played out not only at national and collective levels but also at intimate familial and individual scales.

Even my maternal grandfather, committed to progressive values including women's education, found himself torn between familial and social demands and his own views. The crisis began when a male nephew failed to secure entrance to university the same year as my eldest aunt was to begin her undergraduate

---

[9] Given that colour film stock was produced overseas and was set to primarily white skin tones, Indian filmmakers struggled to render natural skin tones on screen. While the best of technicians evolved techniques to work around the difficulties, it wasn't until the arrival of digital technology in the 1990s that a fuller range of South Asian skin tones could be rendered on film.

degree. She would be the first woman in the extended clan to not only finish schooling but head to university. Under pressure from the male relatives who argued that it would shame the family – and the nephew – to send a young girl to university when young men of the family were incapable, Grandfather inexplicably buckled and announced that my aunt would not be able to pursue further education. Unfortunately, despite a quarter of a century of marriage, he had not factored in his wife or her reaction.

Born in a village in Bihar before Independence, my grandmother had never been to school and had only been taught the rudiments of reading, writing and arithmetic. Over the years, she had educated herself in two languages, learning not only about literature and culture but also nuances of imperial and then postcolonial politics. She was an impassioned follower of the Congress Party, the political organisation led by Gandhi and Nehru that had led mass opposition to colonial rule and held elected office after Independence. She was also a fervent believer in the power of satyagraha, the Gandhian strategy of non-violent resistance, which had been effectively deployed against imperial rule. The same strategy was now brought home as my grandmother declared a hunger strike against her husband's decision. My aunt, frantic at being denied her dream, quickly joined her mother. My mother, younger by a couple of years and still at school, was the next to join the collective action. Soon the younger siblings, even down to my youngest aunts who were still at primary school, had joined the political uprising. In the face of nearly complete resistance from his own wife and children, Grandfather capitulated and my aunt became the first of the family to not only complete her graduate degree but also a doctorate.

The victory also gave fuel to my grandmother, who ensured that all her children and grandchildren – regardless of gender – pursued higher education. During a recent family conversation, my mother and her siblings marvelled at how that one act of resistance had set all of us on entirely unpredictable life paths.

Unsurprisingly, the family – nuclear and extended – became the preferred metaphor of the filmmakers of the era as they tried to represent the new realities, dilemmas and challenges of a new nation as well as to give voice to prior traumas. On-screen intergenerational conflict became a handy stand-in for the wider clash between tradition and modernity, which in films played out as parental opposition to the protagonist's life choices. The conflict would frequently centre on a young couple's quest for love versus their parent's insistence on a suitable arranged marriage that would ensure economic or social stability. The format allowed for innumerable permutations: parents being duped by a conman presenting himself as a desirable match, scheming greedy relatives attempting to defame or falsely accuse the lover of immorality or even crimes, and endless forms of confusion caused by misplaced missives, false impressions, and lack of communication.

Metaphorically placing the wider conflict in familial settings also provided ample opportunities to explore – and perhaps highlight – the risks of premarital sex, a theme that emerged strongly as the decade progressed as a response to growing access to the Pill amongst the middle class and the increased clamour for legalising abortion.

However, the decade's most enduring narrative, perhaps as a wishful response to Partition, remains the lost-and-found trope involving children separated by misfortune – often at a fair or lost in crowds – or by the connivance of enemies – most often represented as a greedy relative – who would grow up to find their way back into the family fold. Although the trope had long been popular in Indian cinema, it fully flowered in the hands of producer and director Yash Chopra with *Waqt* (Time, 1965). The film follows a wealthy man with a loving wife and three young sons who is warned not to take his good fortune for granted. Soon after, an earthquake devastates his lavish home and separates the family. The story weaves through numerous twists and turns until the family is finally reunited. The film's success kicked off a generation of lost-and-found films, each with multiple stars, exotic locations, lavish sets and ever more convoluted plot twists intended to delay the inevitable reunion. Some of these include *Yaadon Ki Baaraat* (Procession of Memories, 1973*)*, *Amar Akbar Anthony* (1979) and *Naseeb* (Fate, 1981).

A sub-genre soon developed around major stars who started playing double roles in films involving identical twins separated at birth and often with diametrically opposed characters. Director Tapi Chanakya remade his own 1964 Telegu film featuring the star (and later politician) N.T. Rama Rao in Hindi as *Ram Aur Shyam* (1967) with Dilip Kumar playing the bumbling, shy Ram and the brave, urbane identical twin Shyam. The film's success kicked off a string of similar movies including *Seeta Aur Geeta* (1972) with the era's biggest female star, Hema Malini, in a similar double role of a shy traditional woman bullied by her stepfamily and the identical but tomboyish street performer Geeta. The format also became a way of asserting star power at the box office, most memorably in *Chaalbaaz* (Trickster, 1989), with Sridevi playing the shy, wealthy Anju and the tough, street-smart twin Manju. The identical-twins or the doppelganger narrative also worked particularly well to showcase superstars like Amitabh Bachchan who dominated the screens at the time. Bachchan played the roles of identical twins separated at birth in films like *The Great Gambler* (1975), the ruthless international gangster Don and the naive Vijay in *Don* (1977)[10] or, adding a third dimesion to the trope, also played the role of the father plus the identical twins in the absurd madcap caper *Mahaan* (Great, 1983). In a daring move, director Rakesh Roshan presented his son Hrithik Roshan in a similar double role in *Kaho Na Pyaar Hai* . . . (Say It . . . You're In Love, 2000) to showcase the rookie actor as both sensitive romantic lead and a chiselled action star. In this case, the gambit was intended to emphasise the range of roles the actor could play.

---

[10] The role was reprised by Shah Rukh Khan in *Don* (2006), with the mob boss role extended in *Don 2: The King Is Back* (2008).

A particularly Indian variation of the doppelganger trope involves the same star playing double roles as a reincarnated soul. Initially attempted – and with great success – with *Madhumati* (1958) starring the actress and dancer Vyjanthimala, who not only played a pair of doppelgangers but also the identical, eponymous ghost. *Madhumati*'s narrative involved an unresolved murder, a haunting, flashbacks to the murdered character's life, and a resolution that not only brings the murderer to justice but also offers a reunion with the earlier grieving family. The success of films as far apart and at least as superficially different as *Karz* (Debt, 1980), *Karan Arjun* (1995) and *Om Shanti Om* (2007) suggests that the reincarnation narrative with its promise of justice delayed but not denied continues to appeal to audiences.

Waqt's impact was not limited to its narrative. The film brought together a glittering array of stars, a decision that would kickstart the 'multi-starrers', or films with ensemble casts. While this involved careful balancing by the filmmaker to ensure each star got their due on screen, it also diminished commercial risk as the film would not depend entirely on the box-office appeal of a single star and instead attract fans of multiple stars. This became the popular strategy through the 1970s and 1980s for filmmakers like Chopra as well as masala film auteurs like Manmohan Desai, the maker of the ultimate lost-and-found movie, *Amar Akbar Anthony* (1977), as well as Ramesh Sippy who, inspired by Sergio Leone's spaghetti westerns, assembled possibly one of the most powerful star line-ups for his 'curry-western' *Sholay* (Embers, 1975). More recent directors continue to use the strategy in films like *Omkara* (a 2006 adaptation of *Othello*) and *Rang De Basanti* (Paint It Saffron, 2006), a film-within-a-film that connects popular figures from the freedom struggle with a group of students who decide to act against government corruption. Casting popular actors across different generations, as in *Mohabbatein* (Love Stories, 2000), about a series of love stories set in a school, and *Kabhi Khushi Kabhie Gham* (Sometimes Happiness, Sometimes Sadness, 2001), a family saga about a divided family, is a variation of this trope and works by capitalising on the transgenerational appeal of the various stars. It also creates space to weave together other popular narrative tropes as subplots, including lovers facing parental opposition, virtuous protagonists cheated out of their inheritance by unscrupulous relatives, and the perennially attractive question of nature vs nurture as often one of the siblings ends up being raised a criminal. The plot also allows for a range of representations of religion, economic status and even choices between modernity and tradition simply by casting stars with particular personas.

The 1960s also saw a plethora of new stars join the industry, expanding audience choices far beyond the ruling star triumvirate of Anand, Kumar and Kapoor. Kapoor's younger brothers Shashi and Shammi had been acting in films for years but found significant and enduring success during this period. Shashi Kapoor had started as a child actor in films before joining the family's theatre company. He found success with Merchant-Ivory Production's 1963 release *The Householder*, making him perhaps the first Indian star to cross over to Western cinema. He continued playing romantic leads in Hindi films and eventually set up his own production house to make films that trod a fine line between commercial and art house. Meanwhile, Shammi Kapoor had gained a youthful fan following with a string of formulaic romantic comedies like *Junglee* (Wild, 1961), *Dil Deke Dekho* (Give Your Heart, 1959) and *Kashmir Ki Kali* (The Flower of Kashmir, 1964) set in picturesque locales and, most memorably, the romantic thriller *Teesri Manzil* (The Third Floor, 1966). Although he continued acting until his death in 2011, Shammi is often remembered by a younger generation of Indians for setting up India's first cyber-café and founding the Internet Users Community of India and Ethical Hackers Association. When the internet giant Yahoo launched in India in the 1990s, its founder Jerry Yang explained that the company name had been inspired by the song '*Chahe mujhe koi junglee kahe*' (They may call me wild) that featured the actor's exuberant cry, 'Yahoo!' from the 1957 rom-com *Tumsa Nahin Dekha* (No One Like You, 1957).

Meanwhile, although Rajendra Kumar had started his career in the 1940s and scored a major hit as the younger son in *Mother India*, he found greater success in the 1960s, playing a string of romantic roles and domestic dramas. Curiously, although he was nicknamed 'Jubilee Kumar' for his ability to deliver blockbuster hits (the term 'jubilee' signifies the number of weeks of continuous screenings by a film, with silver for twenty-five, gold for fifty, and platinum for seventy-five), few of these seemed to have survived in audience memory. Jeetendra, another 'pretty' romantic lead, was headed for a similar fate. However, his career took a turn when he played a secret agent in the spy thriller *Farz* (Duty, 1968), by not only establishing his signature look of pairing white trousers with white patent leather shoes, but also earning him the label 'Jumping Jack' for his energetic dancing. *Farz* made him a bankable commodity for mid-budget films and paved the way for his later work in formulaic 1980s movies with directors from southern Indian film industries.

Perhaps the most significant and enduring star to join cinema in the 1960s was Dharmendra, who in his initial days in the industry had been compared to Paul Newman and James Dean by the country's press for his exceptionally handsome looks.[11] He was also a fine actor – albeit one who performed best for an exacting director – and was cast by some of the finest auteurs of Hindi cinema. Dharmendra appeared in Bimal Roy's *Bandini* (Prisoner, 1963) as a prison-doctor who falls in love with a prisoner convicted of murdering her lover's wife; in Chetan Anand's epic war drama *Haqeeqat* (Reality, 1964), about a platoon fighting in the Indo–Chinese war of 1962; and in O.P. Ralhan's daring *Phool Aur Patthar* (Flower and Stone, 1966) as a criminal who falls in love with a widow. Although the final film is most fondly remembered for the scene where the actor removes his shirt – 'topless Dharmendra' became a favourite on mass-produced

---

[11] Dharmendra has noted his early bafflement at the comparisons because he had never seen films of the Hollywood stars to whom he was compared.

postcards and calendars for years afterwards – it not only explored female desire and love after widowhood but also a relationship between an older woman (played by ageing screen legend Meena Kumari) and a younger man. By the end of the decade, Dharmendra had reinvented himself as a masculine action star, often playing up his physicality and rural origins, a decision that served him well into the 1980s as audiences adored his increasingly hammy macho roles while his shirtless image continued to grace postcards, calendars, and poster stalls in bazaars across the country.

The decade also ushered in a new kind of female star, one whose impact would extend well beyond the screen, or even fashion and style. While the decade would see actresses like Waheeda Rehman, Nanda and Asha Parekh consolidate their star status, a new generation of actresses including Saira Banu, Mumtaz and Hema Malini began their careers. They were joined by actresses from affluent and often convent-educated back-grounds: Simi Garewal was from a military family, Sharmila Tagore from an aristocratic one; Priya Rajvansh had not only been educated at some of the country's finest English-medium schools but also studied at the Royal Academy of Dramatic Arts (RADA) in London. They were not reliant on films for their livelihood, which in some ways empowered them to defy industry practices and wider social norms, which in turn made them both pioneers and role models in and outside cinema.

Sadhana, perhaps Hindi cinema's first fashion trendsetter, fell between the two groups as she was 'convent educated' and had started a degree at university, but a reversal in family fortunes not only ended her education but also led her to seek work, first as a typist and then in cinema. She made her debut with the romantic comedy *Love in Simla* (1960), where she transforms *Pygmalion*-like from a frumpy young woman to a glamorous one. Inspired by Audrey Hepburn, Sadhana opted for a short fringe to mark her on-screen transformation. The hairstyle not only became her signature look but also an instant craze across the country, with millions of women rushing to copy it. Even today, there are likely many in India who have never heard of 'the Rachel' but very few who are unfamiliar with the 'Sadhana cut'. However, the actress set another – perhaps more far-reaching – trend in *Waqt*. Cast as a beautiful heiress, Sadhana sought to modernise the salwar-kameez, the traditional combination of long tunic and loose trousers, at the time mostly worn by Muslim women. She reimagined the tunic in a tight sleeveless version and paired it with the churidar (the form-fitting trousers traditionally worn under long, flared outfits). Faced with a sceptical director, Sadhana asked the costume designer Bhanu Athaiya (who in 1983 became the first Indian to win an Oscar for her work, in *Gandhi*) to create the outfit as she had imagined it. The new outfit – instantly approved by the director and worn by the actress throughout the movie – was seen as the perfect blend of traditional and modern, and became an instant albeit controversial hit especially amongst young women of the newly modernising middle classes.

The outfit was shocking not only for its body-hugging tunic, bare arms and skin-hugging trousers that showed off the legs but also because all the garments – kameez, salwar, churidar – were associated with Muslim women and rarely worn by Hindus. It may seem strange to look back at the time and imagine that clothes (such as the now ubiquitous salwar-kameez) could be particular or even limited to specific religious and ethnic communities. Or that a single film or film star could ever break down long-embedded ideas of community-specific clothing. And yet images from the era show an almost instantaneous change in women's fashion. Within months of the film's release, the traditional sari had been replaced on college campuses, magazine advertisements, on dressmaker dummies and fashion models, and of course on actresses in subsequent films by Sadhana's new version.

Sadhana's impact on fashion also heralded a different kind of fandom and impact of movies. Her female co-star from *Waqt*, Sharmila Tagore, would shock the nation the year after by posing in a bikini for the cover of *Filmfare*, India's major film magazine. She followed this up with a bright blue swimsuit for a waterski sequence in *An Evening in Paris* (1967). By the time Tagore starred in *Aradhana* (Worship, 1969) as an unmarried mother who gives up her son for adoption, her style of glamorously draped sari and tiny blouses became widely replicated across the country as urban audiences turned to films and their stars for sartorial guidance.

By the early 1970s, films and their aesthetic had become so much a part of our lives – fashion, language, home décor – that only the most egregious examples caught our attention. Our neighbours' spectacular new home was one such instance. I do not remember the year, but I know it was sometime between the end of the war that led to the formation of Bangladesh in 1971 and the hushed terror of the Emergency. Dad had returned from the war but he was off again on mysterious 'operations', which meant that my mother and I were back in the plains at my grand-mother's house. There was much curiosity about the neighbours' extravagant new house and I was dragged along when our family was invited over to celebrate the new home.

I have little memory of the visit (my only one), but I remember clearly the pride with which we were led to a new bathroom. It had a sparkling white 'Western style' toilet, a commode with a mechanical flush-tank, which was an anomaly those days in India (where toilets were usually built in the traditional French style that required squatting – though we called them 'Indian style'). Sitting toilets were not common, especially in homes at the time although our old British-built bungalow in the army cantonment up in the mountains had two huge wooden thrones – with brass plaques that read 'Mr' and 'Mrs' – that sat side by side on an elevated platform in the cavernous bathroom. The open seats led to metal containers that had to be slid out for cleaning. They terrified me and never failed to set my mother chuckling, presum-ably at the thought of an English officer and his wife clearing their bowels together, in scatological majesty. But our neighbours' sparkling toilet came with a suspended metal tank with a chain that sent water whooshing into the bowl and down a pipe, removing the need for refuse collectors and water buckets. I was so intrigued by the ingenuity of the contraption that I almost ignored the vast empty, shiny bowl-like object that took up most of the room.

'A bathtub,' someone told me although its purpose baffled me until one of my aunts explained. Adult talk quickly turned to 'bathtub' songs and scenes from the films, and the younger women were soon giggling and singing out lines from *Padosan* (Neighbour, 1968) with Saira Banu and *Abhinetri* (Actress, 1970) with Hema Malini, where the stars cavort in massive bathtubs full of white frothy bubbles. I did not recognise then that the tub was a movie-fuelled symbol not only of wealth but of glamour. Amidst the chatter and singing, I looked to my grandmother and noticed a familiar half-smile lurking on her lips. I edged closer to her, knowing that expression meant she was about to pose a difficult question. I wasn't wrong as an instant later she wondered out loud about the amount of water required to fill the tub. Would running a bath in this house mean that no one else in the neighbourhood would get any water that day? The excitement dampened as she threw out her final question: how could washing in stagnant water make one clean? Silence followed as my grandmother led me out by the hand, muttering under her breath about 'more money than sense' and the 'stupidity of blindly following *fillums*.' Much later, I learned that our neighbours' precious bathtub remained unused as it was meant only to be shown off to guests. Almost like a movie set.

A Heart's Story is Made of
Two Words, Either Love
or Youth[1]

BETTER KNOWN AS A religious centre, Varanasi of my childhood
was – and in many ways remains – a city of constant performance
and spectacle. The city, like most things in India, has had many
names, including Kashi (city of light), Anandavana (the forest of
bliss), and Mahashamshana (the great cremation ground). In
classical Buddhists texts it appears as Benaras or Banaras, a centre
not only of religion but also trade. Its modern and most prosaic
name simply means the city situated between the Varuna and
Assi rivers that flow into the Ganga.

My memories of the city are populated with the colourful
religious processions that regularly filled the streets, their purpose
and affiliation only distinguishable by ecstatic albeit indecipherable
songs for Hindu deities and saints and by the colours – saffron,
white, maroon – worn by the devout. Once a year, these songs
would be replaced by the rhythmic grieving chants for Prophet
Muhammad's grandson Hussain during Muharram.[2] Similarly, the
arrival of the monsoons would kick off an entire month of festivals
to celebrate the rains although in a more ecumenical fashion. Fairs

---

[1] '*Do lafzon ki hai dil ki kahani, ya hai mohabbat ya hai jawani . . .*' from *The
Great Gambler* (1975).
[2] Also known as Ashura and marked over ten days of the first month of the
Islamic calendar.

and festivals would spring up on empty fields and in front of the innumerable temples in the city. Ferris wheels and carousels jostled with loud hawkers selling all manner of goods and hastily thrown-up stages for folk enactments of tales from mythology.

But the city did not only offer religious spectacle. On most days, itinerant entertainers roamed the streets, their voices lifting in equal measures for songs and pleas for alms. When I was a child, snake charmers and bear and monkey handlers would regularly walk through the neighbourhood. As my grandmother disapproved of these, I would have to climb a high window to watch them perform on the street. On one occasion, most likely having noted my curiosity, Dad who was briefly back in town, invited a monkey handler into the garden. I found the tumbles and tricks of the pair of monkeys, dressed in children's clothes decorated with much tinsel, terrifying and unbearably sad and I remained worried about their welfare for days afterwards.

Beyond the ornate metal gates of my grandmother's rambling house, the city teemed with a variety of performances. During summers, we often woke up before dawn to wind our way through still dark streets down to the river. Melodious azaan – the Muslim call for prayer – would mingle with the chiming of innumerable brass temple bells. As we passed particular lanes and approached the river, strains of Bhairavi – the classical raga honouring Shiva and played traditionally at dawn – would join the orchestra in the air with the plaintive shehnai and sitar combination, occasionally complete with a resonant voice. My youngest aunt, closest to me in age, would often walk with me on these mornings, clutching my hand in hers. She was learning Bharatanatyam and would spend hours locked in her room, working on her craft. If I pushed the panels of the door just right, they would open enough space for me to peer in. I would spend hours watching her practice her facial expressions, hand gestures and posture, repeating the sets of graceful movements over and over until she was – inexplicably to me – satisfied with her abilities. On our walks to the river, she would identify the music that rose into the sky around us and explain the significance. Often, she would forget that I was listening and float off into her own mind, imagining dance steps, the fingers of her free hand marking time against her thigh.

In the early hours, we'd run into early risers of the city – a mix of craftsmen, workers, and the devout making their way to the river to bathe and pray or to the mosque for the first prayers. On exceptionally fortunate mornings, we'd run into musicians playing tabla, sitar and shehnai on one of the many platforms at the crossroads, lost to the world and unaware of their audience, the streets usually empty except for cycle rickshaw-pullers and beggars. We would pause to savour the music. Many years later – often in concert halls in places like New York – I realised that those musicians, lost in their own music at street corners and crossroads of Varanasi, counted as some of the country's greatest exponents of classical music.

But I was most intrigued by a more unusual, slightly dishevelled group, often in white muslin kurtas that had been pristine at some point (one could always tell from the finely pleated sleeves that require meticulous ironing) but were wrinkled and stained with paan – the famed betel nut chew – who would be seen on the streets in the fading night. They would often hum and smile while strolling leisurely, as if they were in no hurry to reach a destination. These were the *rasics* – patrons, aesthetes and fans of the many classical dance, music and performance schools that have long existed in the city – on their way home from all-night concerts. I promised myself that one day, when I was old enough, I would join their ranks.

But the year's greatest spectacle occurred in autumn during the ten days of Dusshera, the festival that celebrates the story of the god Rama as detailed in the epic *Ramayana* and his eventual victory over Ravana. Known as the *Ramlila*,[3] literally Rama's play

---

[3] The Ramlilas are performed across India and in various parts of Asia including Myanmar and Indonesia, often without distinction of caste, creed or economic status of performers, organisers and audience. The superstar Shah Rukh Khan has spoken of his first acting role as part of his local Ramlila. They were added by the UN to the list of the Intangible Cultural Heritage of Humanity, with the performances in Ramnagar and Varanasi deemed as some of the 'most representative'.

and based not on the Sanskrit epic but on the *Ramcharitmanas*, a popular vernacular retelling in Awadhi by the sixteenth-century poet Tulsidas, the event turned the city into a giant stage. Episodes from the hero's life were enacted on temporary stages, the costumes and props were all made by local communities, who also acted as the production crew responsible for lighting, stage-craft and make-up. The enactments were free to the public and performed by amateurs selected from the community and trained in their parts over three months. During these months the cast learned to inhabit the characters, even answering only to their assigned character-names, a technique that would have made Stanislavski proud!

Various parts of the city of Varanasi are named after sites from the epic, most famously Lanka, a neighbourhood spread just outside the entrance to the Banaras Hindu University (BHU), one of the country's most important higher education institutions. During the rest of the year, Lanka remained a modern, even affluent, part of the city with shops lining the main road and old mansions and estates secreted beyond hoardings. One of the few cinema halls that habitually played films in English, and was favoured by the university crowd, stood squarely in the middle of this stretch of the city. Yet once a year, for just ten days, the area would magically transform into Ravana's capital and the main battleground for the mythological reenactment. University students with film-inspired haircuts – often worn scandalously long by the men and short by the women – sporting jeans, flared trousers, handloom cotton kurtas and bright floral shirts would mingle with visitors from the rural hinterlands identifiable not only by the old-fashioned printed saris and white dhotis but also by their wide-eyed wonder at the bright lights and busy traffic.

A fairground would spring up almost overnight and the estab-lished shops would recede into the background as makeshift stalls lined the streets, selling clay lamps and firecrackers in anticipation of Diwali (which follows soon after Dusshera according to the Hindu calendar), glass bangles and silk hair decorations, brightly coloured wooden and porcelain toys, and ittar, the traditional perfumed oil. We looked forward to the market particularly for the acquisition of bamboo bows and arrows like those used by actors of the Ramlila for their staged battle. In the days afterwards, we would practise our archery and play at heroes from the epic. We would also secretly sharpen the tips of the arrows into lethal points by scraping them on exposed bricks and rough stones. It's a wonder that we didn't injure someone or ourselves.

The battle was the only part of the Ramlila we ever saw, in part because the stage was closest to both the university campus and my grandmother's house, which meant we could escape the crowds and noise at our convenience. Moreover, Lanka – in the epic and in the city – was the site of the most fun episodes and enactments including the colourful, hilarious arrival of Rama's chaotic monkey army. We'd cheer as Hanuman, Rama's devout simian follower, set the city of Lanka aflame with a torch tied to his tail. And we'd laugh when, unable to identify the correct life-saving herb, he carried an entire mountain to the battlefield. Lanka also hosted the final act of the battle with the destruction of Ravana, achieved on the tenth night of the staging by setting fire to towering effigies packed with fireworks. We never watched the final spectacular act, not only because the final night was a fire and crowd-control hazard but also because my grandmother felt that death of even the 'enemy' was not an occasion for celebration.

The conventions of the Ramlila, the city's many religious processions and the many music concerts and dance shows stretched seamlessly to the films we watched around the year. The acting in dances, folk theatre, movies all seemed to borrow from each other. Stories that we knew from the epics and the enactments from fairs and festivals often moved to the silver screen, at times dressed up in modern trappings and at others as references that we were expected to know. I soon started noticing that the narrative structures for our films were also similar to the many folk and classical theatre forms. Even my aunt's dance and the regular music concerts in the city, although often without an explicit storyline, somehow reflected, refracted and distilled something from other forms of performance.

But most importantly, I began realising that a concert in a cosy theatre or a play on a rickety stage in a field or a movie lighting up the silver screen affected us in very similar ways. That all these different kinds of spectacles were about feelings: expressing emotions in different ways during a performance and evoking them in all of us who attended, listened and watched.

*   *   *

In my grandmother's house, we knew that all answers could be found in books, as long as one found the right book, of course. My uncles and aunts were pursuing higher studies in medicine, literature, law, and culture, and books from their university courses freely mingled with popular novels on the higher shelves while children's stories and comics lined the lower ones. I quickly discovered that the higher bookshelves also included treatises on stories, arts and theatre. One afternoon, browsing through these books, I found a slim volume that explained the origin and purpose of performance. I do not recall the title but it had a library stamp and fragile yellowed pages that threatened to melt under my sweat-damp fingers. And it was short – perhaps just over a hundred pages – so it could almost count as a children's book.

The book contained not only an explanation of stories but also how to stage and perform them. Much of it, like most of the books from the adult bookshelves I read in secret, was well beyond my understanding. However, it explained that two main values or sentiments were most suited for storytelling and representation on stage: vira, or heroic tales about righteous and brave heroes, and shringar or romantic, beautiful stories about love. The very best stories, however, not only contained elements of both but also included a host of other elements. But more importantly, the book told the story of the world's first theatre production.

At the start of the age of silver, humans grew focussed on desire and greed, which in turn led to jealousy and anger and their joys grew dim. Worried about the humans, divine and semi-divine beings, of which there are many in the Indic traditions, including devas (gods), danavas (demi-gods), gandharva (celestial beings proficient in the performing arts), yakshas (nature spirits), rakshasas (shape-shifting malevolent beings) and uragas (powerful serpentine demi-gods) asked for help from Brahma, the creator of the universe. The gods, under the leadership of their king, explained the limitations of the four Vedas, which were not access-ible to all castes and classes of society and requested something that all people could enjoy and benefit from.

In response, Brahma assembled a new art by taking the best from each of the four Vedas: from Rg Veda came the recitation of words (pathya), from Sama Veda music and song (gita), from Yajur Veda gestures and acting techniques (abhinaya), and from Atharva Veda sentiments or emotions (rasa). From this confluence was born natya, or theatre, and formed the Natyaveda, the fifth Veda. Brahma then instructed the gods to put the fifth Veda into practice but when the gods confessed their inability, the task was appointed to the sage Bharata and his sons. Bharata and his sons were instructed in the art of drama and staged the very first play using four dramatic styles: bharati, which is verbal and connected with dialogue, used by men rather than women; sattvati, distin-guished by moral rectitude and exuberance, and best for representing heroism, nobility, enthusiasm and contest; arabhati, for passionate but impetuous situations, especially rage, violence, boasting, deception, etc.; and at the request of Brahma, kaiśikī which is inspired by Shiva's dance and is particularly graceful and suited to the representation of beauty and love. The inclusion of this last in turn led to the creation of the apsaras, beautiful semi-divine women, and of female roles in drama.

Bharata chose to represent a battle between devas (gods) and asuras (demons) in which the former emerge victorious. The gathered audience was delighted and began rewarding Bharata with all manner of blessings and gifts, until the asuras, angered at not being invited to join the audience as well as with their poor representation, brought the performance to a halt by removing speech, movement and memory from the performers. As the contest between the devas and the asuras intensified, Bharata sought a way to protect his work and actors. Brahma again intervened, this time with instructions for the perfect – and first ever – playhouse, which would be protected not only by the gods but by every form of divine and semi-divine being. He also placated the asuras by explaining that drama does not represent the actions of gods and demons, nor does it favour the gods. Instead, it was intended to illustrate the cosmic law by which all beings, even Brahma himself, are bound. It is this cosmic law – of a cycle of actions and their inexorable consequences – that forms the cultural and philosophical mooring of the moral universe represented in classical Sanskrit drama, popular theatre including Ramlila, and our cinema.

While the complexities of a cosmic law were of little interest to me at the time, I was captivated by the tale, not in the least because it seemed to echo some of the modern ideas that percolated in our home, including an emphasis on egalitarianism. I had no idea then of the many ways this origin story would linger in my mind and impact my own developing moral universe. I empathised deeply with the asuras' fury at being left out of the world's first performance even though I felt an instinctive, acute horror at their attacks on the performers and performance. I did not realise then that I had stumbled into my first, albeit abridged, encounter with the foundational text of Indian drama, the *Natyashastra*. Nor did I imagine that I would choose to study the text for much of my adult life. Those age-softened pages told me that I was not alone in seeking answers about drama and film and stories and this knowledge comforted me.

The book also discussed the rasa (essence, flavour) that was indispensable for the intention and purpose of all performance. From what I could understand at the time, each rasa was closely related to an emotional state although how it was created by some mysterious alchemy during a performance and enjoyed by the audience remained a mystery. I would learn much later that the nature of rasa, its creation and mechanics had been subject of centuries of philosophical debate. In the worn pages of that old book, one question stood out: why do we enjoy a performance, and more specifically, why do we choose to watch and enjoy watching acts that would not be pleasurable but terrifying, horrifying and painful in real life?

This is a question I had long intuited at the annual Ramlila performances and more frequent dramatised retellings of the epics. The former often detailed Sita's abduction scene from the *Ramayana*, which I found terrifying, enraging, appalling and saddening in turns, perhaps because the episode makes for an uneasy lesson on the dangers that threaten girls and women. I would feel a combination of rage and shame at her naivety in stepping beyond the Lakshman-rekha, the protective boundary drawn around her, to give alms to Ravana who is disguised as a mendicant. The episode cut particularly close as neither I nor my young aunts were allowed to approach the gate or offer alms to the many ascetics who wandered the city. The brutal murders of teenaged siblings Geeta and Sanjay Chopra in 1978 only emphasised in my mind the dangers faced not only by a mythical Sita but real living women and by extension to the men who loved me, especially my young uncles. Although the adults took great care in hiding the extensive newspaper coverage from me and my cousins, gory details, horrifically embellished, floated all around us, not least from classmates whose families were less stringent in their consumption of media. For weeks, I had nightmares which would only stop when I huddled against my grandmother, clutching the soft muslin of her sari like a talisman.

And yet I listened to every discussion at school and pulled up the horrific information when alone, even when it made me dizzy with fear. Even worse, I would watch every representation of the kidnapping of Sita, my stomach churning to the point of sickness, my heart pounding in terror. Even when I learned that in every version of the *Ramayana*, Sita inevitably, every single time, steps beyond the line, endangers herself, and is kidnapped, I could not – still cannot – look away. The episode is recreated and referenced by filmmakers in many guises, not least because it carries an undertone of victim-blaming and can function as short-hand for feminine defiance that is duly punished, a quick way to provide the male protagonist with motivation for revenge and to establish the immorality of the villain. It shows up in Indian stories, especially on screen, with depressing regularity and varying degrees of explicit or implicit violence. And yet even today, I watch all its versions, each time immersing myself in the terrible churning cauldron of emotions that I would never want to exper-ience in real life.

Fortunately, the old book, quoting philosophers I had never heard of, also emphasised that the consumer of a story should not languish in any single emotion or mood but move smoothly through them, experiencing both negative and positive moods. Encouraged, I reviewed my own reactions to stories that I read or heard or watched and promised myself that I would learn to do this better. For days, I kept notes on my reactions to stories I read or those that my family recounted, films I remembered, and even songs that played on the radio. And for many days, I snuck up to the shelf to consult the strange little book until one day it disappeared, most likely returned to the library where it belonged.

As an adult, I would learn that the *Natyashastra* compares performance to a banquet and offers suggestions for prepara-tion. A 'good' performance is one that offers the rasas – even when one is dominant – in a harmoniously blended whole, producing a pleasure similar to that of tasting a feast that combines the complex flavours of different spices and condi-ments. Even without any textual knowledge, Indian filmmakers often speak of their own films in similarly gastronomic terms, habitually referring to the 'masala' (Hindi for spice) film that must have a finely balanced blend of elements (narration, music, dance, tragedy, action). Again, the annual Ramlila was an early teacher where a performance could move swiftly from

Sita's fear and sorrow as a hostage to her surprise and joy at Hanuman's clandestine arrival with a message and then to the shocking yet amusing moment immediately after when the latter sets fire to the city with a flaming torch tied to his long tail.

The feast of emotions was no different when watching a film like *Aa Gale Lag Jaa* (Come, Embrace Me, 1973), a complicated story that shifted rapidly from a cheerful new romance to sinister plotting that ended the relationship, from challenges faced by a disabled child to the hope offered by a committed doctor, from a terrifying fire sequence to an eventual happy ending. The terror and sorrow seemed as satisfying as the happy song sequences, which included a memorable number set during an amateur roller-skating competition. By the time I re-watched *Parvarish* (Upbringing, 1977) some years later, I had learned to let myself feel terror and horror at two young girls witnessing their parents' murder but relinquish them to enjoy the antics of the same sisters who grow up to be expert pickpockets and the exciting action sequences featuring the film's two suave male stars, Amitabh Bachchan and Vinod Khanna. I had also learned by this time to pull up memories of all I had felt – acute terror, breathless excitement, bubbling laughter, and open-mouthed wonder – in the movie theatre to examine later. I would let myself experience the same emotions again simply by pulling up memories of the scenes but in a more controlled way, often hiding under the covers at night or sprawling on the cool stone floor under high rosewood beds in the afternoons. The latter became the preferred choice for when I wanted to remember and think about a scene that I knew would upset me. My grandmother was particularly careful of me, convinced that I was 'oversensitive' and needed protection from every form of distress. Although this meant a couple of deliberately squeezed-out tears would get me out of trouble, get my cousins *into* trouble and bring down a thunderous scold on my uncles and aunts, it was limiting for my experiments with stories and the emotions they evoked.

Very soon, I realised this strategy of rapidly moving from one emotional state to another, experiencing each fully while being prepared for the next and only analysing each later by pulling them up from memory was also useful for life outside books, theatres and movies. My memories of the decade swing rapidly from the terror of Dad being away at war to relief at his safe return, from excitement over the birth of a new baby to the excruciating pain of an accident that kept me home from school for weeks (which was actually wonderful as I was allowed to play with my aunt's precious dolls and read my uncle's treasured comics collection, much to my cousins' envy). Our family life veered from the heated debates at the dinner table about Jayaprakash Narayan's[4] 'sampoorna kranti' (complete revolution), a promise of full social-political-economic transformation, to the terrifying suspense of the Emergency, the nearly two-year period between 1975 and 1977 when all civil rights were suspended and suddenly some of our university friends were in danger from our own government, to the anguish of an unexpected family bereavement.

The emotional roller-coaster also seemed to apply to the wider reality which swerved from pride at India's first successful nuclear tests in 1974 to the horror of the Chasnala mining disaster that killed hundreds of miners and relentless worries about ongoing food rationing; from the dread of the Emergency to ambivalent optimism – followed quickly by disappointment – about the country's first non-Congress government in 1977. Beyond the salient incidents that made the news was the slow and grating soundtrack of economic precarity, communal distrust and unrest that periodically erupted in violence, and the many armed political insurgencies that were brutally suppressed by the state, including the Naxalbari uprising of 1967 that had led to further

---

[4] Narayan was an independence activist, socialist thinker and leader. Often called 'lok nayak' or 'people's leader, he was one of the key opposition leaders during the Emergency.

93

movements, including the Naxalite insurgency. The ongoing political turmoil churning in Kashmir persisted in the northwest,
creating a volatile mix of precarious geopolitics and local discontent. Meanwhile, the repressive Armed Forces Special Powers
Act of 1958 that allowed the Indian armed forces to maintain
public order in 'disturbed areas', and was first applied to the
Naga Uprising, had slowly spread to all seven states on the
country's eastern flank by the 1970s.

And yet the inexorable march to social transformation
continued, with increasingly numbers of women entering higher
education (including all my aunts, thanks to my grandmother's
hunger strike the decade before) and even more joining the
workforce, especially elite professions including civil services,
banking and the armed forces. An unprecedented movement of
population within India had been prompted by the new market
economy and was slowly transforming social networks and interactions even in the smallest of towns.

In my Catholic school, most of us were Hindu along with
a sprinkling of Muslims and Christians from various sects as
well as Sikhs, Jains, Buddhists and Zoroastrians. But we were
also drawn from almost every part of India, with Bengali,
Gujarati, Tamil and Malayalam as freely spoken in the playground as Hindi and Urdu. Varanasi's small Chinese Indian
community – a legacy of the Empire – also sent their children
to the same school. Very often religious, ethnic and linguistic
identities intersected in complicated ways: one friend was
Zoroastrian by religion, and her father was from Mumbai with
English and Marathi as his first languages while her mother's
first language was Gujarati. My friend moved back and forth
between various linguistic groups but also followed religious
customs that were entirely unfamiliar to us. Meanwhile, our
Chinese Indian friend, with familial roots in Calcutta, spoke
fluent Bengali and was entirely au fait with specifics of a culture
that seemed foreign to me.

It is not surprising that in this milieu, *Amar Akbar Anthony*
(1977) was not only a runaway hit across the country and remains

a cultural touchstone,[5] but was a favourite at school. With no less than six major stars, representing different religious, cultural and ethnic identities, the film offered a vision of India that we seemed to inhabit intuitively. Even the code-switching in the film by Salma (played by Neetu Singh), a first-generation Muslim doctor who dons a burqa only when required, was intensely familiar. We all moved constantly between westernised clothing and traditional wear depending on social context; many of the older women in my own family kept not only their heads but their faces covered when in public; and my grandmother's house had a complicated purdah system with separation of its private and public spaces by curtains that screened off inner doors. All too often, our aspirations of becoming doctors and pilots and, in my case, a university reader – a job that I assumed required nothing more than constant reading – clashed with social expectations and norms that still demanded that women get married young and preferably by familial arrangement rather than through personal choice.

Unsurprisingly, all these ambitions, disasters and anxieties made their way into our movies: the Chasnala mining disaster was turned into the 1977 film *Kaala Patthar* (Black Stone) while *Abhimaan* (Pride, 1973), starring the real-life star couple Amitabh Bachchan and Jaya Bhaduri, examined masculine jealousy and insecurity when the wife achieves greater professional success than the husband; *Ankur* (Seedling, 1974) was an exploration of caste hierarchies that enable exploitation and violence; *Garm Hava* (Scorching Winds, 1973) focussed on the travails of a Muslim family that chooses to stay in India after Partition, and *Aandhi* (Storm, 1975) followed a politician who must choose between her husband and her political ambitions. Even though

---

[5] Shah Rukh Khan referenced the film at a press conference in 2023, noting that the cast of *Pathaan* were like a real-life Amar, Akbar, Anthony as he and his co-stars Deepika Padukone and John Abraham all had different religious affiliations but had joined forces to make the blockbuster hit.

the Emergency almost brought an end to explicit political material on screen, filmmakers remained engaged with social and political issues of the time, with *Sholay* including a subplot around widow remarriage and *Hum Kissi Se Kum Nahin* (We Are Not Less Than Anyone, 1977) referencing the expulsion of Indians from Idi Amin's Uganda.

The Emergency taught even children that political views and affiliations could be dangerous, and, in its aftermath, we quickly learned to identify hidden messages not only in books and films but also in adult conversations. Inadvertently, the country's brief flirtation with authoritarianism had taught us not only to recognise subtext but also to constantly read against the grain. Although I would not learn this until much later, it was similar to the way my grandmother's generation had watched movies, by enjoying the explicit spectacle while also recognising their implicit message.

*   *   *

The *Natyashastra* proclaims itself the fifth Veda, one that concerns drama as a form of education and ritual that can be accessed by all castes of society and is an extensive explanation of theatre, performance and production. Comprising six thousand verses, it emphasises drama's role as a form accessible to all levels of society. The text's principles underlie all forms of classical, popular and, folk performance in India including theatre, dance, music and, in the past century, cinema. They are more practised and performed than studied, passed down as oral and embodied teaching.

Dating back to the second century B.C., the *Natyashastra* also embarks on a sort of survey of theatre conventions across a vast region, most of which is now considered South Asia, distinguishing between Sanskrit drama, often the preserve of the elite, and theatre in other languages across the region, recognising the variations in its discussions of the vrttis (dramatic styles) and pravrttis (regional styles). Interestingly, it emphasises not only the use of many languages across the region for drama but also the use of multiple languages – essentially, a multilingual theatre – in a single performance.

Even after the decline of Sanskrit theatre around the twelfth century, cultural production of the medieval bhakti poets such as Narsi Mehta or Mirabai, who were part of an educated high-caste elite but chose to write/perform in regional languages, continued the earlier performance traditions. Moreover, 'folk' theatre continued conventions and traditions outlined in the text and a line can be drawn from the many forms of performance – including nineteenth-century Parsi theatre – to the *Natyashastra,* beyond the age of 'Sanskrit drama', and into modernity. In an essay discussing *Yakshagana,* a form of traditional theatre from Karnataka, dramatist and filmmaker Girish Karnad explained that most Indian films borrowed their forms from theatrical perform-ances which are part of the audiences' 'living memory'.

Many of these stage conventions can be easily identified, albeit in abbreviated and only thinly secularised form, in cinema. Performance time is divided into several segments, in Hindi cinema perhaps most explicitly by the 'interval' that often separates a film by storyline or mood. Films start with a symbolic construction and sanctification of the performance space and a ritual invocation: generations of filmgoers recognise Raj Kapoor's R.K. Productions by the opening sequence of the family patriarch Prithviraj Kapoor in prayer or B.R. Chopra's B.R. Films by its logo that features a man with a hammer and a woman carrying a sheaf of wheat with words 'ars longa vita brevis' (art lasts long, life is short) while a male voice recites a Sanskrit verse, a combination of the filmmaker's progressive political views as well as more personal expression of identity. More recent and abstract variations include UTV's first logo, which used a woman's finger drawing the company logo in the manner of a traditional rangoli (ritual patterns drawn as a sign of a sanctified space).

This opening invocation need not be prolonged or complex or even of a specifically religious nature. Mehboob Khan's magnum opus *Mother India* (1957) creates a modern version where religious traditions and modern ideology intersect with traditional performance practices. The film opens with streaks of lightning flashing against a dark sky and sounds of thunder that give way to strains of music. A grey cloud appears as a sonorous male voice recites an Urdu couplet: '*Muddai lakh bura chaahe to kya hota hai, wohi hota hai jo manzoor-e-khuda hota hai*' (What does it matter if the world wants the worst for one; only that occurs that God wishes for'). Yet the visual imagery contrasts with the couplet as the grey cloud gives way to the studio logo – a tablet showing a hammer and sickle emblazoned with the letter M and the words Mehboob Productions written underneath. Here the invocation performs a triple task of establishing the filmic artifice within the traditional rules of performance, the recitation of couplet provides a link to Mehboob Khan's own Muslim identity, while the Communist party logo indicates his ideological leanings.[6]

Similarly, numerous filmmakers start their films with a brief still of either a preferred deity or an image of deceased parents invoking their blessings for the performance. One of the biggest grossers of its year, Chandra Barot's *Don* (1978) ostensibly uses Western action genre conventions as its first sequence begins with a long shot of a golden field with a foreign car appearing on the screen. Yet the filmic experience begins with a static shot of a photograph of the producer (who died during the shooting) Nariman Irani posing next to a camera. The photograph is ringed with red and white flowers and accompanied by a text with a dedication that in effect forms a 'secular' invocation.

K. Asif's magnum opus, *Mughal-E-Azam*, begins by thanking the national Ministry of Defence for its assistance in shooting the battle scenes for the film. The second static shot is even more surprising, claiming that 'History & Legend link the Story

---

[6] Gayatri Chatterjee notes that the film was banned by Turkey as a 'communist film'. The studio logo was also excised from the print sent for Oscar nomination. (Chatterjee, 2002: 73)

of our past. When both are fused in the Crucible of art & imagination, the spirit of this Land is revealed in all its Splendour and Beauty.' Both texts are superimposed on a backdrop of friezes representing Mughal-era splendour. The two texts are followed by the credits, this time rolling against a backdrop of friezes depicting battle scenes, military parades, palaces and court scenes. The first shot of the film opens to strains reminiscent of the raga bhairavi, rising over a strangely surreal village-scape, signalling a morning. A huge topographical cut-out map of India rises from the bottom of the screen to loom over the village, as an authoritative male voice begins to speak, '*Main Hindustan hoon . . .*' (I am Hindustan). Here the film elides the invocation required for performance with the role of the sutradhara or narrator to ensure that the ensuing representation is seen neither as history nor as imagination but a subjective representation of the past that freely draws from legend, imagination and facts. In the six decades since its release, the film's opening has grown from pioneering to standard convention, with filmmakers even today using variations of the same.

The musical overtures that accompany the initial invocation are intended to not only attract and settle audiences but also set the mood for the performance that follows. Filmmakers will often use bars from their own 'top hit' movies or songs for this. Yash Raj Films's stylised red-and-gold corporate logo is famously accompanied by the voice of Lata Mangeshkar singing an instantly recognisable fragment from the theme tune of its 2001 monster hit, *Kabhi Khushi Kabhie Gham*.

The use of a ritualised narrator (sutradhara), traditionally the stage manager-director, is also a frequent device and its use has spanned decades in films as varied as *Lagaan* (Tax, 2001), which pits a group of villagers and the local British administrators in a match of cricket, and *Baahubali 2: The Conclusion* (2017), a high-octane historical fantasy set in a mythical kingdom. In classical theatre, this constitutes the pūrvaranga (literally, pre-theatre), a sort of aesthetic prologue to settle the audience, inform their expectations and heighten anticipation, and functions in similar ways in movies. The pūrvaranga can seem similar to elements of western theatre[7] except for one difference: this prologue also signals the dominant rasa to be offered by the performance and creates a space for the spectator to prepare themselves mentally and emotionally.

Without ever having seen Sanskrit plays, most Indian film-makers and their audiences are familiar with its elements: themes of separation and reunion, as well as techniques like using sequences featuring dreams, premonition and flashback that disrupt linear time. There are stories within stories, and one or more subplots. Often a comedic or at least emotionally lighter subplot for a second lead is added to provide emotional relief in a drama or action film. While these devices are recognisable from other traditions, their use and purpose can seem baffling or disconnected to the unfamiliar viewer as these do not provide a psychological motivation or an explanation for a character's actions. Instead, these back-stories, prehistories and depictions of familial and community ties are intended to root the character in their wider milieu and provide moral and socially acceptable motivations. As such any and all action, especially any violence, is attributed to a prior act of harm which must be narratively addressed in the appropriate way to restore order and balance. The hero gains audience sympathy not because they have experienced a prior trauma but by their reaction to the event and often choosing to place the good of their community over personal resentment or interest.

Very often, a film may provide a 'prehistory' as preamble to the main action or through flashbacks. For example, *Amar Akbar Anthony* relies on a preamble depicting the events that lead to the separation of the three brothers from their parents.

---

[7] The similarity may explain the endless adaptations of Shakespeare's plays, initially for Parsi theatre in the nineteenth century and then for cinema. These adaptations are 'Indianised' to the point that they can be unrecognisable to Western audiences. They are also rarely recognised as adaptations of Shakespeare's works by most Indian audiences.

Yet the arrival of the three brothers – as adults and as yet unaware of their relationship – in the sequence that signals the end of the preamble and beginning of real-time action is not causally explained. On the other hand, *Sholay* provides the prehistory in a series of separate flashbacks from points of view of different characters. In popular reincarnation films like *Karz* (Debt, 1980), the prehistory of a previous birth is provided as a combination of a character receiving flashes of memory and a narrative flashback, while in *Om Shanti Om* – an explicit *hommage* to *Karz* – the first half of the film serves as an extended preamble that sets up the actions taken by the reincarnated character in the second half. In each case and despite superficial differences, the objective of the narrative remains to restore balance and order in a world thrown into chaos and which can only be achieved by the actions of the hero.

Scriptwriter Anjum Rajabali noted in an interview published in 2004 that, while James Bond can kill as part of his job, a spy hero in an Indian film requires clearer justification to 'allow' killing and must go beyond a personal quest for revenge or even a political or patriotic explanation. A personal revenge plot as in *Sholay* requires the villain to not only carry out acts of unspeakable violence against Thakur but also to continue terrorising the community. Similarly, even in political or patriotic films like *Mission Kashmir* (2000), about a terrorist who changes his mind, or *RRR* (2022), an anti-imperial historical fantasy about two men resisting the Empire, the protagonists' violence is presented as a reaction to an extreme threat or past acts of violence. Even 'war films', like *Border* (1997), are framed specifically as a martial reaction to an 'unprovoked' invasion. Seen in this light, the final lament of the film – *Mere dushman, mere bhai* (my enemy, my friend) – and the last shot of the national flags of the adversaries side by side indicate a restoration of order over chaos, rather than an overwhelming victory, which would require the total destruction of the enemy and as such would be morally unacceptable.

Nowhere are the classical principles of performance – and indeed the fundamental karmic philosophy that drives them – more evident than in adaptations of Hollywood films,[8] which are almost entirely unrecognisable in their Indian avatars. These undergo what the industry popularly terms 'Indianisation',[9] a process that involves expanding the narrative by introducing additional characters that anchor the protagonist to their community, adding and heightening emotional content, and of course inserting songs. Few Western fans would recognise *Rafoo Chakkar* (Gone in Flash, 1975) as an adaptation of Billy Wilder's *Some Like It Hot* (1959) as the romantic comedy track is reduced to a secondary level while issues of morality, specifically framed to confront challenges of economic deprivation, and crime and restitution are foregrounded. Similarly, *Yeh Dillagi* (This Cheerfulness, 1994) keeps the bare bones of *Sabrina* (1954) while foregrounding dilemmas raised by globalisation and India's policy of rapid economic liberalisation at the time. It also creates a female protagonist who not only refuses entrenched social hierarchies but also succeeds in acquiring her own independent wealth.

Unsurprisingly, Indian filmmakers often express amazement at Hollywood's 'single-track' narratives that simply follow a principal lead. Screenwriter Sutanu Gupta noted in an interview that Indian audiences expect 'everything', including romance, family life, songs while also insisting that films retain a clear focus and not be 'hodge-podge'. Veteran producer and director Rakesh Roshan explains that these structuring choices change the narrative pace as a film must not only establish the lead character but also his background, in essence placing him squarely within a wider community. Scriptwriter Javed Akhtar has routinely pointed to the need for back-stories and secondary or minor

---

[8] This also applies to adaptations of works of Western literature. For example, *Daag* (Stain, 1973) is impossible to recognise as an adaptation of Thomas Hardy's 1886 novel *The Mayor of Casterbridge*.

[9] A very similar process was used by nineteenth-century Parsi theatre for its adaptation of Western plays – Shakespeare was a big favourite – that added not only song and dance but additional characters to embed the protagonists in a surrounding community.

characters that form a social web and give films a 'saga-like' quality. These plot elements are not extraneous as they establish the protagonist as inextricably intertwined with the community and emphasise the emotional and moral stakes of their choices.

As a child, I recognised but could not articulate why I was dissatisfied with single-track foreign films. I wanted to know more about the character's background, relationships and their society at large. It seemed almost impossible that anyone would live out entire lives as isolated individuals. When I first learned that scenes could be cut from films before screening, I decided that British and American films we watched were simply missing these sequences. I wondered if this was because the prints – stored in those enormous circular, black metal cases – were too expensive or heavy to transport across the world and so were made lighter by excising large chunks. Some years ago, I realised that my continued discontent with one-track film narratives is more than just about the storyline. A young cousin was watching one of the *Terminator* movies on television. He suddenly looked up and wondered aloud why Arnold Schwarzenegger's character wanted to save the world given that 'he loves nobody and nobody loves him.' It struck me then that, in contrast, in the Indian tradition, a hero cannot exist without a wider community as any 'restoration of order' plot first requires the hero to care for that world thrown into chaos.

I realised that the prehistories in Indian films function much like a prior existence or a previous incarnation. Although the events included in prehistories are separated from the present by a break in time, they continue to influence the main plot in ways that are deeper and more foundational than more recent events. This conceptualisation is intimately linked to the philosophy of karma, of action and consequence. According to it, human fortunes are believed to depend ultimately on the nature of human deeds performed even across multiple lifetimes. The prehistories in cinema not only ignite a causal process that drives the narrative structure but also explain how current actions are linked to and consequent of prior actions. Moreover, they situate the hero in a socio-familial milieu, emphasising his ties to wider community despite the schisms of time. In turn this not only highlights the hero's enduring moral quality and links their actions causally to a longer series of events but also ties their action and its consequences to a wider community and reality. The hero's fate – and therefore their choices – are inextricably tied to that of their community.

Finally, often the prehistory of a film may only be understood by extra-textual mythological references it invokes, as in the case of the lovers in *Lagaan: Once Upon a Time in India* (Tax, 2001) whose love triangle is explicitly compared to that of Krishna, Radha and Mira, or by the identification of the eponymous protagonist to the epic hero Rama in the action thriller *Main Hoon Na* (I Am Here, 2004). The eleventh-century philosopher Abhinavagupta, whose commentary on the *Natyashastra* is held to be most authoritative, explains that audience involvement can be quickly ensured by deploying familiar characters from history, myths and prior literature. In turn, given that the purpose of any narrative performance such as theatre is didactic, repeated performances of these tales – aimed at representing the cosmic law – become familiar over time, especially to those without access to written literature. Such construction of character not only provides the socio-psychological context for the audience, who recognise the characters in terms of their 'heroic' archetype, driven by bravery, rectitude, compassion or sacrifice, but also indicates the dominant emotion that the audience is culturally educated to expect from a performance.

Over a century of popular cinema demonstrates an inexhaustible inventiveness for metatextual citation where characters reference mythic heroes in a range of disparate situations, even when the outward gloss may appear 'modern' or indeed be set in non-Indian locations. The young lover of the romantic film *Dilwale Dulhaniya Le Jayenge* (hereafter *DDLJ*) refers continually to the *Ramayana*, especially Rama's wooing and winning over Sita in disguise. The action thriller *Main Hoon Na*, where the hero is named after the prince warrior, the finale links the film's protagonist to Rama rescuing Sita as well as defeating Ravana.

From a Western perspective, the two films have little in common, except their leading star. Both have seemingly little 'traditional' content, with the first film set partly in Europe and the second in millennial modern India. For most part, the actors wear Western clothes, except in the second half of *DDLJ* (once the setting moves to rural India). Yet the narrative hook is established clearly for an audience who recognise the metatextual archetypes.

Similarly, romance films evoke a variety of mythological characters, the most popular being Radha from the stories of Lord Krśna, often depicted as the daring but devoted woman who is willing to risk social opprobrium in order to achieve consummation. In contrast, some characters are likened to Mīra, the sixteenth-century poet, as an archetype of a woman who loves selflessly without any hope of consummation of her love.[10] The many versions of *Devdas* posit these two female archetypes portrayed by the two female leads; Paro, Devdas's childhood love married to another man, is reminiscent of Radha, while Chandramukhi, the courtesan in love with Devdas, refers to Mīra with her boundless, selfless love for the protagonist. Sanjay Leela Bhansali's 2002 version makes the reference glaringly explicit partly by dressing Chandramukhi (played by Madhuri Dixit) in the saffron-coloured clothing associated with Hindu ascetics, and via her dialogue and song lyrics. Her transformation into the *bhakta*, a devotee like Mīra, is underscored by her appearance at temples and religious rituals even as she maintains her memories of the single night she had spent with Devdas in carefully preserved rumpled sheets. From the same period, the lavish anti-imperialist cricket saga *Lagaan* uses a similar device to identify Gauri (Gracy Singh) as the protagonist

---

[10] While Mīra as a historic and literary character only dates back to the sixteenth century, it is important to note that she personifies in popular imagination the earlier concept of the *bhakta* or devotee who can long for divine union with eternal hope albeit without necessarily any possibility of the same. Interestingly enough, *bhakta* is also a classical Sanskrit term used to describe a viewer of drama.

Bhuvan's (Aamir Khan) beloved. Her name in turn evokes Lakśmi or the consort of Vishnu (considered by many Hindus as another incarnation of Radha) while the sympathetic English woman Elizabeth Russell's (Rachel Shelley) unconsummated love for Bhuvan is linked to Mīra. Although the two films have little in common, they both follow Abhinavagupta's hook by creating characters who inhabit their own story-verse while also invoking earlier mythological figures that are easily recognisable and well loved by the audience.

Handled well, the narrative construct triggers audience recognition not only of the character but also the most likely plotline, which in turn frees the spectator from concerns of what will happen next and allows them to instead focus on savouring *how* the story will unfold. Over the past century, Indian filmmakers, more by familiarity with performance and narrative traditions than philosophical treatises, have continued to adopt, reference and experiment with such conventions in both religious and secular films.

* * *

As the 1970s came to a close, Dad was assigned to the Indian embassy in Islamabad, Pakistan. My family had been living in a town on the north-eastern border of India. Unlike my grandmother's laughter-filled house in the plains, our home in the hilltown was a baasha, a bamboo hut, with a snake trench dug all around it. A woven bamboo plank was scrupulously placed across the trench for us to walk across each time we had to leave or enter the hut. Our beds were bamboo rafts placed on four living bamboo trees. As the trees did not grow at the same pace, these had to be trimmed every few days to ensure that our beds remained horizontal. One night, a wild pig fell into the snake trench and ran through it, crashing into the mud corners of the trench until the baasha shook and trembled. Dad finally shot it and shared the meat with all our neighbours.

106

At the age of five, my younger sister spoke better Galo than Hindi and believed that our grandmother's home was the only one built of brick and cement and everyone 'normal' lived in bamboo huts. My dad's role at the embassy in Islamabad would not only take the family directly into territories considered hostile but also required us to keep parts of his life confidential. Although my parents decided that I was old enough to be trusted to maintain Dad's cover story, my sister was too young to understand such concepts or indeed be able to differentiate between truth and lie, which made her a security risk. This was when the universe of films collided yet again with real life as Dad, our mother and various members of the extended family embarked on a dangerous plan.

While Dad attended training sessions and briefings at South Block in New Delhi, my mother and other members of our extended family were entrusted to rewrite my sister's memories. My parents may have been initially inspired by *Ram aur Shyam* (1967), but we were all familiar with the storylines of *Don* (1978), *Kasme Vaade* (Promises, 1978) and *The Great Gambler* (1979). Who wasn't, after all? Soon a fictitious identical twin brother was dreamed up for Dad. Next, a fully fledged life story was constructed for this non-existent family member who had migrated to the USA after a stint in the Indian army. As soon as the idea was introduced to my young sister, the entire family collaborated to alter her memories. Events she had experienced with Dad were attributed to this fictitious twin. All photographs of Dad in uniform were re-identified as that of our non-existent uncle. Over six months, my sister's childhood memories were entirely transformed. On the eve of our move to Islamabad, she had no recollection that Dad had ever worn an army uniform or that she had ever lived in a baasha. Instead, she desperately missed Dad's twin brother and wanted to see him again.

I Have Picked Out Dreams of Seven Colours for You[1]

ON A PLEASANTLY WARM day we tramped after my mother through the ruins of Taxila, the ancient Buddhist city not far from Islamabad. It had been at the top of my mother's list of places to visit ever since we found out about Dad's assignment in Pakistan, but the military government's permission was required to leave the capital and General Zia-ul-Haq's regime was less than willing to hand those out. The go-aheads when they did come through were granted capriciously and at the last moment.

I knew that permission for this trip had arrived the evening before because Dad had come home just as the baby needed bathing. He had also been crackling with suppressed excitement but had stopped to make himself a drink, chatting to me about school, studies and my planned theatre production with my friends for which I needed to requisition the garage. Meanwhile, my mother had gathered up the baby and frogmarched my sister up to the bath that adjoined my parents' bedroom. I had played along, extending my conversation with Dad, proposing that a curtain be fixed across the garage to separate the stage from the backstage and begging him to help paint the backdrop. We knew

---

[1] *'Maine tere liye hi saat rang ke sapne chune . . .'* from *Anand* (Joy, 1971).

our house was monitored and technicians from the embassy would regularly sweep it for bugs. The surveillance devices would be back within days if not hours. It was part of the cat-and-mouse game between the two governments in which we, as a family, were at times small but necessary players, at others delectable bait, and almost always dispensable pawns. I waited for a signal from Dad while the squeals and giggles from the bathroom rose above the sound of running water. I knew my mother left every tap running in the bathroom, often placing a metal toy or bowl in the sink to maximise the noise. Finally, Dad put down his nearly untouched drink and slotted the VHS cassette mix of Bollywood party songs into the player. The disco era had begun and in rapid succession, thumping beats from 'Ramba ho' set in a Goan carnival sequence, 'Dil lena khel hai dildaar ka' (The lover's game is to steal hearts) and 'Zamane ko dikhaana hai' (We have to show the world) added to the cacophony of screaming children and whooshing water. Dad and I joined my mother in the bathroom to discuss the permission to visit Taxila – she used the Sanskrit Takshashila, literally the city carved from stone, rather than the Greek name – and I could see her excitement. Dad explained security protocols to me just as he did each time we travelled, even though these were etched deep in my memory by then. My mother added her admonitions, and all the while I hoped that our discussions remained undetected by the bugs hidden all over our home.

I have absolutely no memory of the colonial-era museum building in Taxila except that it had seemed dusty and sadly neglected. But I remember my mother's enthusiasm as she had wandered from one case to another, greeting the many sculptures like old friends. Her voice rose, cracking slightly with emotion, and her words rushed out faster than I had ever heard as she explained the confluence of Greek and South Asian techniques of sculpture that had given rise to the Gandhara school of art over two thousand years ago. My mother had studied art history and specialised in Buddhist art, so this was her domain. I had long known that both my parents painted, although my mother

109

was a trained artist while Dad was an auto-didact who had painted the topographically accurate mountain landscapes on empty cases of land mines that lined the shelves in my grand-mother's house. But now, for the first time in my life, I recognised and admired the precision of a scholarly brain. My mother moved excitedly through the rooms, identifying particularly important pieces, urging me and Dad to notice small details, explaining them, and pulling up vast amounts of information that she care-fully presented with the caveat 'it's not my area of expertise . . .'

The rest of the day, after the museum visit, we wandered through the sprawling archaeological complex, empty but for my family and our habitual surveillance escort from Pakistan's intelligence agency, the ISI, that trailed at a respectable distance behind us. Dad managed my younger siblings while my mother forged ahead, striding around ruins of the stupas, the city dwell-ings and its monasteries, almost breathless as she explained the histories and the art and culture that the silent stones held. As we made our way back to the parking lot that afternoon, the baby was cradled in Dad's arms and my sister pranced about just a few yards ahead, pushing but not breaking the boundaries set by my parents. My mother fell behind, now silent, lingering as if she didn't want to leave. When I turned to look for her, she was standing near the enormous Dharmarajika stupa, bathed in the gold of the setting sun. As always, her beige crochet knit-ting bag was clutched in her left hand, bulging with balls of many-coloured wool, the steel needles thrust through them glinting in the sun. I knew my mother carried a gun and was an accurate shot. It was why the bag went everywhere with us and why none of us were allowed to touch it. Suddenly I realised that she had carried it all day, and not once had I noticed it.

As we drove back to Islamabad, my parents conversing quietly while my siblings slept next to me in the back, I caught a glimpse of the ISI surveillance car that trailed us on the nearly empty highway. Dad caught my eye in the rear-view mirror, grinned and then broke into song: *'Mere sapnon ki rani kab aayegi tu . . .'* (Queen of my dreams, when will you come to me). Smiling and humming along, I looked again at my mother and thought of the many things she had told us during the day about history and art and aesthetics. I wondered if the rasa she had spoken about when explaining the achingly beautiful sculptures and poetry created by the ancients was the same as the one that applied to music and dance, theatre and cinema.

* * *

Rasa appears regularly and in multiple ways in classical Indian literature. The Rg Veda mentions rasa in the context of water, juice, sap or drink while the Yajur Veda curiously deploys the word to signify joy. In the *Upanishads*, rasa is used to denote an 'essential element' or 'essence'. Meanwhile the epics the *Ramayana* and the *Mahabharata* use the word for both liquids including water, milk and liquor, as well as for emotional states, approximating the *Natyashastra* and the thousand years of debate on the nature of performance and aesthetics. Both epics use terms that have come to signify particular rasas to describe specific emotional states, with the *Ramayana* mentioning shringar (love), karuna (sorrow), hasya (humour), vira (heroism), bhayanak (fear) and raudra (wrath) in the *Yuddha Kanda* which describes battle preparations and the war between Rama and Ravana. The *Mahabharata* also mentions the karuna in the context of Uttara's emotions at her husband Abhimanyu's death, and raudra and bhayanak to describe the cremation grounds. However, it is the *Natyashastra* that elaborates the concept as essential to performance, declaring 'there can be no natya without rasa!'

The text first explains that rasa is produced as a cumulative result of aesthetic stimulus (performance, art, music) and the audience's involuntary and deliberate reactions to it. It then switches to an elaborate culinary metaphor: just as various condiments are combined to create an enjoyable dish, elements of narrative, staging, acting, etc. must be brought together in a balanced way to create a pleasurable performance. The gratification of eating the dish is produced by a combination of transitory moods and permanent internal states. Although the dish can be eaten and savoured by many, it is best enjoyed by those with not only a sensitive palate but also a trained one. Similarly, drama includes multiple elements including acting, costume, music, staging, plot etc., which are combined to create a balanced whole. Just as with food, although many can watch and enjoy this performance, only the sensitive and knowledgeable viewer can savour it fully. For this gastronomic metaphor, actors, musicians, scriptwriters, director and all those who work to create a performance are like trained chefs who have learned their craft well enough to prepare and present a complex and balanced feast. In turn, spectators are like consumers of the feast who may be unfamiliar and thus disdainful of the dishes served, or choose to gorge themselves thoughtlessly like gourmands, or in the best of cases have learned and prepared themselves as gourmets to enjoy the banquet sensitively and deliberately and experience its pleasures at emotional, intellectual and aesthetic levels.

Performance thus works like a metaphorical feast, tantalising all our senses and well before the first spoonful lands on our tongues. Before we join a banquet, we prepare ourselves with bathing, special clothes and perfumes. We experience the anticipation not just of partaking of the food but also the environment – candlelight or flowers perhaps, crisp linen and gleaming cutlery – and the company – of friends, romantic partner, family. Each of these factors impacts not only our preparations for the feast but what we expect from it. Simultaneously, an army of experts including chefs, serving staff, suppliers of raw materials, even cleaners prepare not only the food but the conditions in which the feast may be fully enjoyed.

From the moment of our arrival at the feast, our involuntary reactions to the offered stimuli kick in. Do we like the flowers? Is the décor too spare or too extravagant? Is the seating cosy? Is the table pretty and does it enable comfortable eating? Is the company interesting? And are we and our companions in the state of mind necessary for socialising, for celebrations? Our reactions are often instant, involuntary and mostly unconscious and yet a single factor – within ourselves or amongst the external stimuli – can derail our capacity to fully savour a feast or indeed a performance. In the best of circumstances, a small mood change may hamper our full enjoyment; in the worst, it could ruin the entire experience. This echoes the two obstacles to the production and savouring of rasa described by Abhinavagupta: flaws with the performance itself, much like the failure of the chefs in the preparation of food, and the spectator's state of mind which can prevent the enjoyment of even the finest of offerings.

We then anticipate the food itself, listening for sizzling sounds and smelling the first aromas of delicious cooking. If the chefs are successful, these alone are enough to get our mouths to water. As the food arrives, we respond to its presentation, to the colours on the plate, the pattern on and material of the crockery itself. And finally, we try the first bite, not just anticipating but hoping that the taste matches the promises extended by sound, smell, sight and touch that we have enjoyed so far. But our pleasure is not limited to our own individual consumption. We share our joy with others at the table, praise particularly tasty dishes, and discuss not just the food but our entire experience, often by comparing it to other, previous feasts. To our initial involuntary reactions, we deliberately and collectively add memory, knowledge, analysis and critique, all of which enhance our enjoyment. Unlike a purely emotive reaction, a critical process continues well after the meal ends as we repeatedly evaluate and re-evaluate our pleasures, choosing to retain some while discarding others and discovering entirely new ones. This – not just the food itself but the full sensory, emotional and intellectual experience of the feast – is rasa!

For the *Natyashastra* – and the many philosophers of aesthetics who debated the text for the following thousand years – performances work in the same way. The text also categorises the various emotional experiences that can be represented in performance into eight rasas, each with a corresponding 'durable' or permanent emotional state (sthayibhavas) that can be accessed by the spectator when evoked by a good performance. Relying on a culinary

113

metaphor, the specific and enduring taste of an apple or a pepper or a dish made with them is its sthayibhava as it is an innate and permanent quality. Performance, like presenting the apple or preparing the dish, is the means of sharing this quality. The experience of tasting the dish – savouring the performance – is rasa. A great performance is when the sthayibhava or innate emotional states are presented in such a way that both the performer and the viewer can experience them as rasa.

At a more practical, and perhaps popularly recognisable, level, the text also creates an overarching semiotic structure that serves as additional signposts for performers and viewers by linking each of the rasas and its corresponding sthayibhava to a mood, colour and presiding deity.[2]

Rasa	Colour	Deity	Sthayibhava
Shringar (love)	shyam (green)	Vishnu	rati (desire)
Hasya (humour)	sita (white)	Pramatha	hasa (mirth)
Karuna (sorrow)	kapota (dove-coloured)	Yama	shoka (sadness)
Raudra (wrath)	rakta (red)	Rudra	krodha (anger)
		(or Shiva)	
Vira (heroism)	gaura (wheat brown)	Mahendra	utsaha (enthusiasm)
Bhayanak (terror)	krishna (black)	Kala	bhaya (fear)
Bibhatsa (disgust)	nila (blue)	Mahakala	jugupsa (revulsion)
Adbhuta (wonder)	pita (yellow)	Brahma	vismaya (amazement)

Each of these can be created by the performance of distinctive stimuli: hasa, for example, from physical exaggeration or impudence, shringar from beauty and erotic desire, and sorrow

---

[2] This colour scheme is rarely used in modern cinema, although accomplished filmmakers are both deliberate in their use of colours for emotional impact and metaphoric value.

from separation from loved ones or death. These eight rasas may be grouped in two groups of four that are linked with their correlated mental states: shringar, hasya, vira and adbhuta on one hand, with their correlated sthayibhavas of rati, hasa, utsaha and vismaya; and raudra, bibhatsa, bhayanak and karuna with their correlated mental states of krodha, juguspa, bhaya and shoka on the other. The first groups together mental states that are pleasant and desirable while the second those that are unpleasant and to be avoided. In a karmically informed world-view, the two groupings also indicate the consequences of actions informed by the two groups: actions driven by the first are likely to have positive consequence, those by the second, negative ones.

Given the didactic role assigned to drama by the *Natyashastra*, these eight are linked to three of the four purusharthas (goals of human life) dharma or righteous behaviour, artha or material success including wealth and power, and kama or sensory pleasure, which are considered apt for representation through the performative arts. This grouping, described as trivarga, forms the foundation of the type of plays as well as the underlying motivations of the protagonists: heroism (vira) or capable of being motivated by dharma; love (shringar) motivated by kama, which given all humans are capable of desire, makes it the dominant theme of dramatic (and now cinematic) representation; and raudra (wrath), motivated by artha and leading to chaos, war and destruction. While this last forms a frequent basis of narrative, it is rarely represented on its own and is accompanied by elements of vira and shringar.

Nearly a thousand years later, Abhinavagupta added a ninth rasa, shanta (peace/enlightenment), which is often considered the balance/mix of all other rasas. Represented by white and linked to serenity, this final rasa is often regarded as the transcendent one that absorbs all others. Conceptually, even the perfect performance – if it could occur – would not be able to represent this rasa, although it would allow serenity to be experienced fully and simultaneously by both the performers and the viewers. While the three key rasas are linked to corresponding goals of human life – vira rasa to dharma, raudra to artha and shringar to kama – this final shanta rasa may be similarly linked to the fourth, moksha or liberation of the soul.

A connoisseur of this cinema approaches each film like a guest at a feast, prepared to experience the depicted narrative with all the evoked emotions in their full intensity, and recognises that a satisfying performance consists of a range of clearly defined emotional moods placed in an effective sequence. What to the unfamiliar viewer may seem a confused mix of genres (comedy, romance, action-adventure) or abrupt transitions in emotional moods (a glamorous dance sequence ending in a violent fight which then leads to a romantic song) are not only logical to the Indian audiences but even expected. Of course, not every viewer – just like the participant at the feast – experiences the same pleasures or is able to understand and articulate the nature of the experienced pleasures. The enjoyment of a performance depends on two concurrent aspects: the sophistication of the performance, including the setting, narrative and performer's skill, and on the sensitivity and prior knowledge of the spectator – in the best scenario, one with a gourmet-like sophistication. And just like a feast, a performance is enjoyed differently by each person: the higher the level of prior cultural – and filmic – knowledge of the viewer, the greater the pleasure (or disappointment) with the performance. On this sliding scale of pleasure, any film may be seen primarily for their emotional or 'fun' value, or enjoyed solely for the narrative or audio-visual content even as its more complex nuances are savoured differently by a more 'knowing' viewer.

Indian filmmakers not only employ classical principles to evoke strong emotional responses but also to engage in complex political, social or philosophical dialogue with the audience on contemporary issues. This prior knowledge of local history, current events and other socio-political understanding on the part of the viewer not only works to locate a particular film but also activates memories, experience and information of the viewer, ensuring a stronger emotive reaction and commitment. For example, Desai's *Amar Akbar Anthony* tackles not only the trauma of Partition but also more complex politico-social realities including inter-religious harmony. With adbhuta (wonder) as its dominant rasa, the film transforms unimaginable traumas of Partition as well as impossible challenges of the fledgling nation into a narrative that makes both manageable on a human scale. This is achieved by deploying a range of complementary rasas – including shringar, hasya and vira – to provide a 'balanced' feast for the spectator. Despite a deceptively light touch, the film takes up complex political positions, critiquing nationalist heroes including Gandhi as well as other leaders of the past while proposing potential leaders who can not only address past collective traumas but also lead the way to the future.

Similarly, *Om Shanti Om* (2007) provides a good example of how a sensitive, knowledgeable spectator may experience greater enjoyment on the rasic spectrum of pleasure. The film has adbhuta as its primary rasa, even though it switches rapidly to cover seven others: hasya, shringar, raudra, vira, karuna, bhayanak and bibhatsa. The film may be considered frothy or even be written off as a 'brainless' entertainer by an unknowing spectator. However, it is also structured as a tribute to a hundred years of filmmaking in the country and draws in covert as well as overt ways on a host of other cinematic texts. A cinephile knowledgeable about the Hindi commercial cinema tradition would find layer upon layer of intertextuality, with every scene, dialogue, costume and location recalling other iconic moments from cinema history and allusions to their favourite stars. Each bit of additional information would add to the range of emotions evoked by the film.

A deliberate balancing of rasas – created through acting and a host of filmic techniques – also ensures that while the spectator can experience a range of intense emotions, they are unlikely to be swept away by any one of them.[3] A useful example is the *'Tujhe yaad na meri aayi'* (You did not think of me) song sequence

---

[3] Classical dramaturgs used a host of staging and acting techniques along with the changes in rasas to ensure that the spectator could not drift away into an uncritical emotive haze. Many of these are echoed in formal conventions and stylistic practices of Indian cinema even today.

from *Kuch Kuch Hota Hai* (Some Things Happen, 1998), where the sthayibhava being performed is rati (desire). However, as the rasa being evoked is shringar in its vipralambha (love in separation) form, a host of filmic techniques bring together a range of elements: torrential rain that marks the beginning of the song; unlike the warmth of monsoon rains that are linked to romance, the *mise-en-scène* ensures that Anjali's (played by Kajol) surroundings remain bleak, grey and cold; the heart-wrenching song is sung by a group of passing folk singers. As Anjali weeps alone, wandering through a gloomy landscape, intercut shots of Tina (Rani Mukherjee) enjoying Rahul's (Shah Rukh Khan) company heighten the sense of Anjali's loss and sorrow. Although the experience of losing love would not be a pleasant one in real life, its evocation during performance is enjoyable, partly because the sequence simultaneously distances the spectator from a purely emotional response by undermining any reliance on cognitive realism through a series of filmic conventions. These include a rapid change of scenery from Anjali's hostel room to a dark tunnel in a Scottish ruined castle, a filmic choice that comforts the habitual viewer of this cinema but may baffle others. The song's deployment of affective realism also ensures that the sorrow evoked by the song and the sadness experienced in response by the spectator remains manageable. This is further reinforced by film's narrative that has already informed the spectator that the sequence is set in the past and that there is hope for Rahul to unite with Anjali despite their temporary parting. Given the success of both the song and the film, there is little doubt that the sequence succeeds in rasic terms.

*   *   *

Indian cinema was banned in Pakistan when my family lived there. However, the markets were constantly flooded with pirated VHS copies of the latest releases and even General Zia's wife, popularly referred to as Begum Sahiba, was rumoured to be a passionate Amitabh Bachchan fan. When copies of the Bachchan film *Lawaris* were late in hitting the shelves, market whispers blamed Begum Sahiba, who reportedly had the 'master copy' confiscated to watch first. Whatever truth lay behind these rumours, the political situation meant that, although we had rapid access to new releases, these could be only watched at home on the VCR. I desperately craved for the ritual of going to the movies: the excited chatter as my aunts prepared their outfits, the affectionate cajoling by my uncles to get a favourite shirt ironed, my grandmother's half-hearted scolding about being film crazy intermingled with reminders that we were running late. I wanted to watch a film on the big screen, on the '70 mm' that graced our favourite theatre. I even missed the hoots and jeers from the audience and the shower of coins and currency bills that landed at the foot of the screen when a scene or song was particularly good. My favourite aunt had taught herself to whistle like the 'bad' boys, and she'd wait for a particularly loud moment of whistles and hoots to join in, knowing that her contribution would go unnoticed in the mix. A mischievous glint would light up her eyes along with a faint blush and she always seemed slightly shocked at her own daring. But most of all, I yearned for the collective excitement and joy that seemed to run through family, friends and strangers alike during those few shared hours. My parents seemed to miss the same and ensured at least one trip to the movies with the entire extended family and friends on our visits back to India.

A single movie, or rather a single sequence from a film from those years, has stuck in my mind. Director Kamal Amrohi's much awaited 1983 release *Razia Sultan* was a big-budget period film loosely based on India's first empress. We watched the film soon after its release during a trip home from Islamabad. I remember marvelling at our numbers as our family – my parents, uncles, aunts and cousins – stretched across an entire row of seats. The film's haunting songs were already a success. The director was well respected for his debut *Mahal* (1949), widely considered India's first horror film, and the lavish

Pakeezah (The Pure, 1972), a sensitively handled love story between a courtesan and an aristocrat. Despite four decades in the industry, *Razia Sultan* was only Amrohi's fourth feature film as he had a reputation for crafting each of his films with painstaking and meticulous attention. It had been in production for the better part of the previous decade, featuring some of the biggest stars of the time including Hema Malini, popularly called India's 'dream girl', as Razia and the supremely glamorous Parveen Babi as her loyal confidante and attendant Khakun. Amrohi had also assembled a dream team of lyricists, music composers, singers and technicians for the production.

Yet within minutes of the film starting, it was clear that despite the extravagant on-screen spectacle and a few individual scenes, there was little to hold our attention. The first appearance of Dharmendra in blackface – with a strange green tint – as the Abyssian slave-general and Razia's lover had the crowds booing and hissing. It was an early sign that the film would not recover and indeed it bombed at the box office, unable even to scrape together its production costs. It was panned universally by critics and its sole win at the Filmfare awards – the industry's version of the Oscars – was for the art director N.B. Kulkarni, although music director Khayyam had also earned a nomination.

In our theatre, although the opprobrium abated when Razia tried to win herself an empire (even though she spent more screen time pining over her lover), it was clear that the film had been a poor choice. Yet having paid for tickets, we like most of the audience stayed, chatting to each other during the tedious parts, only half-interested in the events on screen and paying attention to only the stunningly shot song sequences.

Perhaps that is why the sudden intense attention of the audi-ence as one song began stands out in my mind. Khakun sings a gentle lullaby – '*Khwab ban kar koi aayega ...*' (someone will come to you in dreams) – to help Razia sleep as the two are rowed on a luxurious swan-shaped boat floating around canals of the palace. The lyrics are erotically charged with references to the scent of silky hair and warm bodies, and descriptions of bodies melting under heated caresses. As she sings, Khakun fans and gently strokes Razia with an elaborate feather fan. The prop instantly recalls the (in)famous scene from *Mughal-E-Azam* where it is used as an erotic aid in a scene between the lead stars Dilip Kumar and Madhubala. Stills of the scene from the older film were featured prominently in magazines, film memorabilia and even on our treasured album of the film's soundtrack. Even an unkissed, prepubescent could hold no doubt of the meaning of the lyrics or the actions of the stars.

As Khakun weaves an ever more elaborate sexual fantasy with her song, Razia's eyes cloud over and she moves restlessly until her toes curl up. The erotic content is undeniable by the time Khakun leans over, takes Razia's chin to turn up her face and moves the fan up to cover both their faces. Any doubt is further removed by the camera instantly cutting to the two women rowing the boat. When one of them widens her eyes in shock, the other holds up a finger to her own lips in admonishment, and then draws the finger across her throat in a clear warning.

I remember peeking at the adults who surrounded me and noting that they were spellbound by the song. Even the usually boisterous men in the cheaper seats who catcalled and yelled crude things at the first sign of an erotically presented female body were entirely silent. I sank back in my seat, feeling suddenly short of breath and unable to look away from the two stars who were often described as the most beautiful women in the country. The sequence was a revelation, temptation and yet also a warning that what had been revealed so sensually on screen was not to be spoken about openly. I sat in open-mouthed wonder and another yet unnamed, unfamiliar emotion. But before I could give myself over to the feeling, an intense fear engulfed me although I did not know for whom. For the women locked in a loving embrace on screen? For the boatwomen who had inadvertently witnessed them? For the two stars who would surely feature in the film gossip magazines after the scene with ever more lurid innuendo? For others who may feel similar desire (I knew that some of our family friends were queer although nothing was ever mentioned)?

121

For others in the theatre with me? Or for myself? For witnessing, feeling, even learning during the song?

When the song ended and the boat with the women slowly drifted away, the audience began moving in their seats again and the casual chatter resumed. It was as if the song – and the captivated silence – had never happened. Afterwards I knew not to ever mention the song, intuiting that something somehow dangerous had occurred on screen and in that theatre. I was not alone in recognising this and some years later when the film aired on the national television channel Doordarshan, the song was mysteriously cropped out. For years afterwards, no VHS version of the film that I found seemed to have the song. None of my classmates, friends or fellow fans remembered seeing it. I even wondered if I had imagined the sequence in all its exquisite, elaborate detail. It was a relief when I found it, over twenty years after the film's release, in a pirated and blurry version online. I have bookmarked various uploads on YouTube even as they disappear regularly. As I write this, it remains unlisted amongst the songs on the film's Wikipedia page.

I no longer experience the same mix of emotions that I remember from that first viewing. After all, rasa creation requires even the sympathetic viewer to be in the correct state of mind. The wonder has faded somewhat, and I recognise that my child-hood reactions were triggered by seeing queer desires represented explicitly for the first time. I now have names for what I could not identify then: sexual attraction, desire, arousal. I even under-stand my fears at the time. It was only in 2018 that the homophobic, colonial-era Article 377 of the Indian Penal Code was finally stuck down after long years of protests, agitations and legal proceedings. However, each time I watch the sequence, I am struck by how well it marshals cinematic and narrative techniques to produce a host of emotions while also ensuring that – even as a young adult – I could not lose myself in any one of them.

This simultaneous evocation and restraint of emotional responses ensures that the spectator retains a critical distance from whatever is represented on stage or screen. This in turn is essential to the Natyashastric concept of sadharanikarana, often translated as universalisation or de-particularisation,[4] which is the mysterious process by which sthayibhava is transformed into rasa. In some ways, sthayibhava can be considered as emotions that are already and always part of the human mind even when an individual may never have experienced them. For example, sexual desire or attraction that underpins the shringar rasa may not be something every spectator has yet or ever experienced. The same may apply to karuna evoked by the death of a loved one or the fear of harm by something that evokes bhayanak. Moreover, the source of the emotions flooding a spectator – grief, love, mirth – may not necessarily be found in the actor's performance or through the writer's narrative or even in a spectator who may have not experienced the situation being depicted. However, we are still capable of drawing on collective memory and knowledge in order to recognise and experience something akin to these sentiments through – and during – a performance. What we feel is not necessarily love or sorrow or fear *per se* but something that approximates the state of feeling these emotions. We do this through the process of sadharanikarana, by moving from the individual to the universal and back again. De-individuation in this manner allows the spectator to participate in emotions that may be unfamiliar or unpleasant in real life by tapping into a generalised and invisible collective. At the same time, knowing that the emotions evoked are not entirely our own also offers the required critical distance that enables a seemingly contradictory pleasure: to fully immerse ourselves in the sensory and emotional experiences of a performance without losing ourselves in it.

*   *   *

---

[4] Although it must be noted here that, while generalisation and universalisation have been used as the most popular translations of the term, these must not be linked in any way to the Aristotelian concept of the 'universal'. (Wadia, 1981:75)

Considering narratives in terms of primary and supporting rasas can help classify films by genre, especially as attempts to map Western film genres onto Indian cinema tend to fail. Even creating 'distinctly Indian genres' such as mythological, social, historical, devotional or stunt applied to pre-Independence cinema by scholars or clumsy portmanteau terms like 'epic melodrama', 'feudal family romance' or, worst of all, 'sentimental melodramatic romance' applied to post-Independence films, do not describe the distinctions between films, nor do they take into account films that pull together elements of more than one of these categories. Instead, using the rasa theory may be better suited to the classification a film like *Chalti Ka Naam Gaadi* which moves smoothly between a romance, social and family melodrama and changes tack in terms of its dominant mood mid-way from a frothy comedy to a suspense thriller with elements of the gothic (complete with a mad woman locked up in the mansion's attic). Similarly, none of the above Western classifications can cover the range of *Naseeb* (Destiny, 1981), which rapidly shifts from romance to social and action to family melodrama, and *Fanaa* (2006), which shifts from romance to suspense and then to tragedy.

If we think of genre as a way of providing the spectator with the means of recognising and describing films and their elements, rasa becomes a useful way of classifying not only Hindi but all Indian cinemas. We would recognise that, despite the many supporting rasas, *Naseeb* is driven by adbhuta which enables the rapid changes in fortunes of its protagonists. Despite the violent and tragic ending and the elements of bhayanaka raised by one of the protagonists being a terrorist, *Fanaa*'s primary rasa remains shringar and all information that precedes the viewing including the titles make this amply clear. Describing a film like *Mission Kashmir* (2000) as terrorist-action-musical-family-drama makes little sense although it features beautifully picturised songs – often reflecting shringar rasa as in case of '*Rind posh maal . . .*' (Flowers will bloom again) and '*Maaf bhi kar do . . .*' (Please forgive me). However, if we notice how both song sequences are followed by scenes of horrific violence (the former is intercut with scenes of a terrorist attack while the latter ends with the murder of the police officer Inayat Khan's, Sanjay Dutt's, wife), it becomes clear that the film has a dominant vira rasa narrative, making these narrative and rasic choices coherent and understandable.

Familiarity with conventions – including the significance of titles and poster design along with a film's key stars and director – means that a knowledgeable spectator, even in a small village, is able to recognise and understand distinct genres before or without ever watching them. A film's marketing apparatus not only clearly identifies its distinct elements but also provides the spectator with clear guidelines of what to expect in terms of the predominant rasa. Critically and commercially successful films across the decades are those that manage to fulfil expectations promised by their publicity material. For example, the poster for the iconic *Deewar*, with the towering figure of Amitabh Bachchan in a bright red shirt in the foreground and a grim-looking Shashi Kapoor in a khaki police uniform, instantly indicates vira as the film's dominant rasa, even though the film includes elements of hasya, shringar and, given its ending, karuna. Similarly, posters for *Jaane bhi do Yaaron* (Who Pays the Piper, 1983) with the lead actors in silly poses and the title in a font that evokes comic books establishes its predominant rasa as hasya despite the elements of shringar, bibhatsa and raudra that mark the film.

Using rasa as the basis for genre would also help identify to a film like *Swades: We, the People* (Homeland: We the People, 2004), about a NASA engineer who returns to India to help impoverished villagers, as a vira rasa film because it emphasises heroic leadership (although in times of peace) and, despite its romantic storyline, devotional sequences and a lack of martial action. Similarly, *Veer-Zaara* (2004) would be instantly identifiable as dominant in shringar despite the political and heroic elements as all those are subordinate to the overarching love story. Finally, *Chalti ka Naam Gaadi* is clearly a hasya narrative despite elements of bhayanak, shringar and vira not only because of its rumbunctious happy ending but because comedy remains the through-thread uniting its complicated plotline and shifting themes. Deploying rasa as genre would merely articulate the knowledge that the primary audience of this cinema already possesses and uses daily to make viewing choices.

Considering films in rasic terms also opens ways of savouring this cinema more like those employed by its primary viewers whose pleasure is rooted in affective or emotional spheres rather than in cognitive realism. The latter requires the viewer to work towards understanding situations, predicting likely outcomes based on available information, and proposing solutions. The primary pleasure of narratives that are grounded in cognitive realism is located in the fulfilment or the subversion of the predicted outcomes. Applied to films, this means the viewer is constantly focussed on 'what next?' In contrast, affective realism focusses less on what happens next and more on how a particular on-screen event 'feels' and the viewer's reward is founded in fully experiencing the emotions invoked by the narrative. This realism is constructed and emphasised by the deployment of a host of filmic techniques and conventions including camerawork, sound effects, editing and *mise-en-scéne* all of which contribute to the building of the sentiment that is felt by the on-screen characters, the actors playing the roles, and the spectator who is meant to experience it.

For example, in the rasic system, the pleasure of a film like *Devdas* – in its many reboots – is not surprise at its ending, or in watching the lovers torn asunder by fate and pride, or the protagonist's determined self-destruction. The audience knows that Devdas will die in the end, but it is the effectiveness of the performance of his decline and death that provides the pleasure. It is one reason that the eponymous role has iconic status in the film industry with some of the best-known actors taking on the challenge. Indeed, the pleasure of *Devdas* lies partly in watching the role performed by some of the biggest stars of celluloid, with their parallel texts reinforcing the power and pleasure of the cinematic performance. At the same time, Devdas as a character evokes karuna (sorrow) not only for the pathos of self-destruction but also through the audience's understanding of the futility of the same. It is this dual response from the partaker – of identification with Devdas's sorrow in performance as well as the recognition of his inherent moral weakness which leads to his unnecessary death – that provides the role with its sustained attraction. Karuna is not simply evoked by Devdas dying, but also from a recognition that he doesn't *need* to do so and indeed that he is morally wrong to do so.

There is no better opportunity for evoking emotions than song sequences. Unlike Hollywood, there has never been a separate 'musicals' category and songs remain intrinsic not only to Hindi but to most commercial cinema in India. There can also be no real comparison with Hollywood or other musical cinema as both song and dance serve specific narrative, visual and emotional purposes.

So essential are songs to cinema in the country that over 50,000 Hindi film songs have been recorded since the introduction of sound in 1931.[5] Filmmakers are clear on the necessity of song and dance to films. Veteran choreographer Saroj Khan noted at the start of the millennium that an Indian audience would likely not even enter a cinema hall if songs and dances were missing from a film. So central are songs to the success of a film that as much as twenty-five percent of a film's budget may depend on the sale of music rights. Not surprisingly then, filmmakers spend a great deal of time, energy and resources creating song sequences as central set-pieces of their films, often even at the cost of other cinematic aspects. For example, Manmohan Desai, well known for memorable music and elaborate song sequences, repeated the background score for his movies at least in part to off-set the high cost of producing the musical score, a tactic that makes any scene from his films instantly recognisable even as

---

[5] Plus many tens of thousands more across over a dozen languages in which the country produces films.

the repetition of sound effects may seem pedestrian. At the same time, film songs also have an extra-filmic life, circulating far beyond the theatre and are often released in audio and video versions as part of a film's pre-release publicity. Their circulation, independent of the film itself, also serves as an additional revenue source that can continue generating income years after the film's release and even when a film fails at the box office.

As few actors are trained singers, Indian cinema has evolved a unique tradition of 'playback singers', who are not only identified in all film publicity material but are often stars in their own right.[6] Famous playback singers like Mohammed Rafi, Lata Mangeshkar, Asha Bhosle and Kishore Kumar not only provided their singing voices to multiple generations of stars and contributed thousands of individual songs to the canon of Hindi film music, but they also retain mass fan followings similar to that of film stars. The convention of playback singing dates to the 1940s, and from the start there was no attempt to hide the artifice of an actor employing another's voice. As early as the 1940s, singers like Shamshad Begum, who sang in multiple languages and had a distinctive and instantly recognisable voice, had reached star status and developed their own following. Instead of hiding the artifice, filmmakers used – and continue to use – playback singers as one of the attractions for their movies, with the names of playback singers well recognised and loved and included on a film's publicity.

In addition to the singers, lyricists and music composers also share prominent billing in promotional material for Indian cinemas, indicating their own star status, and emphasising their importance to the overall cinematic product. Historically, many lyricists have also been established poets who are not only aware of the importance of song but also clear about its use in cinema.

---

[6] Playback singing adds another layer to the visible artifice of cinema, and audience knowledge of it also enables the much desired critical distance from the on-screen spectacle.

According to lyricist and poet Majrooh Sultanpuri, for example, while romantic feelings are better expressed 'musically and poetically', songs should not repeat what dialogue has already made clear in the narrative.

Over time, distinctive functions have evolved for the song sequences. They are most frequently used to: introduce the main star and enable character exposition; reveal key themes as the narrative unfolds; establish mood and heighten anticipation; discuss moral dilemmas; make political statements; express sentiments, especially romantic ones that benefit from poetic language and music; and enhance storylines. A filmmaker may deploy songs towards any, some or even all of these purposes.

For example, *Karz* introduces its star Rishi Kapoor with a disco number '*Paisa yeh paisa . . .*' (Money, this money) that opens with a pair of children's feet walking barefoot across the screen. The feet grow larger with each step, indicating the passage of time, until they are replaced by a pair of tall black boots. The camera pans up to the star with his back to the audience, clad in a gold lamé outfit and holding a revolver. He turns and fires at the camera. The thumping beat of the song restarts as the camera pulls back to reveal an elaborate stage with glittering disco balls and flashing coloured lights. The sequence cuts between the opening credits and the song performance on stage, emphasising not only the star's desirability but also the part he will play – as a singer and performer – in the film. This in turn promises that the film will offer similarly elaborate staged spectacles while the lyrics of the song hint at the motivations driving the plot: monetary greed that led to the character's murder in a previous life.

Similarly, in *Mughal-E-Azam*, the appearance of the female lead, Madhubala playing the courtesan Anarkali, is preceded by a scene where she pretends to be a sculpture that its creator declares is beautiful enough to make 'soldiers drop their swords, kings abandon their crowns, and humans give up their hearts.' She remains unseen by the viewer as Prince Salim, played by Dilip Kumar, defies the warning of the court astrologer to not view the sculpture till an auspicious time. The next scene establishes

Anarkali's romantic disposition and courage as she remains still even when an arrow is fired to remove the covering from the statue, claiming that she wanted to see 'tales become reality'. A captivated Salim declares that she would make a good Radha in the upcoming celebrations, instantly linking the love story about to unfold on screen with the divine love of Krishna and Radha and establishing shringar as the main rasa of the film. Yet even when revealed as human, the actress – renowned for her beauty – remains concealed beneath a layer of plaster, a delaying device that heightens audience anticipation for the song sequence that follows. The song sequence starts with panning on multiple dancers as well as the audience, which includes a fascinated Salim. Anarkali is initially presented seated on the floor with her face covered by a diaphanous veil. The camera pulls up for an extreme close-up as she slowly lifts the veil to reveal her face, enhanced by a wealth of pearl jewellery. Madhubala was often described as having a 'thousand-watt smile', and the lingering close-up is a filmic masterclass in capitalising on a star's particular attraction as well star power. The song '*Mohe panghat pe nandlal khel gayo re . . .*' (Krishna played at the ghat where I gather water) describes Radha's playful annoyance at Krishna's teasing and further emphasises the reference to the mythical lovers. It also moves the plot forward as with each verse Salim grows more enamoured of Anarkali.

The most effective song sequences in cinema combine lyrics, music, on-screen action and extra-filmic star power with an astute placement within the film's narrative. This means that at times a song may not be particularly strong in and of itself or have a life beyond the film but it functions perfectly within the narrative. The peppy '*Maaf bhi kardo . . .*' (Please forgive me . . .) from *Mission Kashmir*, featuring police officer Inayat Khan (played by Sanjay Dutt) trying to tease his wife out of a sulk, is perhaps the least remembered song from the film. In the song, he plays the fool, revealing that the serious, duty-bound Inayat has a private, silly side. He and his wife dance around their home, each picking up or circling around his work briefcase, unaware that a bomb has been placed in it and is counting down to its explosion. However, the audience is not only aware of the ticking bomb – the sound of a clock is incorporated into the score – but also knows that it is likely to go off, harming one or both of the happy couple. The song lyrics, music and acting for the song are firmly rooted in shringar but its placement in the plot and context ensure that the dominant rasa is bhayanaka, moving to bibhasta when the song ends with the bomb going off and followed by karuna as the survivors grieve in its aftermath.

Over the past eight decades since the introduction of sound, precise conventions have evolved to guide the use of song and dance. Playwright, director, producer and actor P. Sambandha Mudaliar, often described as the founding father of modern Tamil drama and whose plays have frequently been adapted for cinema, reportedly recommended that song sequences make up about a quarter of a film's duration. Song sequences also follow specific cinematic conventions regarding their placement and function in the narrative. Using a term from an era when films were still made with stock and their length calculated in feet, screenwriter Sachin Bhowmick recommends keeping a gap of a thousand feet between songs, calculating that the average Hindi film, at fourteen or fifteen thousand feet long, allows for six or seven songs. Director and producer Manmohan Desai would often explain the storyline to his preferred music-composing duo, Laxmikant–Pyarelal, and discuss potential points where each song could be inserted. This meant that the songs were composed and often recorded before the shooting began.

However, the film industry is clear that the primary purpose of song in films is linked to emotions. Music composer Vanraj Bhatia explains that song sequences are often the most dramatic moments in a film where all action stops for a song to take over and express emotions more effectively than dialogue or gesture. Perhaps inadvertently, this echoes the fourth chapter of the *Natyashastra*, which focusses on the role of dance (with its obvious accompaniment of music) in a dramatic performance. Curiously it is also one of the chapters that has raised the least debate, with classic commentators unequivocally accepting Bharata's assertions. The text declares dance integral to drama on grounds that its role is to generate splendour and beauty, being a form that is loved by people and considered auspicious and one that is used during festive occasions to release the tensions that affect the human mind.

Within the *Natyashastric* mode of performance, use of song and dance also helps break the intensity of a narrative. This in turn provides both emotional respite and an opportunity for the spectator to distance themselves from the story. A similar process functions in cinema where a song sequence ruptures the illusion of realism and highlights cinematic artifice. Song and dance not only divert the spectator from losing themselves in a particular emotion but also encourage them to bring to bear a range of other tools such as memory, knowledge and intellect to process the experience instead of relying entirely on the affective.

After more than a century of cinema production, filmmakers as well as spectators are intensely familiar with narrative and aesthetic conventions, primarily through films themselves. A quick shot of snow-capped mountains is enough to signal romance and a single shot of a bee hovering over flowers is instantly understood as erotism. Narrative conventions developed over decades enable audiences to distinguish between the good guys and the bad, between a light-hearted flirtation and 'meet cute' moments that signal true love. The conventions also offer unlimited permutations to filmmakers, the best of whom are able to combine them in a coherent and attractive whole. However, despite the familiar elements, there is no guarantee that any combination can automatically generate rasa and be rewarded by the audience's love and money. The bulk of films produced every year fail at the box office, often for no explicable reason. This neither deters the filmmakers, who incessantly seek the perfect – almost magical – combination of familiar elements to create the elusive blockbuster, nor the audiences who continue to offer their money, time and selves to films.

*   *   *

One freezing Saturday afternoon, at the end of the 1980s, I found a tucked-away table in my university library in Massachusetts. It was February, I would graduate in just a few weeks, and I had no idea what I would do afterwards. I had applied half-heartedly to a handful of graduate programmes and was vaguely considering looking for jobs in New York. Meanwhile, my family was on the other side of the world and, although I missed them, I didn't want to return to India just yet. Worse still, I recognised that I was drifting further and further away from them, and from India itself.

The library was tucked into the side of a hill although the mound seemed a bit too low to be considered as such, at least to those of us who consider the lower ranges of the Himalayas as 'the hills'. The vast glass walls looked out on a snowy landscape worthy of a picture postcard and, although the library was warm, I still shivered and snuggled into my long scarf. It was supposed to be the coldest weekend of the year and the annual tropical party was planned for that evening at the student union. My friends were all busy hunting up plastic flower garlands, gaudily printed shirts and sarongs, weighing up the merits of wearing flip-flops instead of boots, which given the temperature and ice on the paths, seemed like a poor idea. I had told them that I was working on my final thesis, although I had actually sneaked in two VHS tapes of Hindi films. There were dedicated tables in the library equipped with televisions with built-in video cassette players and head-phones. Although these were intended for viewing study material, I figured I could always explain away my movie choices as texts for one of the many courses focussed on foreign cultures.

I still remember that the first film I tried that afternoon was *Parinda* (Bird, 1989), a violent gangster story that had been critically acclaimed and won not only multiple Filmfare awards but also two National Film Awards. It was supposed to be gritty, realist, entirely unlike the usual masala movies. I watched it glumly, repulsed by the violence and gore that not only seemed gratuitous on screen but was all too stark a reminder of real-world events.

We had been living in Islamabad when the Khalistan movement gathered momentum in the western Indian state of Punjab although my attention, like that of my Pakistani classmates, was focussed on the Soviet presence in Afghanistan. In 1984, the escalating cycle of violence culminated with Operation Blue Star when Indian forces stormed the the Golden Temple in Amritsar, considered the holiest site for Sikhs. The operation, intended to remove militants from the religious complex, lasted nearly ten days, sent shock waves through families and communities, and unleashed a wave of brutal repression through the state. The blowback came quickly, with two Sikh bodyguards assassinating Prime Minister Indira Gandhi within the high-security prime ministerial complex. The assassination in turn set off a wave of anti-Sikh pogroms in many parts of northern India. Even before the horror of this violence could really register, the country lurched into another disaster: a poisonous gas leak in the city of Bhopal killed thousands and injured over half a million people. In a strange twist, I found myself feeling safer across the border in Pakistan, where threats were at least clearly defined, rather than in India where the state, communities, lone individuals, even the air itself, could turn murderous.

Dad's assignment and our move to New York just as I turned sixteen came as a relief although I soon found myself floundering in my American high school, not least because my classmates and I shared few cultural memories or references. Our home life was too closely tied up with politics – Indian, American and global – to make sense to either my classmates or my teachers. Family conversations centred around the deployment of Indian soldiers in Sri Lanka. In 1987, we sat in one of the diplomatic booths overlooking the UN General Assembly where leaders from one global south nation after another rose to speak about the existential dangers of climate change. We closely followed the nuclear sabre rattling between the Reagan administration and the Soviet Union. Thanks to the adults around us, we had too much information about nuclear protocols, the load capacity of nuclear missiles, potential targets and the time that a missile required to reach us if launched from across the world. When my siblings and I realised that we lived within a mile of the probable epicentre for a nuclear strike, we came up with an action plan. We knew that there was no way to flee the city, so we made a pact: we would walk down to the UN Plaza, not far from our home. If we were lucky, we would have time to arrange ourselves before the first atomic flash. And arrange ourselves, we would. In shapes that would throw the most beautiful shadows that would remain, as testaments for survivors or perhaps even aliens who stumbled upon our destroyed planet.

In the face of constant specific and generalised danger, I had always found comfort in watching our movies, choosing from our ever-expanding VHS collection and new releases that were circulated by my parents' friends. I had also found Hollywood films on television and grown to love 1930s screwball comedies, 1970s action films and anything at all with Sophia Loren. When Cary Grant died in 1986, I spent the week afterwards binge-watching his films on a classics movie channel. My international film forays were also partly motivated by a change in Hindi cinema: the violence roiling in India had crept into the movies, which had turned darker and cruder, and their most gory violence seemed aimed at women. Even the 1987 superhero caper, *Mr India*, about a street musician armed with a watch that turned him invisible, which was supposedly intended to appeal to family audiences including children, had a disturbing element of extreme violence. Meanwhile, Bachchan, the biggest star of the previous decade, had been tarnished by his brief flirtation with politics and allegations of corruption regarding a major weapons deal. His return to films was *Shahenshah* (The Emperor, 1988), which had been a huge success but mostly bowdlerised his own earlier films and screen persona. I should have loved *Qayamat Se Qayamat Tak* (From Doomsday Till Doomsday, 1988, popularly referred to as *QSQT*), a modern-day Romeo-and-Juliet tale of young lovers divided by a family feud. It was reminiscent of earlier films, including the period dramas based on well-known love stories like *Heer-Ranha* (1970) and *Laila Majnu* (1976) or a contemporary tale like *Ek Duje Ke Liye* (Made For Each Other, 1981) where the differences of language and culture between the lovers were presented as insurmountable. On a trip home, I found my former classmates enamoured of *QSQT* but it had left me unmoved. My friends accused me, only half teasing, of 'turning American', a charge that seemed to extend well beyond my preference for movies.

I had been initially excited by our move to New York because it meant I could access its rich spread of films, not only Hollywood releases in commercial theatre chains but also international cinema at film festivals, cultural centres and diplomatic screenings. My pocket money mostly went into watching the latest releases in movie halls that were the exactly opposite of the theatres I had known: both impossibly luxurious and incredibly tiny, intended only for a few dozen viewers rather than hundreds. They were also strangely prosaic little rooms with plain sound-proofed walls that bore none of the décor including the gilt edges and the velvet curtains that I had come to associate with movie theatres. Worse still, nobody spoke or even made eye contact with each other. Once we took our seats and the lights dimmed, nobody seemed to move. Even in movies like *Back to the Future* (1985) or *Top Gun* (1986), there were no whistles, no hoots, and even friends didn't speak to each other while the film rolled. For the first time, I learned to feel alone, even lonely, in a movie theatre.

As darkness fell on the snows outside the library, I started on the second movie. *Maine Pyar Kiya* (I've Loved, 1989) had been a runaway hit the year before and promised to be a useful counter to the violence of *Parinda*, which had left me feeling bit nauseous and even glummer than before. At least initially, the love story

136

seemed to unfold in ways I had hoped – with melodious songs, bright colours and a tale of true love. As the closing credits rolled, however, I found myself disappointed and discontent, and not only by the absurdity of a carrier pigeon as the hero who saves the day! Either my films were no longer magical or I had stopped being the kind of viewer that the rasic tradition required.

At least one thing had become clear during the afternoon. Although I knew I would not remain in the US after graduation, I would also not return home. The world was a big place, and I would surely find parts of it that would be less painful, less terrifying, and most of all less heartbreaking than India. I packed away the VHS cassettes in my bag, deciding that I was also done with my movies. I told myself that my lingering love for them was nothing more than nostalgia and homesickness, that there were many cinemas in the world and, surely, I would find films to love in another language, from another part of the world. And I decided I would miss neither my country nor my films.

Later that night I walked from the tropical ball to my dorm, my rubber flip-flops slipping and sliding on ice, my bare toes turning blue but still feeling warm thanks to the liberal consumption of contraband vodka poured into the punch. The sky was clear, heaps of banked snow gleamed in the moonlight, and the tall firs seemed to shiver more than I did in my t-shirt and sarong. Somewhere along the way I realised I was humming a song from the second film I had watched that afternoon.

That song had buried itself in my mind, surfacing repeatedly for years afterwards as I wended my way through cities and countries where India was just a name, where there weren't even Indian grocery stores with pirated copies of my movies, and the radio played songs that I'd never heard in languages I didn't yet know. '*Dil deewana bin sajna ke maane na, yeh pagla hain samjhaane se samjhe na . . .*' (Crazy heart refuses to be without its love. It's mad and refuses to listen to reason).

I Remember Your Love
for Me[1]

THERE WAS A NIGHTCLUB in Santiago de Chile, on the far side of the Mapocho river, that I only went to once. I don't remember exactly where it was or even its name. It was one of the many my friends tried out each weekend.

The mid-1990s were meant to be halcyon days, with General Augusto Pinochet's brutal regime finally replaced by a democratically elected government. The Chilean economy was booming even if it was a petri dish experiment for the Chicago School of Economics and despite the bullet marks that still scarred the buildings downtown. My friends and I were all 'expats', a mix of young people from Europe who seemed to all work in technology, Australians and Canadians who worked in mining, and a sprinkling of Americans who were mostly in finance. I was an anomaly and had been told by the immigration officer who stamped my work permit that I was one of only ten Indians to receive it that year. His voice carried a hint of pride as he explained that his people didn't need to emigrate to foreign lands. After an hour of sitting alone in a room with nothing but a massive mirror on the wall (I had been warned by a Chilean friend it was two-way glass), I bit my tongue.

---

[1] 'Yaad aa raha hai tera pyaar . . .' from *Disco Dancer* (1980).

Later, on my daily run, I would peek behind the tall hedges lining the city's wide boulevard heading up to the mountains and would gaze at a valley densely packed with houses. I found perverse comfort in declaring – albeit only in my own head – that at least my country didn't hide its poverty. Then I wondered if that was better or worse.

I found the narrower streets of Bellavista more comfortable, especially beyond the patches intended for tourists. Its homes seemed more human sized and people in bars, shops and even on streets greeted each other, even me, and asked friendly questions. 'It's so far,' they exclaimed, both pleased that I had made the long journey to their land but also worried that I was alone and had no one caring for me. The clubs on this side of the river played a mix of Argentine rock, American R&B and even hip hop instead of relentless Euro techno. People danced instead of standing about posing or shuffling like in a boring MTV video. The club had a neon-lit tunnel at the entrance and a sprinkler system that drenched the dance floor when things got too heated.

I had been on the dance floor for hours and my friends had retreated for drinks at our table. In my wanderings across the continents, I learned to move in new ways: to sensual, joyous salsa and merengue, defiant toyi-toyi, sedate Chilean cueca, and most of all to the free 'club' style that demands nothing but giving oneself up to the rhythm. I found a favourite dance club in every city and made time so I could lose myself in whatever music they played, in beats that were so different from mine. I had learned to love being swept away from myself, even if only for a few hours.

When the DJ began sampling an unknown yet familiar beat, I almost didn't notice. Then a female voice cut through, at a pitch that is rarely used in popular music beyond India. It pulled at me, insistent that I pay attention The song had no words initially and was instead joined by a male voice, both singing out a familiar upbeat mix of musical scales. I stopped moving, suddenly aware of the sweaty bodies pressing against me from all sides, stunned that no one else seemed to have noticed the change in mood. I had never heard the song before but I felt it seep into my bones, insisting that I dance again but in a way that I had forgotten. As I began to move again, I realised that I understood the words. They were not only in my language, but in a cheeky and colloquial variation: '*Tu cheez badi hai mast mast* . . .' (You are a wonderful thing). I froze again, stood still amidst the dancers, feeling in that moment like I belonged.

I had already learned that my attempts to ignore India and my movies were doomed to fail. The cinema near my home in Mexico City screened *Salaam Bombay* (1988) for months on end and years after its release. In a small village of the country's Sierra Gorda, an old woman had held up her equally brown arm to mine and noted that my skin had olive tones while hers was café-con-leche, a difference so subtle that I could not see it. She explained that it meant that I was 'from India' but not 'india', gently parsing the nuances of both Spanish language and our shared yet different postcolonial identities. She had watched *Mother India* decades ago on a trip to the capital and demanded to know if there were more films like that in my country. As she made stacks of corn tortillas on a heavy iron griddle much like the Indian tawa, I told her about my favourite movies. For a few hours, despite the differences and distance, that village, food, even the old woman, felt entirely my own.

Meanwhile Dad had been assigned to Windhoek, the capital of newly liberated Namibia, and I would catch up with new releases on my trips home. Yet it seemed more of a perfunctory exercise, and I found it hard to connect with the films I had once loved so much. Instead, family conversations were now entirely focussed on political discussions as India seemed to stumble from one violent crisis to another. From across the world, I had watched protests against affirmative action by upper-caste Hindu students intent on preserving the historical advantage caste has long granted us with unarticulated unease. Soon after, in 1991, the former prime minister Rajiv Gandhi was assassinated by a suicide bomber while on the campaign trail. The next year, a mob of Hindu far right activists, organised and encouraged by leaders of the Bhartiya Janata Party, demolished the sixteenth-century Babri Masjid in the city of Ayodhya. The event sparked off sectarian violence across the country and to this day continues to feed justifications for terrorist activities offered by violent Islamist groups as well as deliberate and explicit Islamophobia in both national discourse and policy. Amidst my disenchantment, however, I would be regularly reminded of how my movies kept enchanting many others across the world. While working in South Africa as it headed towards liberation in the early 1990s, I had run into a doctor who had recently returned from a conference in Hyderabad. He confessed that he had been delighted with the monsoons and had jumped out into the downpour to dance. He remained deeply disappointed that none of the locals had joined him: 'I always thought dancing in the rain is what Indians do. It's always so in your movies.' I had reassured him that we did, although only sometimes and not generally at the bus stop.

Although living in South America maximised my distance from India in every way, I welcomed the separation. As I worked and lived mostly in English and Spanish, my use of Hindi became limited to phone calls home. Few if any of my colleagues and friends cared about events unfolding across the world, which meant I could worry and fear and mourn events in India entirely on my own. At the time, many cities in the region had few or even no Indian restaurants. In Santiago, there was just one, situated in an upscale neighbourhood. The place was owned by a determined man from southern India who had to import ingredients from as far away as Venezuela, Guyana and Surinam as no local stores stocked them. On my rare visits, he would kindly give me little packages of his precious spices, although they mostly remained unused in my bare kitchen.

And yet that night, somehow a single song sampled by a DJ in a nightclub had suddenly collapsed that geographical, linguistic, emotional distance. For days afterwards, I had puzzled over the moment. The club had only played the refrain and I wondered about the rest of the verses. Which stars featured in the song?

How did they dance to the beats? I could not imagine any of the older stars dancing to that tune. What kind of film used such cheeky lyrics? Without knowing the rest of the song lyrics, I had no way to guess the sort of movie that would feature such a number or where it would be set within the narrative.

Some days later, I checked with the friendly Indian restaurant owner, who not only had heard the song but enthusiastically copied the album on a cassette for me while I ate. He couldn't tell me much about the film, *Mohra* (Pawn, 1994), as he hadn't seen it but he knew that it had been one of the biggest hits of the year and starred some newcomers. He promised to find a video copy on his next trip to Georgetown. While waiting for my cassette, I had examined the CD cover, noting that only one actor was known to me, the veteran Naseeruddin Shah. From the number of images of determined-looking men, I guessed it was some sort of crime thriller and hoped it would not be as tiresomely gruesome as many of the recent films. On the third listen, I decided the song that had so intrigued me most likely featured the pretty woman caught in dancing poses and who obviously played the love interest of one or both the young men in the dark sunglasses. Then I heard it a fourth time.

I may not have recognised most actors on the CD cover but as I heard each song on the album, I could see them in my mind. By the mood, music and lyrics, I could imagine where each song would appear in a film. But I was still curious: I wanted to discover not only how film had chosen to connect the many moods of the actors featured on CD cover, but also exactly how the songs connected to the plot elements – romance, action, drama – suggested by the same images.

* * *

The *Natyashastra* regards plot as merely the body of drama, rather than its soul, and uses the term itivrtta to describe the 'story' (this English word is also used by filmmakers who traditionally did

142

not compile a script in the Hollywood sense but relied on a 'story recitation' around which the film was then built). Unlike Aristotle's *Poetics*, which emphasises clear stages of plotting with a beginning, middle and an end that in turn create a linear progression of action, the *Natyashastric* plot structure is cyclical, based on themes of separation and reunion or mysteries and their revelations, and structured to consistently disrupt the linearity of time. In his novel *Midnight's Children*, Salman Rushdie wryly notes that 'no people whose word for "yesterday" is the same as their word for "tomorrow" can be said to have a firm grip on the time.' Classical Indian philosophers including the *Natyashastra*'s author would have likely argued that a people with the same word for yesterday and tomorrow are perhaps better equipped to confront the vagaries of time.

The *Natyashastra* divides the plot into five sections which are then further classified as primary, secondary and additional sequence of actions. The primary thread focusses on a particular goal – attaining love, winning a war, restoring order and a movement from justice to chaos – desired and strived for by the protagonist, and supported by a secondary sequence of events including storylines for second and third leads and even additional, minor, characters. Moreover, the primary and secondary sequences of events can occur in different times and places while still interacting and supporting each other, and this structure remains deeply familiar to the viewer who may not know Bharata's text but has watched it unfold in hundreds if not thousands of stories on stage and screen. This is also why *Om Shanti Om* can declare, '*Kehte hain agar kisi cheez ko dil se chaho; to puri kainaat usse tumse milane ki koshish mein lag jaati hai*' (They say if you wish for something from the bottom of your heart, the whole universe joins in the efforts to bring it you), and the spectator can accept that, despite the heartbreak and the murder of the protagonist in the first half of the film, his dreams will be fulfilled in the next.

The text lays out guidelines for constructing the story in a sequence of events that are governed by causal – albeit karmic

143

rather than psychological – connections. It also lays out the five stages for a story: first, the desire to achieve an object which Bharata compares to the sowing of a seed; second, making efforts to achieve the desired objective despite no possibility of its attainment; third, the discovery of some means of attaining the object of desire and therefore a growing feasibility of success; fourth, increasing proximity to success, and finally, fifth, its achievement.

The text adds guidelines for structuring these five stages effectively by offering five key junctures that can be loosely compared to plot points which serve as transitions from one stage to another. The first, compared to the birth of the seed, is triggered by the activation of the protagonist's desire to attain a primary objective, for example the first sight of the beloved or an act of injustice that must be avenged. The second is compared to the emergence of the first visible roots and shoots as the efforts to obtain the objective, despite its seeming impossibility, grow stronger. In the third, the seed begins to bloom as the objective seems initially within grasp but then recedes and requires further effort. The fourth stage is marked by unforeseen external obstacles and/or internal doubts until the fifth stage, when the objective is achieved. Each of these is aided by transitions in rasa while maintaining and emphasising the dominant one. For example, a love story may move from the protagonist's first meeting with the beloved (shringar), pursuit of the lover which may involve comedic situations (hasya) or acts of courage that impress the lover who eventually responds positively (vira), and move through raudra, bhayanak, bibhatsa as the lovers encounter obstacles and to shringar again, either on its own in the case of a happy ending or mingled with karuna if the lovers can only be united in death.

The *Natyashastra*, as well as later philosophers and practitioners, are clear that while the beginning and the end are necessary to all dramatic performance, the other stages can be condensed, extended or even excluded as necessary for a script. These choices can either produce a slow and complicated epic drama or a fast almost unilinear action, such as in comic plays where neither great depths nor moral stature are required.

Bharata also provides guidelines for structuring a play with multiple streams of actions, creating a scaffold for multiple plots and subplots, again using the metaphor of the seed or a small, initially invisible, element that grows and culminates in the fruit or result. While the seed provides coherence to the protagonist's quest, motivations and actions, an additional structural principle of the bindu – literally a dot, and metaphysically the point where creation begins[2] – also comes into play. For the purposes of the plot, the bindu is a fixed point around which the various streams of a story are organised. These two structures act together to enable a play to retain an inner coherence that binds its protagonist to the other characters as well as to the narrative and its evolving situations. Moreover, the main storyline – of the hero's pursuit of goals – may be supported by two kinds of subsidiary sequences: a subplot that helps the main storyline, and a subordinate storyline that has no distinct narrative purpose of its own but can provide either supporting information or opportunities for spectacle such as song and dance.

Elements of this structure can be identified in works of directors as diverse as Mehboob Khan, Gulzar and Yash Chopra, and even when directors are visibly influenced by non-Indian cinema. Ostensibly influenced by Italian neo-realist films, Bimal Roy's *Bandini* (Prisoner, 1963) opens with the static shot of a church clock tower – a device which simultaneously acknowledges its Western realist influence while also signalling the more traditional

---

[2] Indic philosophical traditions have debated the nature of the bindu for centuries. It is often described as the symbol of the cosmos in its unmanifested form. In Buddhist traditions, bindu is the point around which the mandala, or the ritual circular pattern representing the universe, is created. The twentieth-century Indian painter S.H. Raza described the bindu as the point where life begins and 'attains infinity'. His paintings are instantly recognisable not only because of their use of colour but also by the use of the dot as their central metaphor.

145

ritual invocation – with the production house logo superimposed on it before moving to a shot of women prisoners arriving at a jailhouse. The female protagonist, Kalyani (played by Nutan), is identified in the first scene amongst the new arrivals by the police officer who is impressed by her beauty and demeanour. The following sequences establish the characters of the sympathetic jailer and the idealist doctor Devendra (Dharmendra) who falls in love with Kalyani.

Although Kalyani's emotional state is declared as that of repentance for the murder for which she has been sentenced, there is little else to indicate the mood of the film. The initial fifteen minutes of the film provide the 'realist' character exposition and the dominant mood or sthayibhava is not revealed until the first song begins, telling of the loneliness of a woman separated from her family and pleading for her brother's visit. The song recalls the tradition of *teej* or the annual visit by the brother to a married sister bearing gifts. This first song establishes the dominant mood of the film as the vipralambha form of shringar (love) or love experienced as sorrow of separation from the beloved. The viewer knows that Kalyani as a convict cannot possibly be united with the doctor who loves her; nor can she possibly find happiness with the man in her past whose wife she has murdered. Yet the desire for a lovers' union is signalled by the song, which forms the first stage of the plot. At the same time, the dominant sense of the vipralambha rasa is emphasised: Devendra's love for Kalyani is hopeless and, although he may love her, she does not reciprocate his feelings. Similarly, despite their reunion, Kalyani can never reach the kind of love she desires with Bikash (Ashok Kumar), a fact underlined by the pathos of the lyrics and music of the final song. The film's ending is often characterised as hopeless, yet within the rasic logic the final song emphasises and heightens the primary mood of the film: of vipralambha with clear tones of karuna (sorrow).

The interior logic of the film is driven by presenting Kalyani in the mode of classical female protagonists reminiscent of *Shakuntala*, a minor character in the *Mahabharata* where she appears as the semi-divine mother of Bharata, the founding father of the dynasty that produces the Kauravas and Pandavas whose fratricidal war the epic recounts. She is also the eponymous heroine of Kalidasa's fourth-century Sanskrit play about a beautiful maiden who is loved, abandoned and then restored to her husband after a series of mishaps, miracles and revelations. Like Shakuntala, Kalyani is initially the young ingénue who falls in love with a sophisticated outsider (in this case, Bikash is a freedom fighter). Her subsequent fall from grace and search for the lover who has abandoned her echo the classic love story.

Of course, *Bandini* is not a straight-forward adaptation of the classical story. Instead, like much of the commercial cinematic tradition, it relies on hooking the viewer by evoking recognisable characters and then adds a narrative twist. Kalyani is no Shakuntala; she kills Bikash's wife in a fit of madness. Within the neo-realist tradition, this revelation would have sufficed as the climax of the film. Yet within the *Natyashastric* logic, the murder forms neither the climax nor the finale of the film. Narrated by Kalyani in a flashback sequence, the murder scene is followed by Bikash's recognition of Kalyani, his explanation of his choice to abandon her as well as his repentance. Kalyani's confession of her crime and the events that led to it absolves her morally if not legally for Devendra's mother, who accepts her as a suitable daughter-in-law. This marks the second recognition, this time social, of Kalyani's inner heroic worth as that of a heroine.

The film ends with Kalyani recognising a dying Bikash at a port scene and choosing him over Devendra who loves her. However tragic, pessimist and irrational this final choice may appear, Kalyani's decision emphasises both her position and power as the heroine and affirms the vipralambha form of shringar as the main rasa of the film. Moreover, Kalyani's choice, despite Bikash's imminent demise, cannot be considered tragic as it reinforces the balance required by classical principles of narrative and performance. In the final sequence, Roy abandons all attempts at cognitive realism and chooses affective realism with the plaintive sounds of the steamboat overlaid with S.D. Burman's pathos-filled voice singing '*Le chal paar . . .*' (Take me across).

Released four decades later, *Veer-Zaara* (2004) serves as a neat counterpoint of how a dominant rasa, this time the sambhoga form of shringar, or love that ends in union, is rapidly established by an initial song sequence and maintained through the narrative. Directed by Yash Chopra and written by his son Aditya Chopra, the film opens after its initial credits with a long sequence of landscape shots – rivers, flowers, waterfalls – while a voiceover recites a love poem. The poem gives way to a low-angle long shot, focussing on the male protagonist Veer (played by Shah Rukh Khan) who walks through a bright field ready for harvest. His song speaks of a growing desire for something unnamed and unseen and links it to the pregnant fruitfulness of the nature around him. Shots of the protagonist are intercut with images of an unidentified but obviously desirable woman, who is framed as the object of his yet undeveloped desire and love. This song also functions as the *Natyashastric* first stage, ensuring that the audience has not only been attuned to the predominant mood for the film but also been introduced to the protagonist who is prepared for love.

The song ends with a long shot of the protagonist and the unidentified woman running towards each other. A gunshot rings out and the woman falls to the ground just before she reaches Veer's arms. The sequence cuts to the sweating, panting close-up of a much older Veer who has obviously been dreaming. As the following sequences unfold, the audience savours the vipralambha form of love as there appears to be no hope for an imprisoned Veer of ever reaching union with his unidentified beloved. However, while the narrative weaves through multiple decades and expands to include violence at various points; however, the dominant rasa for the film remains shringar in its sambhoga form – established by the initial song sequence – and the viewer can draw pleasure even from sorrow and fear evoked by the lovers' travails, knowing all the while that they will eventually be reunited.

*   *   *

I arrived in New Delhi just in time for the biggest movie the country had seen in decades: *Dilwale Dulhaniya Le Jayenge* (The Bravehearted Will Take the Bride, known popularly as *DDLJ*, 1995),[3] a contemporary romance between a young couple raised in London and set between Europe and India. The film offered a happy middle path between tradition and modernity, and launched the stereotype of the non-resident Indian (NRI) who lives far from the homeland, flaunts flashy cars and designer clothes and moves smoothly between cultures of East and West while also holding on to old-fashioned values. The film had already been declared a mammoth hit in the weeks before my arrival and it seemed that every restaurant, shop, café and, worst of all, long-distance overnight buses incessantly played its soundtrack or pirated DVD copies. I had heard the soundtrack while making my way across the globe and the melodious '*Ghar aaja pardesi tera desh bulaaye hai . . .*' (Come home stranger, your country calls you) had stayed in my mind, perhaps because it so closely chimed with my personal version of the prodigal's return. Although my trip home was meant to be brief, intended only to see family, I found myself unwilling to leave.

The India to which I returned was entirely unlike the one I had left or remembered. For the first time in our lives, Dad was based in the capital, New Delhi. My siblings, who I always thought of as children, had mysteriously turned into young adults,

---

[3] The film was the highest-grossing Indian film for the year, picked up ten Filmfare Awards, and has been screened every day, without a break, since its initial release in October 1995 at Mumbai's Maratha Mandir theatre. For Valentine's Day in 2023, producers Yash Raj Films re-released the film for a single week across cinemas in India.

no longer so different from myself. The loss of my grandmother, my personal lodestar, was both a reality I refused to accept and an aching void that I could not ignore. When I walked through her house in Varanasi, the only building that I had ever considered home, it was shadowed and emptied, as if her death had taken all the laughter and joy it had held. My friends and classmates were gone too, emigrated for work or marriage to Bombay, London, Singapore and New York. I learned that even the principal of my old school, a Catholic priest from Kerala, had died. Although I didn't think of him often, he had been a constant throughout my peripatetic childhood as I moved schools depending on the availability of education wherever Dad was assigned. He had been a tall, kind man with twinkling eyes who would gently rebuke my tomboyish ways, ruffle my short hair and wonder if I ever planned on growing it 'like all other girls'. My hair now hung well past my shoulders, and I wondered if he would approve of it or be disappointed. Oddly, I suspected the latter.

At least my uncle still growled at priests at the ghat who cajoled the devout into unnecessary, expensive rituals and threatened karmic retribution to any that refused. I grinned at their hurried retreat, comforted that some things at least remained the same. However, I quickly realised that my compatriots had as little idea of me as I did of them or my country. Most people assumed I had returned for an arranged match, an idea which infuriated me, caused endless hilarity for my siblings, and shocked Dad. Thankfully, my mother rejected offers of potential matches with such brutal but polite efficiency that I didn't learn of most of them until years later. My explanation that I was working on a novel – my first – caused greater bewilderment: 'You sent her to an American university to become a writer?' was the response of most of my parents' acquaintances. It was a valid query as few women studied overseas at the time and even the men who went abroad studied something useful like engineering, science or medicine. I learned of a nastier assumption when a US-educated man my own age informed me that girls like me had been spoiled. Initially I thought he meant pampered but then realised that it was code for presumed sexual promiscuity due to my stay in the immoral West.

It became clear that I had to re-learn India, and I chose the same process that had worked well elsewhere: grabbing a backpack to travel the country, criss-crossing across the land without any plan or rush, hopping onto the next available train, bus and ferry. Despite the distances, the changes in cuisine, language and culture, *DDLJ* kept me company. Fellow travellers played its songs on cheap boomboxes on the slow train from Thiruvananthapuram to Kanyakumari. The soundtrack ran on a loop despite loud complaints by the passengers on the quirky overnight 'sleeper' bus from Goa to Mumbai. I despaired at the repeat viewings on a tiny but loud television mounted at the front of a bus from Chennai to Madurai, where the driver paused the third successive show at dawn to switch to a recording of exquisite classical Carnatic vocals. At a tiny hotel in Chittorgarh, the restaurant was full of drunken men, all of whom seemed to have drawn sartorial inspiration from too many movie villains. They broke off their overly curious staring to break into a collective, out-of-tune rendition of '*Tujhe dekha to yeh jaana sanam . . .*' (When I first saw you, my love) from *DDLJ*. The manager frantically ushered me out of the room, following with a tray with my unfinished dinner. He assured me that he would post a guard on my corridor. I slept uneasily, with a chair propped under the doorknob, that night. However, when I saw the manager at the front desk while checking out in the morning, we both giggled long and loud at the memory.

At the time, few Indian women travelled on their own, even fewer before marriage, and almost none at all with a backpack. This last raised grumbles from porters at every train station as they informed me that carrying my own luggage was unseemly and also robbed them of their livelihood. Mostly I was met with a mix of kindness, curiosity and a host of amusing or infuriating assumptions. A priest in Madurai asked me kindly if I was there to plead for a husband, the only explanation he could imagine for a woman travelling alone and without any matrimonial markers: I wore no bracelets on my arms or vermillion in my hair or a thaali (the traditional gold necklace that married Hindu women wear) around my neck. In Goa, my dark skin and curly hair made me invisible in a crowd, but my clothing rendered me hyper-visible, and I only realised after days of simmering fury at incessant unwanted male attention that few of my female compatriots wore as little at the beach. I eventually found a quiet beachside bar run by a local man whose Ethiopian wife quickly took me under her wing, explaining social – and sexual – codes of her adopted, and my natal, country. In Khajuraho, an older stranger walked up, addressed me with an aristocratic title and then berated me – albeit politely – for behaving in ways that 'dishonoured my family'. I didn't understand if it was my patronage of the rooftop bar, my battered clothing or my half-drunk cold beer that was the cause of this dishonour. I explained that he had mistaken me for someone else and, in any case, India no longer had any hereditary titles. He stomped off, grumbling about young women who didn't respect traditions, but not before bizarrely bowing to me. By the time a camel driver in the deserts near Jaisalmer attempted to confirm my caste, I was troubled but no longer surprised. He seemed to find my answers sufficiently explanatory, nodded to himself as if slotting me into some category known only to him, and told me that he had guessed the same because 'women from other castes could not behave' like me.

I learned quickly that the south of the country, despite my inability to speak the languages, was far more welcoming of women travellers. But movie theatres even there were not spaces for lone women, or at least not with any degree of comfort or safety. In contrast, the spaces for innumerable classical, folk and popular performances of drama, dance and music were oddly welcoming. More importantly, these seemed to happen everywhere: on beaches and riverbanks, at temples and fairs, in town centres and street corners, and sometimes even in formal concert halls and theatres. They also appeared, as if by magic, from thin air, as it seemed when my bus from Bangalore to the eastern coast broke down on an empty road in the middle of a forest. The afternoon stretched into dusk while the driver and his assistant tinkered with the engine and the passengers waited on the side of the road. Suddenly the sound of reed instruments and drums rose into the air and a troupe of people appeared at the turn in the road. They were carrying a statue, a local deity that I didn't recognise. All of them wore brightly coloured costumes and some had masks on. They paused before the weary passengers at the side of the road to suddenly break into a performance. I didn't understand the nuances of their narrative or the form of their performance, but I recognised that they were enacting the story of a bride – perhaps the elaborated dressed and decorated deity they were carrying? – making her way to her husband's house. The actors moved in ways that I knew signalled the bride's anxiety and excitement at meeting her new husband and the joy of the many who made up her wedding procession. The narrative switched to introduce the powerful but loving husband awaiting her and the battles he had fought and won, the many ways he cared for the people. Was it an enactment of Shiva's wedding to Parvati, a popular theme for folk performances? Or that of Sita's wedding to Rama? Or something entirely different? It didn't matter. There was enough that was recognisable, meaningful, beautiful in the range of graceful movements of the actors to keep us all captivated.

The bus was fixed by the time the performance ended, although the driver was in no hurry to start moving again. We all fished out money from our pockets and added it to the brass bucket one of the actors took around our group. We were smiling as we reboarded the bus, peering out of the windows and craning our necks to watch the troupe disappear into the gathering night.

I thought of that roadside performance some years later while watching John Matthew Mathan's debut venture, *Sarfarosh* (Willing to Die, 1999). There is little on the surface that is similar between the two. The film is a slick, big-budget action thriller, and yet its structure echoes not only that performance in the forest but many dozens I have attended since. Later I realised that although elements from the *Natyashastra* are identifiable in every movie, the entire recommended plot structure can be mapped onto this film.

Sarfarosh begins with a list of acknowledgements that runs over a minute and then is followed by a quick cut to the production logo and finally a shot of gold coloured sand-dunes. The camera closes in on a bird that rises in flight towards the left of the screen, indicating the national borders with Pakistan. The background twitter of birdsong and wind gives way to a solemn voice reciting a poem with its final word forming the title of the film. The next shot shows a caravan of camels, moving from left to right, clearly in response to the message that the bird had carried, and is accompanied by a song whose lyrics serve as a warning. The song sequence intercuts static credits with shots of the caravan that is transporting smuggled weapons. The weapons are carried through India, from the arid desert to the verdant south where they are used to murder a wedding party. The opening is intended to signal that vira (heroism) is the dominant rasa of the film. Within minutes of its start, the film not only establishes its sthayibhava but also that the protagonist's main objective is to defeat a threat to the country and its people.

Although the film sets the stage for action, it delays the introduction of the protagonist, Ajay (played by Aamir Khan), who is initially presented as young man fond of romantic music and entirely unlike the feared police officer discussed by other characters. Shringar aspects of Ajay's personality are emphasised with attention to his family life, memories of a college sweetheart Seema (Sonali Bendre) and interest in romantic Urdu poetry. This series of events – weapons smuggling, dangers to first unidentified members of Ajay's country and a flashback that reveals that his brother too was killed by terrorists – makes up the first stage or sowing of the seed where the protagonist's main objective is identified and his commitment to achieving the goal established.

The second stage – or where the primary objective appears impossible – is emphasised by revelations of the power and influence of the criminals. Although these are intercut with romantic and domestics aspects of Ajay's life, his heroic side is revealed in a short sequence where his arrival at the police station establishes him as the feared officer ACP Rathore. This revelation establishes Ajay's capabilities for achieving victory despite the magnitude of the threat. The viewer is also introduced to a secondary narrative with Inspector Salim (Mukesh Rishi) a Muslim cop who is mistrusted by his fellow, Hindu, policemen. The second stage is where the seed becomes visible as the protagonist's efforts gain strength. In the film, this involves revealing Ajay's true self to Seema, not just as her poetry-loving former classmate and current suitor but also the heroic and dedicated police officer. It also entails a confrontation with Salim about the latter's bitterness about the suspicion with which he is regarded. Both revelations help Ajay form a 'supporting' team and link him more closely to his wider community.

In the third stage, Ajay's investigation throws up new leads, leads to confrontations with the criminals, including one where Ajay is wounded, and indicates that his goal requires much greater effort. The alternating success and failure of Ajay's investigation and the growing love between him and Seema form the fourth stage where unforeseen complications and doubts arise, including the revelation of Gulfam Hassan (Naseeruddin Shah), a ghazal singer and Ajay's friend, as the criminal mastermind, spy and the main villain.

The fourth stage offers a space for expressing and overcoming doubts, raising and clarifying moral dilemmas and seeking clarity, and often forms the most emotionally charged and verbal of the five stages. In *Sarfarosh*, this fourth stage intercuts Ajay's developing investigations with a series of emotionally complex moments, including Ajay's sorrow at learning that Gulfam is involved with the crimes, an intensifying conflict between the criminals, and his father's silent benediction before he leaves for his mission. The film cuts rapidly from an emotionally charged

155

shot of Ajay's worried father to a song-and-dance sequence which is further spliced with scenes of Ajay's team of policemen arresting members of the criminal gang and finally reaching Gulfam's desert estate.

This song is the second of the film's staged or performed spectacles, often described as item numbers[4] which are used to heighten anticipation of the dramatic action that the viewer knows must follow. However, the two songs that would in another film be presented as lavishly staged spectacles are quite perfunctory in *Sarfarosh*. Despite their setting – the first in a dance bar and the second in a mansion in the desert – their erotic lyrics and sexualised dance movements, the camera doesn't focus on the glamour factor. Nor do the two songs attempt to create a sense of anticipation or heighten tension. Featuring unnamed, unknown dancers, the songs instead serve as means of character exposition and extending plot information. The first song reveals Salim as a loyal and effective policeman and leads to an emotional confrontation between Salim and Ajay, while the second is intercut with long sequences of the raids carried out by Ajay and his team. Ajay's successful confrontation with Gulfam marks the final and fifth stage, where the narrative's main objective is achieved. While the ending appears upbeat and positive, the audience is reminded of the film's main rasa of vira with a reprise of the music from the first song.

The film's plotting also coincides with the second set of structural elements where a bindu or fixed point serves to join the various subservient rasas and subplots into a coherent whole. Ajay's main objective forms the bindu connecting the various diverse streams, including his romance with Seema, the collective

---

[4] Item numbers are deliberate spectacles often set in nightclubs or a stage performance and can feature either one of the main characters or at times an actor particularly popular for their dance performance. Actress and dancer Helen – of European and Burmese heritage – remains perhaps the most well known and beloved of these and few major films of the 1970s did not feature her in a dance sequence.

grief of his brother's murder as well as Salim's story as a Muslim policeman, and even the minor comic part played by the informer Phatka (Anil Upadhyaya).

These overlapping concepts create an architecture which is both rooted in and reflects the philosophical principles encompassed by karma that asserts that all actions have inevitable and unavoidable consequences. However, although the consequences of characters' actions occupy centre-stage, the structure also takes into account punishments for social, political and ethical transgressions as well as rewards for righteous actions. This philosophical underpinning also means that neither classical Sanskrit drama nor India's many folk traditions – nor indeed the thousands of films produced in a dozen languages – can be strictly classified as comedies or tragedies.

This is not to say that there is no conception of tragedy in the *Natyashastra* or that its principles only cover comedies. Instead, according to the text, the overall mood of a play does not depend on catastrophe but on the seriousness of the theme, manner of presentation, and emotions involved. In addition, given the concept of reincarnation, the death of a protagonist does not necessarily signify a tragedy and indeed the death of the hero is often constructed as a sacrifice or as martyrdom that benefits the wider community. While the deaths of lovers in romantic stories lack the same social significance, their love is seen as having overcome the obstacles and they are united in death. This is echoed by Javed Akhtar who notes that the hero can make failure look so magnificent that audiences admire and envy him. As part of the scriptwriting duo Salim-Javed, one of Akhtar's best-known films is *Deewar* which culminates in a protracted sequence of the protagonist's death.

In the rasic tradition then, a 'tragedy' would require an irreparable destruction of the social – and moral – order which can only be brought about by a complete rupture of the cosmic law. Curiously, in all my reading and viewing, only one work stands out as creating such a rupture: Guru Dutt's brilliant but flawed *Kaagaz Ke Phool* (Paper Flowers, 1959), which revolves around a film director Suresh Sinha (played by Dutt who also directed and produced the film) making a version of *Devdas*. It was the first Indian film to be shot in Cinemascope and the last film that Dutt would officially direct. The film faced scathing criticism and extremely negative box-office response at its release, although it is now considered a classic of global cinema. However, it still makes for uncomfortable and ambivalent viewing.

Constructed as a flashback, the film follows a famous film director, Suresh, who is making an adaptation of *Devdas*. He meets a young woman Shanti (Waheeda Rehman) and decides to cast her as Paro, the beloved from the famous novel (and its many film adaptations) which metaphorically links Paro and Devdas to the divine lovers Krśna and Radha. Suresh's film and its new star become a huge success. Shanti and Suresh, who is already, although unhappily, married, also fall in love. When Suresh loses custody of his daughter and Shanti not only leaves him but also entirely withdraws from acting, he takes to drinking. By the time a series of events brings the couple back together, the situation has reversed, with Shanti becoming the big star and Suresh the alcoholic, a failed director.

Kaagaz Ke Phool's film-within-a-film device provides a brilliant insight into filmic creation and viewership. It also draws several links with *Devdas*, the text familiar to the viewer if only through its film adaptations, including Suresh's relationship with Shanti (the actress he casts as Paro in his film) which echoes the one between Devdas and Paro. Suresh, like Devdas, becomes an alcoholic when he loses Shanti. Shanti's love for Suresh is shown as similar to Paro's love for Devdas, and in turn evocative of Radha, the mythical beloved of Krśna. However, unlike Devdas who seeks Paro even when he knows their love has no future, Suresh chooses his pride and rejects Shanti. Indeed, *Kaagaz Ke Phool* works hard at establishing the comparisons, which make Suresh's inexplicable rejection of Shanti at the end of the film shocking and horrifying. Some of the commercial failure and vociferous critique at the time of the film's release, as well as the uncomfortable viewing it makes even six decades later, can be attributed to its distressing ending. Although *Devdas* also ends with the hero dying, it is only after fulfilling his promise to Paro. However, *Kaagaz Ke Phool* ends not with lovers continuing to love each other despite their separation but with Suresh's incomprehensible rejection of Shanti. Given the metatextual comparisons evoked by the film, this refusal of Shanti by Suresh turns into a symbolic – and psychically impossible – repudiation of Paro by Devdas, of Radha by Krishna. If a tragedy in the rasic tradition requires an irreparable destruction of the moral order, *Kaagaz Ke Phool* provides it by rejecting the eternal love symbolised by Radha and Krishna that is incessantly replayed in human lives and in performance.[5] Moreover, given that Radha, as the human beloved of the deity, symbolises all of humanity, Suresh's final abandonment also signals god's rejection of a devotee.

I had watched the film multiple times before, the first time with my mother who found it both beautiful and disappointing although she never explained why. A French acquaintance in Mexico had loved the film before meeting me and not only insisted that we watch it together, frequently pausing the DVD to swoon over its technical aspects – the proficiency of the exquisitely lit shots, the strange yet effective shot composition that renders its female lead breathtakingly beautiful at times and disturbingly unappealing at others – but also sighed repeatedly that 'Indians are so romantic.' Back in India, and as I struggled to make my first novel work, I found an old VHS copy in a local shop. The sound and image had degraded on the tape to the point that parts of the film appeared as nothing but electronic frizz on the screen, and my repeat viewings made it worse. It struck me that, although the film's primary rasa is karuna (sorrow), the ending pushes it over into bhayanak (fear) and finally vibhatsa

---

[5] *Sahityadarpana* suggests that invoking tragedy is to create it and thus restricts its depiction in literature and performance. This is not to say that the four 'unpleasant' rasas are not performed or narrated, but that the negative extremes of human experience are not to be depicted in performance.

(distaste/disgust) as it posits the impossibility of a cosmic, incess-antly recurring love between not only the divine lovers but also between humanity and divinity. This rupture not only creates an irreconcilable dilemma in aesthetic and performance terms but also on philosophical and psychological levels where an entire cultural worldview is challenged and finally rejected. The horror here is not just the heartbreak faced by Shanti and Suresh as individuals, which could be psychologically accounted for, but rather the rejection by Suresh (as the symbolic representation of Krśna) of Shanti (as Radha, the archetypal lover and devotee). This makes *Kaagaz Ke Phool* not a love story but perhaps one of the very few true constructions of horror in Indian cinema. It is psychically and emotionally bearable only because its film-within-a-film device explicitly and insistently reveals the artifice of cinema in each frame and by doing so distances the viewer from its overwhelming, comprehensive horror.

The insight brought a more difficult recognition, this time about my own craft. The novel I was writing at the time, despite being written in English, was not rooted in the Latin American magic realism that I admired or in the European and American literature that I had read at school and university. Instead, I had somehow reverted to telling the story the way I had learned as a child. Suddenly the roller coaster of moods, disunities of time and space, and characters who did not follow the rules learned in my literature classes, began to make sense. What I was trying to create was not fantasy or magic realism or any other genre named in my literature classes, but all my Ramlilas and favourite movies turned into text on the page. I just had to figure out how to write it!

*   *   *

Given that the *Natyashastra* resolutely opposes any identifica-tion by a spectator with characters and represented situations, and rejects any drift into a non-discriminating sentimental haze, it is unsurprising that realism, at least of the material kind, is not an aim or priority. Classical philosophers actively warned against seducing the spectator's consciousness into accepting an illusion of reality in performance or creating an identification with the performance or its performers. Abhinavagupta suggests the use of *natyadharmi* – or stage specific – conventions to ensure that the audience remains critically distanced from the performance. For cinema, this means that techniques which not only reveal the artifice of filmmaking but also emphasise the artificiality of cinema are preferred over the 'invisible' style preferred by classic Hollywood or European cinema. Fantastic *mise-en-scène*, exuberant and visible use of camera, obvious sound techniques and flashy editing create this artificiality.

Recognising this underlying principle, familiar to Indian film-makers less from texts and more through living, embodied performance traditions, goes a long way towards explaining conventions that are often read by the Western viewer as naive or shoddy. Instead, their refusal of Hollywood conventions including the use of an unobtrusive camera, continuity of image, shot centring, frame balance and sequential editing, serves a particular purpose: ensuring that the audience is always aware that whatever is shown on screen is a deliberate and artificial creation rather than any representation of reality.

Bimal Roy, one of the major auteurs of Indian cinema, explained that the goal of realism was not necessarily 'the scientific understanding of the human condition at a particular time and place but a knowledge of self,' a view that may leave many realists outraged. Roy's explanation echoes the opening chapter of the *Natyashastra* that describes the purpose of perform-ance as not a depiction of material reality but a representation of an inner reality. His view that realism was 'not interpretation but the creation of a mood' is amply visible in the sequence in Roy's *Bandini* where Kalyani murders Bikash's wife. The sequence follows Kalyani, who is already in shock after her father's death, when she discovers that the abusive patient she is assigned to serve is her ex-lover's wife. The camera closes in on Kalyani's face to the sound of a high-pitched buzzing which gives way to the insistent clanging of an ironmonger at work. The camera cuts rapidly and repeatedly from close-ups of an expressionless Kalyani preparing tea, to close shots of a bottle of poison and the silhouette of the ironmonger swinging his hammer, sparks flying each time it strikes iron. The clang of the hammer is intercut with shouts of Kalyani's name by the wife and sounds of Kalyani lighting a stove to prepare tea. The murder remains off screen and the viewer is only informed by the terrified screams of a nurse who is shown entering the room but never actually discovering the corpse. The sequence is more expressionist than realist, with camera, lighting, sound and editing all marshalled to enhance the viewer's enjoyment of an act of terrible violence rather than to provide any coherent account of the murder.

As a filmmaker, Manmohan Desai stands at the opposite end of the spectrum from Roy yet he made a similar case for this deliberate artificiality, explaining that the events shown on screen may have been shot in very different conditions and enhanced by clever editing. He questioned the need for making films that looked anything like reality and instead suggested a film could represent anything 'as long as it touches a chord'.

The creation of artificiality has been a favoured convention of Indian cinema from its earliest days with Phalke's *Kaliya Mardan* (Slaying of the Serpent Kaliya, 1919). In the film, a title card identifies Mandakini as playing the role of Krishna, followed by a slow dissolve where the young actress's face morphs into that of the deity. The sequence ensures that the audience recognise that the images on screen are not magical but created by human skill. From the very beginning, filmmakers not only established cinematic artifice as a cornerstone of the filmic conventions but also pushed boundaries in terms of *mise-en-scène*, setting, even stars. The early mythological film *Savitri* (1924) not only cast Italian actors, Rina De Liguoro and Angelo Ferrari, in lead roles but was entirely shot in Rome. The film's publicity emphasised that the scenes had been shot 'amidst the world-renowned cascades of Tivoli in Rome'.

Similarly, audiences knew that Madhubala, the star of *Mughal-E-Azam*, was unable to dance kathak even though the role demanded proficiency as a dancer. However, the role of Anarkali is performed in the dance sequence by the actress in close-ups and by various male members of the choreographer Lachchu Maharaj's troupe in the long shots, most of which do little to hide the switch. In addition, the film makes no attempt to conceal the changes in technology and technique, including improved cameras and lighting that occurred over the fifteen years during which it was made. Shot mostly in black-and-white, it switches over to colour for the final thirty minutes, allowing Asif to dazzle the eye with the colour shots of an immense Sheesh Mahal (Hall of Mirrors) that showcases Anarkali's defiance of the Mughal emperor as well as the emotive climax. Ironically, the impact of Asif's choices is lost in the digitally coloured version of the film (released in 2004). In the decades since *Mughal-E-Azam,* a vast range of filmmakers continue to emphasise the artificiality of their on-screen narratives with repeated use of conventions and techniques that are familiar to their viewers and form a unique film style.

The *Natyashastra* differentiates modes of representation between natyadharmi (or following the conventions of theatre) and the lokadharmi (or following the conventions of the material world) and recommends the former as a form more suited to performance. This does not mean that Bharata or his successors ignore or reject material reality but that they simply consider conventions of theatre more appropriate for conveying an inner reality. In fact, social representation – lokanukarana – is a considered primary object of drama. The text also describes the role of anukrti (or imitation) as an element of staging and acting. However, this imitation is not to be confused with the Hellenic concept of mimesis as anukrti refers to speech, gestures, manners, appearance and dress of actors which conforms to whatever is current in society (lokavrttanukaranam) rather than referring to any specific actuality. For example, our use of contemporary idiom is not imitation but rather conforming to social usage in order to communicate with each other. The same applies to performances where actors, scriptwriters, directors and producers deploy familiar conventions of language, gesture, staging in order to communicate more effectively with the audience.

Furthermore, this worldview is not driven by any socio-historical determinism but takes the social order for granted and instead focusses on moral roots and implications of human behaviour. For Bharata, like many classical Indic philosophers, human society or loka is best understood in terms of cosmic and moral laws and constraints instead of the transitory practices of historical, political and economic interstices. Unsurprisingly then, drama – or indeed cinema – need not present a documentary account of material reality, an idea that may explain why there has been little need or impetus to develop any form of realism in the arts. Curiously, classical philosophy emphasises that any narration of facts may well be untrue, a view that finds much resonance in postmodernist ideas.

This explains why classical drama, folk theatre as well as modern films rely on expansive conventions of signs, symbols and conventions of representations that can only be described as natyadharmi or 'belonging to the stage'. Dance and music, as well as backdrops, stage settings and properties can be quickly indicated by natyadharmi conventions, familiar to the audiences from prior performances and collective knowledge despite ignorance of specific forms, plots or storylines. This shared recognition means that audiences do not require or demand material realism as a precondition for the performance of a narrative. Instead, narratives on screen are understood as affective rather than cognitive realism and familiar conventions can be efficiently deployed so the performers and the spectator alike can instead focus on rasa creation. Like that roadside performance I saw in the forest, the attuned spectator of Indian cinemas already has the knowledge to not only recognise, understand and appreciate a performance but also anticipate it even before an actor enters the stage (or screen).

* * *

Despite my love of Hindi movies, I first arrived in Mumbai as a crew member for an amateur theatre production at the close of the twentieth century. By this time, I knew that the key to understanding cinema and my country lay in learning how we told – and performed – our stories. I had learned that India's contemporary theatre was vast, mindbogglingly varied and incredibly welcoming, and that was how I found myself as part of a production team for a retelling of the *Mahabharata* from the perspective of its female characters. Nearly two dozen of us including actors, puppeteers – the staging required giant faceless puppets which occupied their own sleeper berths, much to the ticket collector's consternation – and production crew had piled into the train for a two-day journey from New Delhi to this city of dreams for a limited run at the famous Prithvi Theatre. We were a motley bunch, drawn from a dozen states across the country, with English our only shared language. The playwright and director was an academic while the lead actor – the only person I knew before joining the production – was perhaps best known as the voice of the country's Republic Day parades on the national television broadcaster, Doordarshan. Most of the young men in our team were chasing the dream of making it big in the movies. Shah Rukh Khan, the superstar who had also been part of Delhi's amateur theatre scene not too long ago, was discussed repeatedly on our journey. For hours, we lurked near the open doors of the train, smoking cigarettes, discreetly sharing a bottle of Old Monk rum and watching villages and fields whoosh past. We loudly sang songs from movies during the endless rounds of antakshari – a memory game centred around songs – we played to while away the journey. One of the young men looked around with wonder and a hint of envy as we finally arrived in the heaving city. 'Shah Rukh had once said he would rule this town and now he does,' he repeated as our taxi wound its way to Prithvi.

The theatre is in Juhu, not only one of the poshest parts of Mumbai but one littered with homes of movie directors and film stars. The boys, as our lead actress had named the starry-eyed young men, hastily dropped their bags before racing out to see Amitabh Bachchan's house that stands around the corner. That house is a landmark by itself and the street vendor who supplied us at every odd hour with vada pao and super cheap tea was happy to regale us all with stories of the great man himself. Going by his many stories, the vendor not only practically lived in Bachchan's mansion but was the star's indispensable aide and confidant.

I was more fascinated by the theatre. The entrance was both grand and intimate, with a touch of old-school movie glamour I hadn't seen elsewhere. There was a café that spilled into the open air and not only served a mean keema-pav, a sort of spicy mince sandwich wrapped in a bun, but also incredible Irish coffee. A bunch of us quickly fell into a routine, arriving earlier than we were expected to cheekily sip on the coffee, telling each other that it was necessary for the hangover we were nursing from the night before. And we each kept a running list of all the stars we spotted in the café and the favourites we hoped would eventually drop by. We wondered which actors had used the Prithvi green rooms that seemed to take up almost as much space as the theatre itself. These were more luxuriously appointed than any we had seen so far, with state-of-the-art lighting, flattering mirrors, and sweeping countertops that no amount of our paraphernalia was able to fill. We took turns sitting on the sumptuous make-up chairs, striking poses from our favourite films in the lit-up mirrors and feeling like the most glamorous of film stars. I realised that, for the first time, I was in a theatre designed for and by actors, and every other element – the incredible acoustics, the extraordinary light rig, the magnificent green rooms – was intended for one single purpose: to showcase the actor.

However, it was the Prithvi stage that filled me with awe. The stage juts out into the centre with audience seating rising sharply on all sides. At the rear of the stage, a small open-ended space functions as background and entrance. The design made it possible for an actor placed downstage to stand within an arm's length of the audience, a fact brought home sharply when on our first night, one of the actresses misjudged the distance and almost ended in the lap of a spectator. Backstage, we worried that the design of the theatre meant the audience could hear our horrified giggles and we ended up stuffing drapes from the giant puppets in our mouths to stifle the sound.

One night we finished our technical check earlier than planned. The theatre emptied out as the crew headed to grab food before the performance. I lingered until I knew I was alone. Even the house lights had been dimmed and I knew that the doors were locked. I sat for a long time in the front row, staring at the stage and craning my neck at the light rig. Finally, I took a deep breath and took the single step up from the floor to the stage. I walked slowly to the centre of the stage, clenched my eyes shut and turned to face the shadowed seats that rose above me. A strange magic thrummed and filled the emptiness around me. I thought that if I opened my eyes I would be surrounded by gods and demi-gods, spirits and demons. With my eyes closed, cool air filling my nose, silence filling my ears and every hair standing on end, I could taste rasa. Not only the rasa which we hoped to create with our performance that day, but of all other performances this stage had seen. And perhaps even every performance in every time, everywhere. When I eventually opened my eyes, there was nothing to see but the empty, dimly lit stage and beyond, rows of seats lost in the dark. But somehow the magic lingered.

My Heart Loves You But Dares Not Tell You[1]

THE BEAS RIVER FLOWS through some of the most beautiful mountains that make up the Himalayas. It marks the easternmost end of Alexander's (the Great) conquests. I knew this but the mountains are not visible in the darkest hour before sunrise. And I am sure that the biting cold, even though it was almost summer, had been the reason the conqueror's soldiers – having fought through thousands of kilometres from Greece – decided they would not go farther. 'I would turn back too,' I heard someone mutter in the dark, 'straight to my warm bed.' However, our cameraman insisted that there was only a forty-minute window for the perfect light at dawn and reaching our chosen location required a drive through the mountains followed by a trudge along the riverbed. Many of us had hoped to snooze on the bus but the driver preferred careening down the winding roads and taking each hairpin bend at speeds that left the end of the bus hanging perilously over the cliff edge. When we disembarked, we were shaken and nauseous. The frigid night air slapped us awake and we plodded single file, lugging unwieldy cases of equipment and bags of props through the

---

[1] '*Mera dil bhi kitna paagal yeh pyaar to tumse karta hai . . .*' from *Saajan* (Beloved, 1991).

rocky riverbed, hoping that none of us would break an ankle. I was bone-cold and car – or is it bus? – sick, and knew that even when we arrived at our destination, we'd need to unpack and set up for filming only to pack up again when the light changed and race to our second location of the day. I glanced at the dark that surrounded us and blew on my hands to warm them. It would be a long, busy, punishing day and yet I had never felt so alive in my life.

Months of planning, organisation, waiting for requisite permissions and funding, and assembling a crew had preceded that shoot along the Beas and then the Ravi, a sister river that runs westwards from the mountains of Himachal Pradesh, through Punjab and across the border into Pakistan. Work on the film had started before India's second round of nuclear tests in 1998 and had pushed forward despite a shoestring budget and innumerable delays.

I had signed on early in 1998 as the assistant director for the documentary, although my job title reflected neither my responsibilities nor my (lack of) experience. Most of my job involved ensuring everyone reached the filming location ahead of time and the schedule stayed on the clock, neither of which were particularly onerous given the relatively small size and passion of the cast and crew. Instead, I spent my time soaking up knowledge that floated freely among the crew. I would absorb the discussions between the cameraman and the director as they planned a shot. Next, I would follow the cameraman as he conferred with the lighting technicians and watched them set up the equipment. Then I'd race along to the costume and make-up team, managed by two men who cheerfully alternated between complaining that our film had no women in the cast to showcase their skills and boasting how they were earning money for doing very little on the shoot. The latter would be greeted by hoots, jeers and strings of exuberantly graphic but good-natured abuse from the rest of the crew.

Very soon my favourite part of the shoot became the arrival of our production team. They would go ahead to set up on

169

location before anyone else arrived, vanish for a few hours, and reappear as if by magic at some point to spread out a hot meal. I knew they carried the folding tables and eating implements and organised catering from the nearest town or village, and somehow managed to show up with hearty meals or thermos flasks full of tea and bags of sandwiches at the exact moment when the crew started flagging and tempers began to fray. This was also mysteriously just as the director called 'cut'. We all ate together, around tables when there was enough space for them, spread out on the ground when possible, or on nearby rocks. Despite the pressures of keeping to schedule or the stress of a shot that just would not come together, our meals were shockingly relaxed with conversations flowing easily. The cameraman would talk about camerawork from Indian, Italian, Soviet films; the lighting technician would marvel at the way part of the studio roof had been removed to create the perfect light for *Kaagaz ke Phool*, the envy at such freedom – and budgets – clear in his voice; the make-up man had a small album that functioned as a portfolio with the same model – his wife or sister or girlfriend depending on the day – made up like stars of the past and present ranging from Meena Kumari, Vijayashanti and Madhuri Dixit to Madhavi, Sridevi and Karishma Kapoor.

Gradually, I realised that the crew were generously teaching me the contours of film style. More importantly, with experience in multiple film industries of the country, they were teaching me Indian film style.

* * *

Film style describes recognisable cinematic techniques including *mise-en-scène* which covers all that is before the camera but specifically setting, lighting, costume and performance, cinematography which includes perspective, framing, camera choices, etc., sound design and its connection to images, and editing or how shots are connected to form a whole. Individual filmmakers may have a distinctive style based on how they use some of their preferred cinematic techniques over more than one film. Similarly, film industries can also develop a particular film style if several filmmakers choose to repeatedly deploy particular techniques. Over time, these techniques form a set of stylistic principles that become instantly recognisable to their habitual audiences. These principles are not eccentric aesthetic decisions but are grounded in the wider culture that produces and consumes the cinema. As such, film styles not only help identify and recognise distinctive cinematic traditions but also offer an insight into the culture that produces and consumes the movies.

Classical Hollywood film style, which continues to guide many contemporary filmmakers in the global north, employs chrono-logically arranged narrative with an explicit cause-and-effect relationship between the events. The key guiding principle in such cinema is continuity editing where elements like camera, sound and editing are rendered invisible to the viewer. Although filmmakers do experiment with rupturing this classical style, either by rearranging the chronology of the narrative or by making the cinematic artifice visible, the overarching principles remain the same: the audience is expected to suspend disbelief and accept what is on screen as a representation of some form of intellectu-ally coherent reality. The cinemas of India have also developed their own styles with cinematic elements that are shared across the various industries but also quite distinct, depending on their intended reach and primary audience. Despite the variations of style, Indian films share one characteristic: unlike Hollywood, they are guided by a deliberately constructed artificiality that exposes cinematic techniques and even draws attention to them instead of rendering these invisible. This in turn means that the spectator is not expected to consider the on-screen narrative as 'real' in any cognitive sense. Instead, this film style demands an affective response from the spectator while also ensuring that they are never fully swept away by the evoked emotions.

The constituent elements of this film style, developed over a century of filmmaking, are rooted in and reference earlier performance traditions including non-chronological narrative structures that reject unities of space and time, and render any discussion of continuity irrelevant. Extravagant, often ahistorical, costumes, acting that draws attention to itself, dialogue and delivery that is deliberately exaggerated, and flashy use of camera have all grown to be hallmarks of Indian – and especially Hindi – cinema's signature film style. It's a style that is almost entirely antithetical to not only classical Hollywood but also most European cinema. Unconsciously or perhaps out of habit, the country's earliest filmmakers chose to privilege the natyadharmi – or stage specific conventions – over the lokdharmi or conventions of material reality, with the *mise-en-scène* of even the earliest films constructed in ways that remain recognisable to viewers today.

For cinema, a central element of *mise-en-scène* is how objects and figures are located with regard to the viewer's gaze in terms of cinematic time and space. This is also where the first distinctive element of Indian film style emerges, and with the country's very first feature film. Described as frontality, the technique often frames the actor centrally in a momentarily static tableau. Identifiable even in the few surviving reels of Phalke's *Raja Harishchandra*, the technique is frequently used to not only centre a character who may be human, semi-divine or divine but is in that moment framed and presented as if in some elevated, idealised and ideal capacity.

Historically, this convention can be traced to Indian visual cultures formed in the nineteenth century and informed by colonial contact, changes in technologies and the development of urban industrial art, the arrival of photography, new printing techniques of the chromolithograph, woodcuts and the news sheets. Simply put, frontality means placing the camera at a 180-degree plane to the figures and objects that make up the frame. In turn, this affirms and emphasises the iconic stature of the character – much like popular representations of deities – and/or the actor as a way to reaffirm their star status and power. This mode of framing also allows for frontal, direct address by the character/actor on screen to the spectator, which ruptures the narrative and reinforces audience's awareness of cinematic artifice. It creates a moment of communication not only between the character and the audience but also between a star and their fans.[2]

Decades after Phalke, filmmakers continue to use frontality although in increasingly sophisticated ways. The final sequence of *Coolie* (1983) uses frontality to emphasise the immense star power of its leading actor, Amitabh Bachchan, who had been severely injured during production. Director Manmohan Desai not only changed the ending to let Bachchan's character live – the nation would have accepted no less! – but also a coda was added that constructs the star in iconic terms. In the final scene, Bachchan appears on the balcony of the hospital where he had been treated to thank his supporters both within the film – depicted as a crowd gathered outside the building – and beyond it. The sequence stands at the interstice of cinematic spectacle, audience involvement, national discourse and Bachchan's own star persona, collapsing all these categories into a single moment of direct address by the actor to a rapt nation.

Two decades later, a scene of *Swades: We the People* exemplifies a sophisticated use of frontality where song lyrics, storyline, camera angles, cultural references and stardom combine to render a single figure as the devotee as well as a momentary embodiment and icon of Rama.[3] The same scene brings about a complex conflation of star persona, cinematic narrative, and audience's knowledge of the epic and Hindu philosophy. Set during a Ramlila performance, the sequence

---

[2] While this anticipates the Brechtian principle of breaking the fourth wall, it is worth noting that Indian theatre and indeed any of its performance traditions have never *had* the imaginary fourth wall dividing the action on stage from the audience.

[3] The personality of Rama here becomes not only a focus of contemporary nationalism but also a symbol for the ideal man, providing additional politico-social symbolic significance to the sequence. In a subtle elision, the protagonist's name is Mohan, linked to the youthful Krishna.

focusses on the protagonist Mohan (played by Shah Rukh Khan) who initially forms part of the audience as the female lead Gita (Gayatri Joshi) acts out Sita's part in the epic. Enacting the episode when Sita is held captive by Ravana, Gita sings of the troubles that beset Sita who pleads for Rama to come save her, simultaneously voicing Sita's lament as a captive, her own love for Mohan, as well as symbolically embodying the call of the 'motherland' that needs Mohan's skill and expertise to flourish. Ravana (played in the sequence by a minor character) makes an appearance to taunt Sita and asks where Rama can be found and why he has not yet saved her. As Gita/Sita articulates her faith and love for Rama, saying he can be found in her every breath, the scene cuts to Mohan who spontaneously takes over the narration, explaining that Rama can be found everywhere. The camera initially catches Mohan in a long shot and then zooms in for a medium shot that positions him simultaneously as of and yet apart from others on screen, and remains focussed on him as he sings to the on-screen audience. However, given the framing and camera choice, this moment also functions as a direct address to the off-screen spectator.

The sequence functions on multiple levels: assuring Gita that Mohan, like Rama, is worthy of her love, that he has heard the simultaneous calls from the motherland/Sita. It also symbolically connects Rama's quality as the 'best amongst men' to Mohan, and by extension to the star himself. The camera focusses on the star as he addresses the on-screen and off-screen audiences directly, affirming Mohan's role as a righteous leader and indicating the qualities associated with the deity. As he moves through the crowd, the cinema audience recognises the ritual of Dussehra enactments where the actors are treated and worshipped as living embodiments of the deities. This knowledge ensures audience recognition of the celluloid narrative, as well as of wider symbolism. The *mise-en-scène* ensures three simultaneous effects: the framing identifies the protagonist as a worthy devotee and leader, signals a recognition of Mohan as the momentary embodiment of the deity by the on-screen audience of the Ramlila, and affirms not only Khan's star status but his off-screen persona as apt for this on-screen link to Rama for the film's audience.

Mise-en-scène also extends to setting, costume and performance by actors, and over time a clear film style has developed where the artificiality of all these elements is emphasised. Of course, as with theatre, these elements in cinema also draw freely from the lokadharmī so that material reality is simultaneously represented, simplified, exaggerated, parodied and inverted on screen. Every element of the real world – homes, villages, prisons, court-rooms – is altered, reshaped and somehow made 'more'. Nightclubs and parties are more glamorous, urban slums are grittier and bleaker, family homes are warmer and cosier regardless of class. The same applies to natural settings, where waterfalls overflow with spectacular abundance, forests appear in lusher green tones than any available in nature, the ice on mountain tops is more blindingly bright. Furthermore, with the introduction of every new technology, filmmakers find new and creative ways to create this 'more'. Nikkhil Advani's *Kal Ho Na Ho*, (Tomorrow May Never Come, 2003), a love triangle set in New York City, for example, digitally heightens colour quality and lighting, bathing the city in a hyper-real glow, while colours are repeated, co-ordinated and echoed constantly to link the main characters together. Although released before the advent of image-based social media, the film's setting and costumes nevertheless unfold like an extended, impossibly beautiful, Instagram reel.

Considering film setting in symbolic terms rather than any 'realist' depiction of a time and place is a more useful way of understanding setting in Indian cinema. For example, *Sholay* constructs an idealised village, with familiar elements, including the central well, narrow but neat lanes and picturesque but simple huts. Three elevated structures loom over the village and suggest social, political and religious authorities and include Thakur's rambling house, the mosque, hinted at by a steep set of steps, and a water tower which serves as setting for Viru's (Dharmendra) comic half-hearted attempt at suicide. Similarly, Manmohan Desai's multi-star extravaganza *Naseeb* (Destiny, 1981) constructs a fabulous if wholly improbable glass house that is destroyed by gun fire in a spectacular action sequence.

The underlying principle of the natyadharmi also conveys that settings do not follow unities of time or space. This means the palatial residence of the wealthy Raichand family in *Kabhi Khushi Kabhi Gham* is both recognisably a British stately home and located at a stone's throw from an elaborately artificial rendering of New Delhi's Chandni Chowk. Similarly, in *Dil Se* (From the Heart, 1998) the female protagonist's journey from Assam in the northeast of India to New Delhi requires a geographically impossible detour via Ladakh in the far north. On the opposite end of the scale, non-glamorous settings are also exaggerated for visual and emotional impact. The urban 'gangster' films of the 1990s and early 2000s, including *Satya* (1998) and *Company* (2002),[4] are characterised by exaggeratedly gritty urban settings which simultaneously reference 'real' locations and reflect the fury and terror of the characters. Even the bridge that shelters a young Ravi and Vijay in *Deewar* is darker and more menacing than any real bridge, and the passageways and roads that Vijay (Amitabh Bachchan) must navigate in the final sequences are rendered darker, emptier, longer and more winding than any 'real' passages. The mansion of *Nau do Gyarah* (Nine and Two Make Eleven, 1957) is gloomy and foreboding despite its elaborate gardens and enormous windows. It draws upon familiar elements of Indian gothic, and echoes elements from the 1949 classic *Mahal*, including shadowy corridors, darkened interiors and winding staircases. Moreover, given the emphasis on affective realism, despite the range of films, genres and period, in all of the examples, setting functions more as an indication of a character's inner state than any realist depiction of a particular time and space.

---

[4] Curiously, while these 'gangster' films often purport to provide a 'realist' Western-style experience, they still follow the stylistic conventions of Hindi cinema.

Similar principles guide decisions regarding costume and therefore films do not attempt to create either realist costumes in historic or social terms, or even to maintain costume continuity within the narrative. Although cinema has long functioned as the country's fashion arbiter, within the filmic narrative, costume functions much the same way as setting does: to simultaneously provide visual pleasure, reflect a character's inner state and reinforce recognition of the cinematic artifice. It's therefore not surprising to see Roma (Zeenat Aman) of *Don* (1998) sporting short hair while playing the avengeful karate expert and switching to long hair once she learns Vijay's (Amitabh Bachchan) secret and is convinced of his love. Curiously, the climax of the film requires Roma to display her martial arts skills, and once again, and without any explanation, she reverts to short hair.

As with sets, costumes do not necessarily reflect the reality of specific characters or indeed their position in the narrative but rather provide a symbolic nod to the emotional aspects of the character. They also often reference a star's off-screen persona which may in turn impact their costume choices over a number of films. For example, Dev Anand's suave suits in the 1950s, Helen's cabaret costumes outrageously overloaded with feathers and sequins in the 1960s, or Amitabh Bachchan's flamboyant, fetishist white suits and shoes of the 1970s are not only instantly recognisable but also inextricably linked to the actors in audience memory.

In addition, within a film, costumes may provide a passing nod to the period, as they do in *Mughal-E-Azam*, or recreate a fantastic version of the past while wholly privileging aesthetic over historical accuracy, as in *Asoka*. A film may rely on a combination of realist and fantasy wear, as in *Dayavan* (The Kind One, 1988) where Shankar (Feroz Khan) and Shakti (Vinod Khanna) alternate between contemporary urban wear and explicitly fantastic 'costumes'. Or the fantastic may be limited to specific song sequences or scenes which may not necessarily be differentiated from the rest of the narrative, as in the case of Desai's *Naseeb* where outfits for the final song sequence reference disparate influences including the Cossacks and Audrey Hepburn's iconic white and black outfit for the races in *My Fair Lady* (1964).

*   *   *

If *mise-en-scène* determines style for presenting what is before the camera, cinematography is the mechanism for delivering this to the audience and includes choices regarding the size and shape of the image, the frame, type of colour, camera choices such as depth, angle, height, movement, etc., as well as speed and perspective. It is also the most easily recognisable element of film style, and in the case of Indian cinemas, the most obvious component of the studied artificiality or natyadharmi convention that are their hallmark. Flashy camera use is an instantly recognisable characteristic of the country's films and serves not only as a showcase of the cameraman's skill – with use of extreme camera angles, close-ups and rapid zooms – but also draws attention to cinematic artifice.[5]

The noted auteur Guru Dutt is well known for his complex lighting and shot composition and distinguished by a coherent visual style across his films. For most of his career, he worked with the same team, which may partly explain this visual coherence. It is, for example, easy to note a *noir* styling to his shots, where the lighting throws ominous shadows across the screen, long vertical bars are replicated to imply imprisonment and repeated even through strings of flowers, and close-ups add to the sense of frustration and entrapment. *Pyaasa* (Thirsty, 1957) and *Kaagaz ke Phool* both employ these techniques to create a melancholic mood, while the thriller *Aar Paar* (Once and For All, 1954) uses them to emphasise elements of suspense. However,

---

[5] Unsurprisingly Shekhar Kapur's *Elizabeth* (1998) was panned by a number of Western critics for his use of this film style which they described as jarring and distracting.

even the comedy, *Mr & Mrs 55* (1955) deploys light and shade to work camera angles in creative ways, using the contrast in tones to heighten the social differences amongst the characters, highlight their temperaments and showcase the physical spaces they inhabit.

Within Dutt's oeuvre, the sequence marking Bhootnath's (Guru Dutt) first meeting with Chhoti Bahu (Meena Kumari) in *Sahib Bibi aur Ghulam*[6] (Master, Mistress and Slave, 1962) perhaps exemplifies one of the most complex uses of the subjective shot. Although Dutt – like other filmmakers of his time – uses the technique to establish subjective gazes, these work more on symbolic and emotional levels rather than on a cognitive one. At this first meeting, the camera establishes two clear subjectivities – that of the shy newcomer Bhootnath and the beautiful but tragic Chhoti Bahu. Summoned to her chamber, Bhootnath is unable to look up or meet her eye. The camera emphasises the artifice of cinema through quick interchanges of high- and low-angle shots with zooms, close-ups and extreme close-ups.

Initially, a low-angle shot reflects Bhootnath's view, noting only the chess-board floor, the rich carpet and finally, in a medium shot, the hem of her rich sari and heavily adorned feet. As he seats himself on the floor, the camera catches in close-up what he sees – the adorned feet of a deity-like Chhoti Bahu. Her gaze, in contrast, constructed through high-angle shots, places Bhootnath in a subservient position. Yet as the dialogue shifts, the camera angles not only reflect the developing rela-tionship between the two characters but also emphasise the precarious – gendered and classed – balance of power between them. As Bhootnath's gaze, surprised by Chhoti Bahu's comment, rises up, the camera frames his face in a close-up. While his

---

[6] The film is officially credited to Abrar Alvi's direction but has always been subject to debate. With many of Dutt's signature elements, many critics include this film as part of Dutt's oeuvre, especially in light of his refusal to 'direct' cinema after the failure of *Kaagaz ke Phool* the year before.

first glimpse of Chhoti Batu is through a low-angle shot, emphasising her higher social standing, Bhootnath's gaze quickly takes on a sexual charge as the camera moves to a close-up, first noting her heavily kajal-rimmed eyes and the vermilion mark on her forehead, and then her dark-painted lips. Bhootnath's confusion between reverence, shyness and incipient desire is contrasted by the insistence of the camera continuing to construct Chhoti Bahu's gaze through high-angle shots, remaining that of a higher social being or even deity under whose regard Bhootnath must lower his. The fleeting instant of Bhootnath's confusion and potentially transgressive desire is quickly replaced by the first balance of gaze and when the camera cuts back to Chhoti Bahu again, still framed as a subjective shot through Bhootnath's eyes and seen through a low-angle shot. However, as she leans forward to voice her request, the camera again catches the subtle shifts of power between the two. While Bhootnath continues to be seen through high-angle shots, the camera begins to shift to a more frontal mode for Chhoti Bahu, highlighting her attempt to bridge the gap and foreshadowing her eventual downfall.

Dutt was not alone in his generation to use the camera in innovative ways. Vijay Anand's *Guide* (1965) uses the camera to not only establish the estrangement between Rosie (Waheeda Rehman) and her husband but also her lack of agency by placing her in the background for her initial appearances. As the wife of a noted archaeologist, she is nothing more than the background scenery and the camera initially only catches her in long and medium shots. It is only Raju's (Dev Anand) subjective gaze that establishes her centre-screen. Rosie's first definitive close-ups only occur during her first dance sequence, and even in this scene she is initially placed in the background. The scene also locates Raju within the film's narrative and their future relationship. As Rosie loses herself in dance, Raju is pushed to the background, foreshadowing their future relationship where she will become a star and he her behind-the-scenes manager.

Rosie's confrontation with her husband, Marco (Kishore Sahu), showcases Anand's complex camera use. Much of the sequence is shot using medium shots, and even the close-ups highlight the emotional distance between the characters by rendering at least one of them out of focus. The sequence opens with Marco hearing the sound of dancing bells coming from a cave. Rosie is then seen mostly through shadows or through body parts, her arms or hands peeking from behind darkened statues and niches. When Marco finally sees her in her entirety, she is positioned high above him, dressed for dancing, tapping her foot to sound the bells. In the subsequent shots, as the two argue, Rosie remains in the background, physically and emotionally overshadowed by her aggressive, successful husband. However, the camera reverses their positions the moment Rosie asserts herself, placing her in the foreground and zooming in for a long close-up when she accuses her husband of adultery and marital rape. For the rest of the sequence, Rosie remains either the focus of the camera or foregrounded physically, reversing the earlier power balance, while Marco is steadily relegated by being filmed in medium-shot and only in profile for close-ups. The sequence ends with a close-up of Rosie slapping Marco and then cuts abruptly to a high-angle close-up of feet clad in red shoes and jangling with dancing bells (reminiscent of Dutt's use of a similar shot from *Sahib Bibi aur Ghulam*). The camera stays on Rosie's figure as she walks away, cutting to a medium shot of Marco one final time.

Compared to Anand and Dutt, Manmohan Desai's films seem to use the camera not only more simply but also more playfully. Desai credited his cinematographers, including Peter Pereira and N. Satyen, for shot composition and lighting, insisting that he liked handling everything in film except the cinematography. At the same time, he was clear that the camera was to be used simply, not as a gimmick. Despite his claim of simplicity, Desai's films deploy the camera in creative ways that emphasise the cinematic artifice. For example, an objective shot of an actor peering drunkenly into a post-box in *Naseeb* is constructed from within the mail-slot, mischievously placing the cinematic audience in an obviously impossible location. However, *Parvarish* (Upbringing, 1977) uses a similar technique to chilling effect by constructing a subjective shot from the point of view of children hidden inside a drum who witness their parents' murder. The event is presented as the memory of the witnesses, but the camera shifts rapidly between objective and subjective shots, moving the points of view between the hidden children, the murderer, the parents, as well as an unidentified spectator who not only knows the children's hiding place but can zoom in for close-ups through the cracks in the drum. Although the scene is intense and terrifying, the camera use ensures that the audience can neither fully occupy one point of view nor ignore the artificiality of the on-screen narrative.

This emphasis on symbolic content and affective rather than cognitive realism is visible even in Desai's first film, *Chhalia* (Conman, 1960), about a criminal who helps a woman caught up in the Partition and abandoned by her husband. Desai is often credited (or blamed) for many elements that make up Hindi film style, and his debut suggests these were part of his own directorial repertoire from the beginning. In the climax scene, the camera sets up an effigy of Ravana during Dusshera celebrations as the presiding gaze through extreme low-angle shots. However, unlike the benign gaze of a deity, Ravana can only preside over injustice and misery. During the sequence, all characters except Shanti (Nutan) are caught in high-angle shots, showing their submission to the forces of injustice. As the climax unfolds, the effigy is ritually set aflame, although still filmed in low-angle shots, and slowly falls to the ground. At the same time, Shanti is brought together with her estranged husband (played by Rehman) and the camera switches to filming the couple frontally, establishing their parity but also the husband's letting go of the suspicions he had harboured towards his wife. In contrast, when the camera cuts back to Chhalia (Raj Kapoor), Shanti's rescuer, he is framed in a slight low angle, evoking his link to Rama, as the vanquisher of Ravana and establishing him as the upholder of virtue. Later cuts to Chhalia, again in low angle, indicate the restoration of the cosmic order, with evil vanquished and justice re-established.

The camera is used in very different and innovative ways for the modern film *Kal Ho Na Ho*. Here, the camera not only captures the 'missing' bits of reality but also provides an internal – and extremely explicit – counter-narrative within the film. These are aided by the editing techniques which in one instance replicate a single event from various perspectives. Although the film purportedly tells Naina's (Priety Zinta) story from her perspective, the point of view shifts from one character to another, providing a far more ambiguous and multi-perspective narrative. However, two sequences emphasise how camerawork can enhance cinematic artificiality. Both narrate the same event, Naina and her friend Sweetu (Delnaaz Irani) discusssing marriage. The first is ostensibly an objective shot of the two women walking through a train station when someone jostles Naina's coffee, spilling it over her clothes. As she cleans herself, the shot remains an objective one. However, the camera shifts quickly to a subjective shot from Sweetu's perspective as she is distracted by a passing man. Her interest in the man sparks an outburst from Naina during which the camera again switches to an objective position. The sequence also plays on a familiar device, a character's direct address – verbal or silent – to the audience, as Sweetu appears to suddenly notice the extra-cinematic spectator. She holds the spectator's gaze for a brief moment before turning back to the cinematic narrative. The second sequence is framed as Naina's memory of her conversation with Sweetu, but this time her focus is on the man who had jostled her arm. The camera remains objective, even though this second narrative is from Naina's point of view. However, this time the camera follows the man as he gathers napkins and returns to the two women, arriving just in time to overhear Naina's outburst. The camera remains objective, with two women in the foreground. Although the stranger remains in the background, the camera focusses on his expressions. As he chuckles at Sweetu's response, the camera catches her turning to him, reversing the earlier version where she had locked eyes with the spectator.

The repeated scene retroactively informs the viewer that the sequence was in fact the stranger's point of view. The second sequence retains the objective shot, despite being Naina's memory. Together the two scenes colour in characters and information that were primarily 'missing' to the main narrative, with the second sequence also explaining gestures and reactions that were opaque in the first. The sense of artificiality is further heightened by Sweetu's entirely different responses in the two sequences: in the first sequence her face remains sober as she holds the spectator's gaze, while in the second she smiles and acknowledges the stranger.

* * *

Given the passion for cinema in the country, it is no surprise that the technology for the sound film or talkies arrived in India soon after the release of *The Jazz Singer* (1927). Filmmakers began experimenting with synchronized sounds quickly, and in early 1931 Madan Theatres released two short films featuring skits and scenes from popular plays and heavy use of music with orchestral performances, tabla and sitar solos, and a range of song-and-dance sequences. It was followed within weeks by *Alam Ara*, the country's first feature-length talkie, which kicked off a second gold rush of film production.[7] Curiously, sound films were slower to take hold in much of Europe or even Japan while

---

[7] Like the first movie gold rush, prompted by the success of Phalke's *Raja Harishchandra*, this too brought a wide range of people into the industry. Moreover, the expansion of filmmaking in multiple languages, regions and cultures also created a vast, diverse work force of directors, writers, actors, technicians and experts across the country.

India's commercially driven filmmakers and viewers alike were quick to adopt them.[8]

The arrival of sound comprehensively transformed Indian cinema, not only splitting filmmaking along linguistic lines but also leading to a rapid expansion of cinema production and viewing in multiple languages across the country. Talkies also kicked off an irreversible decline in consumption of Hollywood films in the country which, despite occasional blockbusters dubbed into Indian languages, persists today as audiences choose cinema in their own languages. Many conventions of the use of sound, including but not limited to song-and-dance sequences, were developed in this period and often drew from theatre traditions. Of these, perhaps the most recognisable are 'sound effects' which are used to disrupt the background soundtrack, emphasise the artificiality of the narrative and heighten the emotional impact of a scene. These range from the whirr and the clap that accompanies the toss of a coin in *Sholay*, the jarring clang when Vijay loses his precious amulet in *Deewar*, to the crack of thunder that punctuates Narayan Shankar's recognition that he has lost all that he held dear in *Mohabbatein*.[9] The use of the sound of thunder to mark a dramatic discovery, or drums and bells for divine intervention, or a furious lashing of rain on tin roofs for growing passion and love, all draw on earlier stage conventions. However, after their repeated use in nearly a century of talkies, most viewers in India know – and have learned – them not from stage but cinema.

Indian filmmakers also rejected the Hollywood style of using diegetic sound or sound that originates within the video or story

---

[8] Indian cinema and Hollywood – the two most commercially minded film industries in the world – were the most enthusiastic in adopting sound. Both industries, despite frequent financial constraints faced by Indian filmmakers, appear to share a passion for new cinema technologies that is not limited to the case of sound.
[9] All three roles are essayed by Amitabh Bachchan and reflect not only the star's longevity but the ways conventions guiding the use of sound stretch through decades of filmmaking.

space such as characters' voices, music from instruments or noises made by objects which are produced at the time of filming. Driven partially by material constraints as films could rarely be shot in sound-proofed spaces, Indian filmmakers quickly adopted dubbing where actors added their speech after a film had already been shot and edited. Until recently, and the introduction of digital technology, dubbing was carried out in special recording studios where actors would watch their performance on screen and repeat their dialogues to match their lip movements. The dubbing process also meant that actors would re-enact their scenes entirely by themselves as dubbing was done individually instead of in groups. This meant that actors would perform their roles first before the camera and while interacting with fellow cast members and then again a second time, entirely by themselves, in the dubbing studio. At the same time, dubbing also allowed filmmakers from industries across the country to cast actors who did not necessarily speak the language used in a film. Professional dubbing artists or actors – including very well-known ones – who were fluent in the language would do the voiceovers. These dubbing conventions also extended to 'playback singing', where professional singers provide their voices to actors for the song sequences.

These practices mean that an actor's on-screen body can be different from their speaking voice, which in turn may be different from their singing voice. This can seem fractured to an audience unfamiliar with these conventions. However, even the earliest talkie audiences had few qualms, familiar as they were with other forms of performance where sound and action do not necessarily emanate from the same physical body.

Music and song were already an intrinsic part of silent cinema, which in turn had incorporated them from popular forms of theatre. Even in the early days of cinema, Indian audiences not only accepted and expected but also demanded song and dance as an element of performance. However, after the inception of sound, it is nearly impossible to point to a single blockbuster hit that does not contain songs. Not only do a film's songs contribute to its box-office success but often these can become more popular than the film itself. Even when a filmmaker chooses not to incorporate music and song in a film, this is a deliberate opposisitional choice intended as a statement.

While many of the structuring techniques for including song and dance in films are based on earlier traditions, filmmakers have evolved complex structuring and cinematic conventions. Throughout the 1950s, Raj Kapoor deployed Soviet-style montage, a style developed in the 1920s that combines shots to create meaning without attempting to hide the cuts,[10] for his song sequences. He would also intercut song with voiceovers and sound effects to heighten the aesthetic and emotional impact, although these techniques also emphasised the artificiality of the cinematic narrative. Similarly, Guru Dutt would cut directly from dialogue to the first line of a song, skipping over any opening bars. This technique turned the songs in his films into extensions of a character's speech. More recently, Karan Johar repeats, adapts and references quickly recognisable fragments of music from title tracks not only within a single film but across his movies. So the insertion of a fragment from a popular song from *Kuch Kuch Hota Hai* into a scene or song for *Kabhi Khushi Kabhi Gham* provides a continuous self-referentiality. It also indicates an extra-cinematic reality that filmmakers and stars inhabit beyond the screen and where films are conceived, planned and made. A similar device is used by Siddharth Anand in *Pathaan* (2023) to introduce the antagonist Jim (played by John Abraham). Jim's villainy has been signalled well before the scene which follows a high-speed chase through Dubai but the viewer first sees his

---

[10] Developed initially by Lev Kuleshov of the Moscow Film School in the 1920s, Soviet Montage Theory is best exemplified by Sergei Eisenstein's *Battleship Potemkin* (1925) whose influence on film editing is global and enduring. Brian de Palma's *The Untouchables* (1987) deploys not only many Eisensteinian editing techniques but also riffs on the earlier film in the sequence of the woman struggling with a pram on steep steps in the run-up to the shoot-out between the mobsters and the lawmen.

complete face when he removes his helmet. The use of electronically distorted strains of '*Ae mere watan ke logon zaraa ankh mein bhar lo paani* . . .' (People of my country, fill your eyes with tears), the patriotic lament recorded after the 1962 Indo–Chinese war, is jarring yet effective, hinting at Jim's character and back-story as well as evoking a complex reaction from a viewer familiar with the song, its history and place in contemporary culture.

A unique corollary to the introduction of sound is the link forged between poetry and cinema. Early talkies had turned to regional literary traditions for material that was at once recognisable and loved. Poets, past and present, found their works transferred to the screen as lyrics for songs, with some of the country's leading poets collaborating with commercial cinema to write dialogue, song lyrics and screenplays as well as taking up film direction and production. Kavi Pradeep, Sahir Ludhianvi and Kaifi Azmi are some of the poets who have contributed not only lyrics to film songs but also story ideas and scripts and, as in the case of Gulzar who also directs and produces, two dozen films to the Hindi film canon.

*　*　*

In the summer of 1999, time became plastic, stretching to endless hours of night as I watched my mother tracking the news with the same rigour as she had through my childhood, switching between multiple national and international television channels. Dad would be working long hours and so our landline was off limits to my siblings and I, in case of emergencies. For the first time since 1971, India and Pakistan were locked in a significant military confrontation in the brutal high altitudes of the Himalayas. Although the combat was restricted to Kashmir, armed forces were ready to mobilise along India's entire western border and were on high alert along its even longer northern one with China.

My mother seemed to know not only the topographical specifics of every peak, every point, where the fight was taking place but also every detail of Indian troops, including the positions of every army unit involved at any given hour. She knew the altitude, temperature, incline, ground conditions of every point where troops were locked in battle and had endless information on places I had never heard of until the fighting began. Her knowledge of the country's security apparatus nearly matched Dad's and she was more than willing to talk to me and my siblings, explaining political strategy and even military tactics. As the war lengthened from days to weeks, I was stunned by the accuracy of my mother's analysis and predictions. I began to see that Kargil, Dras, Batalik, Tololing and Tiger Hill were not just points on the map to her but embodiments of worries she had buried deep within herself.

I also started noticing that far too many people and places that made up my family's life were related to the armed forces. The building next to our flat was named after an officer killed in independent India's first war of 1948. My mother's concerns had transferred from Dad's safety to that of the sons of friends who were in the army. A cousin in the medical corps was moved up to Srinagar in Kashmir, and word floated down through the familial pipelines about casualties and injuries. A neighbour was part of the welfare association of army wives, an organisation that supports spouses and children of army personnel, and seemed overwhelmed by the scale of support that was required for families. News came that a childhood friend a few years younger than me, who I only remembered as the kid who was exceptionally sweet to my dog Atom, had been moved from Jammu up to the frontline in Dras. By the fifth week of the war, even the men we had filmed just months ago for our documentary were being re-deployed and I found myself terrified for them and their families.

Time strangely collapsed in on itself as my mind began reaching back to memories from my earliest years: of pretending to sleep while my mother pored over newspapers in Hindi and English, often going over the same report repeatedly and then crosschecking it with others from papers saved from previous days; of waking

189

up to find her staring anxiously at lists of names that I only learned much later were the names of those killed in battle; and most of all, of the overwhelming terror I felt watching her. One image lingered in my mind: of snuggling in her lap while she studied a detailed map, tracing blue rivers and green jungles with a single, elegant finger. Nearly three decades later, as another war raged on, I finally understood that gathering and analysing information was my mother's way of managing worries about Dad's safety.

The realisation did little to help my own anxiety. My mind had resurrected nightmares from my childhood, particularly one about a sniper that had haunted me for years. As a toddler, I had heard adults talking about the men in Dad's unit who had been killed by snipers. At the time, I had no idea what the word meant except that it was dangerous. My imagination had conjured a giant shadowy figure who could appear anywhere at any time and snatch people away. With war permeating our lives again, that nightmare returned except this time the shadow snatched away not only Dad but also my siblings, friends and the many people I loved. In this reprise, my adult self still could do nothing more than clutch my mother and watch in horror as the sniper picked everyone we loved one by one.

Then my director friend – perhaps recognising the fraying thread that held together my increasingly sleep-deprived mind – asked me to join them in editing the film we had shot just months ago. For the remainder of the war, I trooped daily to a tiny studio tucked away in a cramped neighbourhood of South Delhi that was reached by a narrow set of uneven steps. A huge diesel-fuelled generator took up most of the landing next to the door and ensured that our work was not interrupted – or, more importantly, lost – by a power cut. However, the generator could not power the air-conditioner as well as the editing deck and the latter took precedence. One afternoon when the generator ran out of fuel, we had to abandon work as the studio had turned into a sauna.

My role in the editing studio was supposedly advisory and my friend would regularly ask for my views on the length of a dissolve parsed to the precise fraction of a second or the choice of a jump cut over a morph. These would sometimes turn into a discussion with the editor, who would gesture me to wheel my chair closer to the editing deck and give me a lesson on editing techniques and technology. My friend would call for a tea break and we'd spend some time talking about our favourite films before returning to work. When we emerged from the studio into the night, my eyes would be unable to bear even the dull yellow streetlights.

I knew that my role was superfluous and that my friend's film would be completed faster without me, but I was grateful for any distraction from the insistent dread that seemed to follow me around. I quickly learned that even though the war waged on and the reports from the front remained as shattering and painful each day, I could withdraw – at least temporarily – into thinking about cross-cuts, fades, wipes and everything else I had learned. And if I tried hard enough, I could even jump cut my thoughts from fear to calm.

Editing at its simplest level involves selecting and arranging shots based on their place in the narrative, their role in establishing or enhancing the mood of a particular scene or the film as a whole, their impact on the film's rhythm and pacing and their ability to articulate and emphasis the film's themes and deeper meaning (if any). In many ways, editing is perhaps where a filmmaker's intent takes its final shape. My growing collection of books on filmmaking – mostly published in the UK and the USA and focussed on Hollywood and European cinemas – emphasised the value of continuity editing, a style that helps a viewer suspend disbelief and immerse themselves in a story without any disruptions or distractions. This style of editing uses a variety of techniques – eyeline matching, 180-degree axis of action and match cuts – to blend shots taken at different times or locations and even by multiple cameras in a seamless narrative. It is essential to cognitively realist film narratives that are clearly grounded in time and space. This style of editing does not call attention to itself and is intended to ensure that cinematic artifice be rendered invisible.

I had realised even before my first day in the editing studio that this was another aspect of film style where Indian cinema followed an entirely different set of rules. Its editing conventions used completely different techniques that not only made the cinematic artifice visible but actively called attention to themselves. However, these conventions were also unlike the Eisensteinian montage where editing also calls attention to itself. Like other aspects of film style, it was clear that, given the exposure to Soviet cinema, Indian filmmakers had incorporated some of its elements. However, the key principle at the heart of Indian editing conventions was again the construction of a visible cinematic artifice. This was used, like other elements of style, for enhancing the *emotional* experience of the film while also ensuring that a viewer could be absorbed in the on-screen spectacle but not be swept away by it.

Editing is deployed in Indian cinemas to collapse narrative time and space and to disrupt any possibility of a linear narrative. This disruption of time and space can be most easily spotted in song sequences where characters not only change costumes but also move from one location to another in quick succession and without any explanation. A single song sequence can move from a village in Punjab to the mountains of Switzerland or a market in Delhi to the Egyptian Pyramids or the ice floes of Alaska. However, these choices are not limited to song sequences but extend to all parts of the cinematic narrative where editing conventions use familiar techniques such as dissolve, freeze-frame, superimposition and fade for completely disparate purposes and with entirely different impacts. These editing choices create a narrative structure where time functions in circular or spiral rather than linear manner. Films as varied as *Mother India*, *Awara*, *Deewar* and *Kal Ho Na Ho* along with many others use editing choices to elide, inverse or even collapse time. A particularly curious instance can be observed in *Saudagar* (Merchant, 1991), where editing allows the young lovers to sing their first duet prior to their first meeting without raising any eyebrows from the audience. Instead, the style suggests that love does not follow from an initial encounter but has always and already existed.

Similarly, Aditya Chopra's *DDLJ* not only bridges time and space but also uses editing to create imaginary realities that only exist in the characters' minds. When the main characters Simran and Raj go their separate ways after their Europe trip during the duet '*Ho gaya hai tujhko to pyar . . .*' (You have fallen in love), the editing allows the characters to sing to each other, bridging the growing physical space between them with a fantasy communication. Similarly, while the second duet, '*Tujhe dekha to ye jana sanam . . .*' (When I saw you, my love), depicts Raj and Simran's reunion in India, the editing reprises their European journey, cutting to events and places that the audience has already seen. However, in this reprise, the two revisit the locations as lovers rather than strangers. These choices can seem entirely baffling, even illogical, to a viewer more familiar with Hollywood conventions of continuity editing but are better understood when considered as continuities of a film's emotional reality rather than disruptions of the material one.

A more explicit use of editing can be found in films that combine apparently realist elements with symbolic ones, as can be observed in the climactic sequence of *Mother India*. Mehboob Khan edits the final sequence as a series of shot and counter-shots between Radha (played by Nargis) and her son Birju (Sunil Dutt).[11] With each return to Radha who has fired at Birju, the camera grows closer and her image increases in size to heroic proportions until she discards the gun and runs to her son. At this point, as Radha embraces her dying son, Khan reverts to emphasising the intimate mother/son dynamic by focussing on

---

[11] The actors began a relationship during the shooting and married soon after. An apocryphal story claims that Nargis fell in love with Dutt during a scene where his character saves hers from a fire. Apparently the fire on the set had actually got out of control and endangered the actress. The story, regardless of truth, remains in popular imagination and was included, albeit with tragi-comic effect, in Farah Khan's 2008 homage to the film industry, *Om Shanti Om*.

the mother's palms trying to stem the blood from wounds she herself has inflicted. However, Khan disrupts the emotional devastation of the filicide by moving from an extreme close-up of Radha's blood-drenched hand to a quick dissolve and a shot of floodgates of a dam letting out much needed water into agricultural fields. For an instant, Radha's palms and the floodgates are superimposed, linking the two inextricably. At this point Khan abandons any form of cognitive realism. In the following high-angle shot, villagers line the newly built canal and watch as blood-red waters from the dam begin to irrigate the green fields.

Rang de Basanti (Colour Me Saffron, 2006, hereafter *RDB*), a film-within-a-film that links a group of revolutionaries from the colonial period to a group of students who are inspired to act against the contemporary government, exemplifies the ways Indian conventions of editing can be deployed to simultaneously construct, reveal and even revel in the artificiality of the film narrative. The film constructs itself as a complex and layered artifice with an opening sequence in sepia which places the action in the past but switches rapidly to the present. A third layer is added soon after, with the narrative switching to the film one of the characters Sue (Alice Patton) is making about her grandfather who had served as a jailer in colonised India.

RDB uses elements of classic Western 'continuity editing' to not construct a seamless cinematic reality but to emphasise the artificiality of whatever is unfolding on screen. As the film proceeds, sequences are repeated either in sepiatone or full colour, and the narrative jumps between the past and present, the diegetic reality of the film in the present and the cinematic reality of Sue's film-within-the-film. After the Sue's friends organise a protest at India Gate[12] with their fellow students, *RDB* begins to fully merge

---

[12] In a strange case of life following art, the shots of the student's vigil at India Gate in *RDB* were replicated by protesters calling for a retrial of model Jessica Lall's murderers a few months after the release of the film. The photographs of the protest as well as television footage eerily echoed the composition and visual style of the protest in the film.

the various narrative strands and time frames, conflating the characters of the present with those of the past and the roles they play in Sue's film. So Bhagat Singh's (played by Siddharth, who also plays one of Sue's friends) memory of the massacre at Jallianwala Bagh is entirely in black and white but, as the sequence unfolds, the British officer shouting orders to shoot is replaced by the current Defence Minister (Mohan Agashe). The victims of the massacre are also replaced by Ajay (Madhavan), the present-day pilot (and Sue's friend) killed in an air crash. The entire sequence remains in black and white, not only collapsing time frames but also merging various narrative realities of the film. It is only when the sequence ends with a cut to Karan – who has been cast as Bhagat for Sue's film – that the viewer realises that they have watched a dream sequence and not a historical depiction of the massacre or an episode from Sue's film.

* * *

War loomed large as I once again prepared to move out of India. The terrorist attacks on the USA on 11 September 2001 had resulted in a concentrated military campaign by US-led forces to overthrow the Taliban regime in Afghanistan and had a wide-ranging impact in South Asia. The Indian government under Prime Minister Atal Bihari Vajpayee had already been reeling from the devastation caused by the Bhuj earthquake in January 2001 that had left tens of thousands dead in the western state of Gujarat and from multiple charges of corruption, especially in the defence procurement process. On the other side of the border, in Pakistan, General Pervez Musharraf had seized power after a dramatic coup in 1999 but struggled to consolidate his authority. The two countries, both with significant nuclear arsenals, were locked in a cycle of failed diplomacy and limited border skirmishes even before the 9/11 attacks. Both now attempted to use the rapidly shifting geopolitical situation to further their own domestic and international agendas.

195

The situation changed dramatically with a terrorist attack on the Indian parliament in December 2001, just days after the Taliban collapse in Afghanistan. The event kicked off a cycle of escalation as the two nations squared off against each other. For months, tensions simmered, never quite coming to a boil but also never settling into calm. In the heart of Delhi, my siblings and I realised that our home was once again within a mile of the most likely hypocentre of a nuclear strike. This time we knew there would be no time to prepare, as the missile would be launched from just across the border. There would be no place this time to cast beautiful shadows in case of a nuclear war.

Violence simmered within the national borders too. In February 2002, fire gutted a train in Gujarat, killing dozens of Hindu travellers and triggering a wave of violence against Muslims in the state that lasted nearly three months, killed and injured thousands, and destroyed hundreds of mosques and shrines. While the country had seen riots before, something about the nature of the violence had changed. When apparent calm finally returned, it was clear that India too had been irrevocably altered, that there would always be a before and after Gujarat 2002 in the country's history. While descriptions of the events vary depending on political affiliations – from riots to ethnic cleansing and genocide – what is clear is that over a hundred thousand people were displaced by the violence, many of whom never returned home.

By this time, I had finished my first novel and published a second book. This time it wasn't despair or discontent that was leading me away from the country. Instead, India had offered up enough material for an entirely new novel. However, I had learned the story, setting, themes and characters so intimately that I could not write it anywhere in the vicinity of the familiar sugarcane fields and mango orchards of north India. I realised that I would have to leave India so I could write about her!

Like the last time, I turned to movies again, deliberately choosing those that offered a brief respite from relentless reports of political violence on the news channels. Thankfully, the film industry obliged with a feast of films: the stunningly shot period drama *Asoka*, about an emperor who was key to the spread of Buddhism through Asia; an eye-wateringly expensive – and loud – adaptation of *Devdas*; *Dil Chahta Hai* (The Heart Desires, 2001), a modern coming-of-age film about three friends set between India and Australia which assuaged some of my own doubts about leaving the country; and *Kabhi Khushi Kabhie Gham*, a lavish family drama with a tagline that can only work in India: 'It's all about loving your parents.'

One baking summer afternoon as I planned my move abroad, my friends and I carried flags to watch *Lagaan* (Tax, 2001), a period film about a group of villagers who challenge the British colonial administrators to a game of cricket. Power cuts had been particularly frequent that year and a visit to the cinema not only offered entertainment but also a few hours of air-conditioned comfort. Tickets had been hard to acquire as the film was running to packed theatres even weeks after its release. In the parking lot I realised we weren't the only ones carrying national flags. Most were small, easy enough to hold up and wave, but a large group of excited students behind us carried a full-sized one. Two young men held the flag up while the rest of the group fell into rows behind them to walk into the theatre as a united team. The audience had people sporting team t-shirts and dupattas in the saffron, white and green colours of the Indian flag.

The second half of *Lagaan* is an extended cricket match full of references to sports trivia and is peppered with superstitious belief about why the Indian team might win or lose. As the rival teams faced off on screen, I found that fellow filmgoers had brought in not only flags but also drums and whistles. Soon the theatre sounded like a cricket stadium as we shouted and jeered, groaned and cheered along with the action on screen. We bit our nails as the last balls were bowled even though we knew that, unlike a real cricket match, the movie could only end one way. Then the whole theatre erupted in cheers at the finale and

197

strangers turned to congratulate each other. We walked out smiling and laughing in a moment of mass camaraderie.

I knew that I would miss many things about India when I left. But this shared magic of sitting in the dark to feast together on a film? This, I would miss the most.

We are Worshippers of Love, We are Beggars of Rasa[1]

IT WAS 2015 AND I was researching a story in Jordan. Abdel, my guide through Wadi Rum, had a loud belly-laugh that erupted each time his trusty white Toyota truck bounced over a sand-dune. He teased me for wearing the seatbelt and mocked me for clutching the sides of the seat. He had grown up in this desert, showed me his favourite spots, and took more photographs on his phone than me. 'Every time I look, the desert has changed,' he explained, more in love with his land than anyone I have met. Abdel also drew detailed, evocative pictures in the sand with nothing but a stick, sketching scorpions and birds, hills and oases, and on one occasion Alexander's horse Bucephalus, with sharp quick strokes. Each line in the sand was accompanied by part of a story: about kings lost in history, djinns that guarded a water source, about his grandfather who had fought in the war. When he finished his story, we would stare for some time at the pictures he had drawn. Then he would sweep the sand with his hand, leaving the ground as pristine as before and we'd clamber back into the truck for another bone-rattling drive through the desert.

I discovered that he loved Hindi movies when he jumped out of the truck at a derelict train station in the middle of the desert.

---

[1] *'Prem ke pujari hum hain, rasa ke bhikhari . . .'* from *Prem Pujari* (Worshipper of Love, 1970).

'Straight out of *Sholay*,' he called as I clambered onto the rusted locomotive, abandoned decades ago after another failed attempt to revive the old Hejaz Railway. 'OK, then I am Jai,' I shouted back. He grinned and pointed to himself 'Veeru!' naming himself as the other hero of the film. For a few hours, we reverted to becoming children, running along the tracks, jumping off the carriages, joking and clowning. Abdel shot a video of me acting out Amitabh Bachchan's dialogue from the movie, '*mujhe toh sab police waalon ki suratein ek jaisi lagti hai . . .*' (Faces of all cops look the same to me). The light was fading when we headed back to the camp.

As we drove through the desert, the bright stars and the truck's headlights the only points of light in the pitch-dark night, Abdel had a question for me. 'You know what is Shahadah?' he asked me. 'Yes,' I said, although I could see he didn't believe me. 'I will teach you so speak after me,' he insisted and recited the first part of the verse. Then his eyes narrowed when I followed him with the second part. 'So you learned about Islam?' he asked. 'At school,' I said without telling him more. He smiled and said, 'Good, good.'

I had almost fallen asleep when Abdel spoke again, laughter in his voice. 'You Hindi!' he scoffed, using the Arabic word for Indian. 'Did you learn it at school? Or you just watched *Coolie* many times?' I smiled at the twinkling stars above, delighted to have found another fellow fan of my cinema on my travels.

The *Natyashastra* emphasises that natya (theatre) is for everyone, which means that all of us are capable of partaking of rasa created by performance, regardless of our background, language or provenance. This in turn implies that there is a sliding scale of pleasure that depends on two concurrent aspects: the quality of the performance, including acting, setting, narrative, etc., and the sensitivity and prior knowledge of the spectator that helps derive maximum enjoyment. Later philosophers, especially Abhinavagupta, examined the role of the audience, how they impacted a performance, and theorised the qualities of an ideal spectator. Given that the concept of rasa extends to all arts, these questions regarding aesthetic pleasure go beyond theatre. The ninth-century philosopher Anandavardhan examined the role of a reader or listener of poetry, positing that a poet creates not a description but a suggestion of emotions that can only be fully enjoyed by someone who is open, prepared and attuned for receiving these.

The rasic tradition classifies spectators into three categories: preksaka or an observer who derives some pleasure from a performance but lacks full empathy or knowledge to savour it fully; samajika or someone part of a social group, and better prepared, more informed and likely a regular consumer of the arts; and finally, the sahriday – literally the one with a heart – or the ideal partaker who is able to fully immerse themselves in the rasas evoked by a performance, retain a critical distance, and simultaneously enjoy and critique a work. The sahriday is someone who is not only open-hearted but has also prepared themselves for a rasic experience through the study of the arts.

If, like all performance, a film is a metaphorical feast composed of numerous narrative, stylistic and technical ingredients, then the ideal spectator is one who does not only enjoy it at a purely sensory level. Instead, the sahriday viewer is one who can marshal a wealth of information to make sense of not only the 'menu' on offer but also the ingredients of the dishes, the provenance of both, the order in which the meal must be consumed, and the reasons for the order. However, this awareness is neither egregious (as it enhances the pleasure of the feast) nor should it be grounds for snobbery which would mean a close-heartedness that would hamper our enjoyment. Instead, our prior knowledge helps build expectations and anticipation. So the recognition of the ingredients, either from prior information or experience, and the way they are used in a dish helps us anticipate its flavour. Repeated tasting of the ingredients combined in similar or different ways trains our palate, improving our abilities to discern subtle differences in scent and taste. In turn this knowledge helps prepare us for a dish that we may never have tasted before but can identify, anticipate, understand and enjoy based on our prior knowledge. Anandavardhan points out that merely stating that a newly wed couple are in love reveals nothing about the state or quality of that love. However, if that love is effectively expressed in poetry – or, in this case, film – it can suggest the emotions experienced by the newly wed lovers to an empathetic listener or viewer. The ideal consumer – sahriday – would not only be open to the suggested emotion but also be able to draw on their experience and knowledge to recognise and appreciate the form in which these are expressed. Moreover, this ideal audience would be already prepared to experience and savour the poem or play or film even before it began. This is because fully savouring rasa is not based on surprise but on a set of expectations about the dominant rasa. These in turn are based on a spectator's individual recognition and understanding of the information made available by the creator such as the cover of a book, the opening notes of a melody, or posters and other publicity material for a film.

Since the inception of sound, the songs of a film (and in the past three decades, the video clips of the song sequences) have formed a key part of film publicity and promotion. These are disseminated by radio, music video channels and recently via YouTube. They contribute not only by building the film's marketing hype but also by signalling the themes and moods of the story. Posters, hoardings and film trailers (the latter a relatively recent phenomenon in India) are similarly deployed. For example, for a film like *Mangal Pandey: The Rising* (2005), it is clear from the first instance that the dominant rasa will be vira as the title itself points to the revolutionary hero of the Indian uprising of 1857. Its martial theme song exhorting people to '*Jaago re . . .*' (Wake up) was released as part of the film's pre-release publicity campaign. The video clip accompanying the song shows an elephant rearing its head and then cuts to a young man with long hair, a red tilak on his forehead, bare-chested with his hands tied behind his back. His walk – linked by the rhythm of the song to the elephant – signals the film's dominant rasa, although the lyrics along with the visuals also clarify that the story will not end in victory. The posters of the film depict the lead star Aamir Khan holding a rifle, his hair flowing in the wind, dressed in the identifiable red uniform of the British East India Company. The background of yellow and orange, with a halo of light behind Khan's head, points to the film's theme of sacrifice and valour. The period aspect of the film was also emphasised by Khan's press appearances where he kept intact his character's old-fashioned moustache and long hair. In comparison, the publicity campaign for *Asoka* (2001) relied on songs and video clips that focussed on the lead pair expressing their love, either in union or in separation, and highlighted its dominant rasa as shringar (love). Despite its explicit reference to the historical figure of Emperor Ashoka, the film's publicity created the expectation of a narrative emphasising love over war-like heroism. Similarly, although the poster for the film features the face of the protagonist, the eponymous Ashoka (played by Shah Rukh Khan) at the top right corner, clad in armour and holding up a sword, it also foregrounds the film's glamorous female lead, Kareena Kapoor, who plays the love interest, Kaurwaki. The lead pair are separated on the poster by soldiers on horseback with swords drawn, indicating that the film primarily deals with war as a challenge to the lovers rather than the historical Ashoka's military conquests and his eventual conversion to Buddhism.

At times, the songs and their video clips that are released for publicity can seem unrelated to the film's dominant theme, especially to an unfamiliar viewer. These are often particularly catchy dance tunes, often set in exotic locations or lavish bars and shot as extravagant spectacles. Within the film itself, these song-and-dance sequences are transitional scenes intended to prevent the dominant rasa from becoming overwhelming. They may also introduce shringar (love) to a primarily vira (heroic) rasa narrative, albeit fleetingly, and be used to lighten or delay the cumulative violence within the narrative. Often called the 'item number', these songs are edited with images of action or violence for publicity video clips and bookended with film title, credits and publicity stills. The habitual spectator is able to quickly recognise that such a video clip is highlighting a particular rasa and is not an indicator of the primary rasa itself for the film. *Sholay* (1975), for example, uses the '*Mehbooba, Mehbooba*' (Beloved) song with the dancer and actress Helen to build suspense before the protagonists destroy a cache of weapons acquired by the villain. Yet the song does not dislodge the film's primary rasa of vira emphasised on the posters and hoardings. These focussed mostly on images of the male protagonists, armed with rifles and placed against a backdrop of lurid reds and yellows. Similarly, *Kaante* (Thorns, 2002), a remake of Quentin Tarantino's *Reservoir Dogs* (1992), used two item numbers for its pre-release publicity. Both songs are set in nightclubs with a heavy rhythm component and feature sexualised visuals of glamorously dressed women. However, the film's poster featured fragments of facial features of the six male protagonists alongside overtly phallic images of handguns and cigarettes, signalling that the dominant mood is vira. Moreover, the songs feature male and female voices, and the lyrics are laments for separated lovers, making it clear that the narrative will not end well for the protagonists.

Film titles add to this anticipatory information as these are often metaphorical and more likely to indicate the dominant rasa rather than the storyline or themes. So a film with a modern setting like *Dil to Pagal Hai* (The Heart Crazy, 1997) is not only instantly identifiable as shringar by its title but also by the posters with the three lead actors, Shah Rukh Khan, Madhuri Dixit and Karishma Kapoor, placed in close proximity to each other and smiling, which promise the story will end happily for all of them despite indications of a love triangle. Similarly, *Sholay*, meaning embers, refers to the film's predominant rasa of vira while *Waqt* (Time, 1965) signals adbhuta (wonder). At times a subtitle is added to indicate the use of a familiar title for a new film but also to clarify a change in the dominant mood, as in the case of *Khamoshi* (Silence, 1969) which hints at the karuna (sorrow) of silence. However, when the same title was re-deployed for *Khamoshi: The Musical* (1996) the additional subtitle emphasised music and suggested an altered emphasis on shringar. An interesting dissonance arises when a film carries a title such as *Fiza* (Atmosphere, 2000) which provides no clue to the dominant rasa of the film. In such a case, pre-released songs, video clips, hoarding and posters, star personas of the main actors, and the director's prior movies help identify, even if ambiguously, the subject matter and dominant rasa of the film.

* * *

When the insistent 'India? Indian?' questioning first hit my ears, I was half-blinded by the bright sun outside the photography museum in Saint-Louis, Senegal. It was 2016 and I was tracing the footsteps of the pioneering aviator Jean Mermoz and one of the earliest airmail routes between Africa and South America and had passed mostly unnoticed till that point. 'India?' the question came again as a dapper older man slowly took shape before me. When I nodded, he switched to flawless Hindi. 'You like films? You like Bollywood?' he grinned and insisted on escorting my friend and I through the old town, guiding us to unmarked workshops of artists and to picturesque stretches along the Senegal river lined with colourful fishing boats. 'Like the boats on the Ganga,' he noted. I had to agree. The brightly painted wooden boats, despite their loud outboard motors, were very like the ones I remembered from my childhood. He sang Hindi film songs from the 1970s as we wandered through the streets, asking for my favourites and rendering each one flawlessly. He had studied in Calcutta as a young man, learned Hindi and Bengali although he had mostly forgotten the latter. And he had fallen in love with Indian cinema, he explained with a cheeky wink, mostly for the actresses. 'My favourite is Neetu Singh,' he announced and was delighted when my friend pointed out that I had the same last name. 'Do you know her? She is so beautiful.' Sadly, I had to disclaim any link with his favourite actress.

He dragged us to an abandoned ochre-coloured building with rusted, arched gates flanked by two tall palm trees. To our north, the monumental arches of the Faidherbe Bridge gleamed in the sun, in far better shape than this forgotten pleasure palace. The box-office window looked exactly like the ones I knew from home, with its diamond-shaped metal grille and a small square at the bottom to allow for the exchange of tickets and money. Bits of rocks and rubble had been left in front, most likely by bored neighbourhood children, and looked like offerings to some long-departed god. Above the window, ticket prices were painted in blue. Like the cinemas of my childhood, stall tickets were cheaper than balcony seats for the matinee, although unlike India they cost the same for evening shows.

'I used to come here every day before it closed down,' our new friend mourned, gesturing till we joined him in peering through the grille. The foyer was dusty and little piles of trash – plastic water bottles and empty chip packets – had collected in heaps, likely pushed in by the same people who had piled the stones at the box-office window. Broken display cases lined the walls, some still cradling faded, torn film posters. These were mostly of old French movies, not the arty kind that make the festivals and film-school lists but cheaply produced, commercial fare, their content made clear by images of bikini-clad women and flashy sports cars. One case held a poster for an Indian film I recognised but had never seen, *Julie* (1975), a romance about an interfaith couple, premarital sex and unplanned pregnancy. 'Julie, I love you . . .,' the old gentleman warbled as we walked along the river gleaming in the afternoon sun. 'My Indian friends taught me to watch films,' his voice was thoughtful. 'They taught me a different way to see.'

Films deploy three mechanisms of the gaze: of the camera that frames and guides our perceptions, of the main character, and finally of the spectator. The first mechanism is constructed by filmic techniques which are guided by cultural ideas, principles and conventions. This culturally grounded deployment of filmic techniques informs the way the camera 'sees' the characters on screen.

The second mechanism is introduced by aesthetic conventions that establish the gaze of the main character and construct the point of view in a film. In cinemas such as classic Hollywood, this is not only bound by realist conventions of presenting a seamless, invisibly constructed narrative, but is also most frequently presented from the point of view of the main character. For many cinemas across the world, this main character is most frequently male, although principles of film style can emphasise, undermine or subvert the authority of this gaze. Conventions of realism, including classic Hollywood's invisible style which present films as seamless narratives covering a sequence of events, are likelier to entrench the male gaze. In contrast, Indian cinema with its constantly shifting points of view and the deliberately constructed artificiality not only rejects any notion of performance as 'real' but also challenges, subverts and overturns the authority of a single, hegemonic gaze. This in turn is grounded in earlier cultural practices and philosophy. Indian epics as well as their performances have long incorporated not only the possibility of multiple points of view regarding an incident but also multiple ways of seeing the world, divine image and even cosmic truth. Moreover, the tradition thrives on not privileging a particular point of view as the most authoritative, valid or true.[2]

Finally, the third mechanism refers to the gaze of the spectators which – like that of the performers creating the narrative – is embedded in cultural practices and beliefs, and informs the reception of cinema. Realist cinema, which renders cinematic artifice invisible, assumes a spectator who is isolated, individualised and engaged in an act of voyeurism: essentially watching events unfold without the knowledge of those involved in those events. A key part of the pleasure of such voyeuristic spectatorship is based on

---

[2] One indication of this multiplicity is that Indic traditions do not rely on a single religious text, instead offering a range of texts, myths and explanations, none of which can occupy a definitive hegemonic position. This means that there are many versions of the story of Rama, for example, told from various points of views. It also means that, unlike most traditions, there are even numerous 'origin' or creation myths of the universe and each of them holds equal validity.

anonymity as this viewer can see the people on screen (or stage) but is not seen in turn. Such voyeuristic spectatorship also encourages this viewer – alone in a dark room – to identify with a figure, mostly likely the film's protagonist. In contrast, Indian films not only emphasis the artificiality of the cinematic narrative but also repeatedly acknowledge the viewer through multiple elements of film style and demand a different kind of spectator. It is not surprising that in India, film viewing is considered a social, familial and communal activity. To this day, I cannot bring myself to watch an Indian film on my own, although I have developed the habit of solitary viewing of Hollywood, European, South American cinemas into a not-so-guilty pleasure.

However, the pleasure of watching films as a shared activity goes beyond dragging a companion to the movies. Instead, it requires taking a viewing position that is not of a voyeur but a participant in the spectacle presented on screen. This, of course, is aided by film conventions and techniques deployed by Indian filmmakers, including multiple – and constantly shifting – points of view, the refusal to retain a single hegemonic gaze and an ongoing acknowledgement of the viewer by actors on screen through a series of well-recognised conventions of visual interactions. This does not mean that the voyeuristic pleasures of cinema are not evoked by Indian filmmakers, but these are neither the main form of spectatorship nor sustained through an entire film.

Instead, the most frequent form of film spectatorship is deeply rooted in cultural, religious and aesthetic traditions. While most film fans or creators and performers are unlikely to have considered the principles that inform how we *see* performances, or indeed how the performers invoke distinctive ways of *seeing*, most of us are not only familiar with viewing practices but also use them consistently. For the Indian viewer, this is primarily rooted in darshan, a term that is used for looking at not only deities but also other personages, often (although not always) in positions of authority. The term is colloquially used by Hindi speakers for seeing friends, colleagues and families. And it is also used by movie fans for 'seeing' their favourite film stars on screen.

At its simplest, darshan is a way of participating in ritual, which is often but not always religious and grounded in the practice of 'seeing' a religious image as part of worship. However, this worship is not centred around paying homage to a superior being and instead encompasses a wide range of intimate and ordinary acts by the worshipper, including the rituals for welcoming, feeding, dressing the deities. A worshipper may thus approach a deity as a friend or child or lover and, in each case, their act of worship will not only include an aspect of respect, awe or honour but also affection, love, even desire. This is why Meera, the sixteenth-century poet, expresses her devotion for Kṛṣna in eroticised love poetry and is popularly perceived even today as an idealised lover. Religious festivals re-enact not only the story of Rama in Ramlilas but also celebrate the wedding of Shiva and Parvati and the birth of Kṛṣna with practices that echo rituals of marriage and childbirth. In each case, the practice of darshan constructs the relationship between the devotee and the divine as one based not on hierarchy but on intimacy and familiarity.

Without darshan by at least one worshipper, an image of a Hindu deity, whether in a temple or at home, has no divine power, just as a spectacle of secular power or splendour means little without a witness to view and appreciate it. Darshan is not a one-directional act of gazing upon a religious icon or a powerful authority figure. Instead, it requires a gaze that is returned as it is not just seeing but the act of being seen that creates a reciprocal and reciprocated relationship, and which leads to a transformation in *both* the icon and the worshipper. The icon is imbued with divine power by the worshipper's gaze, and the act of worship in turn heightens spiritual awareness and approximates the experience of the divine in the devotee. In religious terms, darshan describes the process of constant transformation that must occur during the worship, in both the deity and devotee.

This concept extends also to viewing performance of music, dance, theatre, and of course cinema which demands not voyeurism but a mutually shared connection between the performers and the spectators. This shared visual connection removes and reverses the power structures of voyeurism. The spectator is actively acknowledged by actors on stage or screen, and an active connection is forged between the performance, extra-filmic lives and personalities of the actors, and the consumer.

Anurag Kashyap's short film *Murabba*[3] (Preserve) is one of the most explicit and nuanced explorations of darshan as a religious, secular and cinematic viewing practice. Released as part of *Bombay Talkies* (2013), an anthology of short films named for the historic, pre-Independence film studio to mark the centenary of Indian cinema, it explores trans-generational cinephilia, the power of stardom, and the complex relationship between stars and their fans. The film opens in the north Indian city of Allahabad, associated in popular imagination with the star Amitabh Bachchan, where the protagonist Vijay (Vineet Kumar Singh) makes money persuading pilgrims to take darshan of a powerful ascetic. His long hair, flared, faded jeans and check shirt recall Bachchan's signature look from the 1970s. Even his name is one used for Bachchan's characters in multiple films.

Vijay's father (Sudhir Pandey) recalls that his own father had requested him to carry a jar of honey to Dilip Kumar so the star could bless it by dipping his finger into it. Blessed by the star, the honey had extended the ailing man's life for years. He requests Vijay to undertake a similar task: of carrying a single preserved gooseberry fruit (murabba) to Bachchan, to be tasted and returned as a cure for his illness. The use of food, to be blessed and returned, is an overt reference to the Hindu concept of prasad, the devotional offering made to a deity and then consumed by devotees. *Murabba* links fandom to ritual practices of pilgrims who undertake long and arduous expeditions to sacred sites. Vijay's journey to Mumbai, his many difficulties and prolonged wait outside Bachchan's home, the final summoning

---

[3] Murabba in north India is generally a sweet fruit preserve, with the most popular version using whole gooseberries.

by the star, and his entry past the closed gates to finally see his idol all replicate the motifs, rituals and stages of a religious pilgrimage.

Vijay's travails are finally rewarded with a meeting with his idol. In a Bachchan film, the scene's soundtrack would require temple bells, bhajans or other devotional material; for Vijay the star's appearance is accompanied by his most famous dialogues. His quest completed, Vijay heads home with the murabba, only to have a passenger in the train break the jar and another step on the remains. But unlike films, Vijay cannot and does not resort to violence. Instead, he procures another jar and gooseberry to fool his father, even carefully biting into the replacement fruit to imitate the teeth marks left by the star.

His return home is anti-climactic as his father challenges him on his tale, confessing that he too had lied about his own trip to the city. The film ends on a cryptic note with the father noting that *Achaar ki botal mein murabba nahin rakhna chahiye* (One should not keep sweet preserve in a pickle jar). Vijay, recounting his journey to his friend, explains that Bachchan had 'blessed him', but follows it up with his father's quote.

Murabba explores the many forms of darshan as a nuanced mechanism for the visual interactions between the intra-filmic deity, Bachchan, and Vijay and it deploys a host of cinematic techniques to forge a visual and emotional connection between the on-screen star and the on- and off-screen spectator. It most explicitly mobilises this spectator–star connection when Vijay finally sees Bachchan. The shot sequence recreates the entrance of the devotee into a temple, with the focus on Vijay's face as he veers between disbelief, awe, fear and gratitude. Initially, the camera shows Bachchan obliquely, with each reverse shot moving the star more firmly into Vijay's view. The low-angle camera positions Bachchan in iconic terms. Yet this is not simply a deity being honoured by a worshipper or a king being adored by subservient subjects. Instead, each reverse shot draws Vijay closer to his icon, emphasising a momentary but powerful intimacy. The darśanic is mobilised at multiple levels: Bachchan's generous welcome of Vijay also functions as an on-screen acknowledgement of the spectator watching *Murabba* without whom neither the film nor the star would have any meaning.

The sequence also uses a host of techniques including camera angle, sound and editing, to emphasise the egalitarian complicity between the spectator and the star, reinforcing the complex transformation required and produced by darshan in Vijay, the star, and the crowd watching their interaction within the film as well as the spectator of the film. Vijay's insistence that the star taste the murabba in his presence not only evokes the tradition of cajoling, even hectoring, a personalised deity, but also gives physical form to the ritual of presenting prasad to be 'tasted' by a religious icon. Bachchan's obvious relish as he licks his fingers clean signals the star's acceptance, acknowledgement and appreciation of not only the offering but also Vijay's – and by extension – his fans' devotion.

Darshan is similarly activated in *Swades: We, the People*, where the protagonist Mohan (Shah Rukh Khan, hereafter SRK) spon-taneously answers the question about where Rama may be found.[4] The scene brings about the complex conflation of star persona, performance, cinematic narrative and techniques, audience gaze, epic metatext, and Hindu philosophy and ritual of embodying divinity. Towards the end of the enactment, approximately thirty-two seconds explicitly mobilise darshan to construct multiple layers of potentially contradictory meanings, both within and without the film.

The short scene works on three levels simultaneously: Mohan articulates his devotion for Rama; the on-screen crowd recognises him as a momentary embodiment of the deity; and, finally, the film's audience is reminded of the way the star's on-screen persona over multiple films has been linked to characteristics of the ideal man (Rama). In the scene, the camera position reinforces this transformation as it first frames the star from a high-angle shot,

---

[4] See the previous chapter.

hinting at a divine gaze that looks beneficently on him. As Mohan continues to describe the omnipresence of the deity, the camera comes in for a close-up but also moves to a frontal shot. The gaze is no longer of the deity but of an equal – encoding and including the spectator – in the process of divine embodiment, a transformation that is instantly, if only subconsciously, recognised by the knowing spectator.[5]

The practice of darshan is not limited to such explicit moments and is easily recognisable, even if briefly, in almost every film. Darshan also informs many of the aesthetic conventions and stylistic techniques developed by Indian filmmakers. For example, iconic framing that characterises aesthestics of frontality is often deployed to emphasise dramatic impact in a scene or to highlight an actor's star status and quality. At the same time, the shot/reverse shot convention has proven a particular favourite of the country's filmmakers because it enables the simultaneous presentation of both positions of a darśanic exchange and can occupy multiple points of view in a single scene. The device is most frequently used to depict lovers or an emotionally intense exchange between characters. Unsurprisingly, a combination of iconic framing and shot/reverse shot has been a distinct characteristic of films dating back to *Kaliya Mardan* (1919) to depict characters in relationships with a marked difference in power (or indeed a character and an image of a deity).

Since the silent era, the concept of darshan has also been mobilised in secular ways in cinema. A single scene from *Amar Akbar Anthony* exemplifies the way darshan can be deployed without any religious intent or meaning. Towards the end of the film, Anthony (Amitabh Bachchan) minces up a winding flight of stairs, delicately holding his flowing priest's habit between his fingertips. He briefly holds the audience's gaze and

---

[5] It is a measure of the strength of SRK's star narrative that his Muslim identity does not disrupt audience identification, although it definitely complicates the reading of the sequence as an assertion of 'Hindu nationalism'.

waves his hands like a conductor leading an orchestra, gesturing at a pair of curtains which magically swoop shut. The scene follows the film's title song, where Anthony repeatedly addresses the camera. He winks, smirks and performs other comically exaggerated gestures in the song to create a humorous complicity, especially as the other characters in the scene remain unaware of his clowning. The magically closing curtains work especially well as the film's myriad twists and turns rely on the adbhuta (wonder) as the dominant rasa while racing through romance, action, drama and tragedy at breakneck speed. Bachchan's gaze lock with the spectator is simultaneously solemn and comic. More importantly, Bachchan's repeated direct address is also intended as a recognition of the spectator's willing participation in what is unfolding on screen. The brief sequence mobilises darshan as a culturally specific viewing practice that simultaneously acknowledges the presence of a spectator rupturing any notion of voyeurism, establishes a visual connection that recognises the on-screen spectacle as a crafted performance instead of a depiction of reality, and ensures that the spectator cannot be swept away by the spectacle but remains actively engaged.

* * *

The Valley of the Kings was scorching in August 2013 when I visited. I was travelling through Egypt for research and, given the political situation since the popular uprising of 2011, there were fewer than a dozen visitors on the entire site and the staff seemed delighted to see anyone at all. The euphoria that had followed the fall of Hosni Mubarak had settled into grim stoicism on all sides as another dictator consolidated power with brute force. While I was still in Luxor, the forces of General Abdel Fattah el-Sisi raided two protest camps in Cairo, killing nearly a thousand people and injuring many more. The tension had been building for weeks and it was clear that most Egyptians I met during my travels were expecting greater brutality and state repression than ever before.

And yet I was consistently greeted with the smiling query of 'alhind?' – the Arabic name for India – followed by 'do you know Amitabh Bachchan?' and enthusiastic discussions of favourite movies. I had found myself at the top of a minaret of Cairo's al-Azhar Mosque hearing the gatekeeper rave about *Ganga Jamuna Saraswati* (1988), a forgettable film from Bachchan's low period in the 1980s. At a seafood restaurant in Alexandria's market, a waiter wanted to know when Bachchan would make another film with Shah Rukh Khan because he loved *Kabhi Khushi Kabhie Gham*. A stranger had walked up to me in Hypostyle Hall of the Karnak temple to ask if Shatrughan Sinha, a star from the 1970s and 1980s, continued to act, and had been deeply disappointed when I informed him that the actor had moved into politics.

I wasn't surprised when a pair of guards lingered nearby as I made my way through the tomb of Seti I. The conversation soon opened with the usual 'alhind? India?' At my confirmation, the older, mostly bald, man pulled out his phone to show me a photograph of a much younger version of himself with Bachchan. Going by the wide shirt collars and the hairstyles on both men, the photograph had likely been snapped some time in the mid-1970s. 'I kept my hair like him,' he explained, running his hand over his smooth pate while the younger guard cackled with laughter. 'Me, I like Shah Rukh Khan,' he declared between giggles and demanded to know when Khan would visit the Valley. 'This is umm-al-duniya,' – mother of the world – 'he has to come here.' I promised that if I ever met the star, I would pass on the request. The two guards grinned and left me to wander the tomb alone.

The younger guard was waiting at the exit later and thrust a small plastic bag at me, indicating that it was a present. The bag held fresh green dates from the tree in his house. I suspected they were meant for his lunch and tried to refuse. 'Just something for the heat, not a full meal,' he insisted. Then he smiled widely, 'but they are fresh and sweet and also a bit sour. Just like your films.'

For any performance to succeed, there must be rasa. However, the bulk of the films produced in India every year fail commercially, suggesting that most of them somehow fail to generate rasa. Abhinavagupta identifies two types of obstacles to the production and savouring of rasa in performance: flaws with performance itself, and those that depend on the spectator's state of mind. These suggest that a film's success depends on a conjunction of a narratively and technically proficient product as well as a receptive, knowledgeable viewer.

However, this mysterious balance is only achieved when a spectator responds to the performance in the way intended and indeed expected by its creators. While part of the failure of rasa creation may lie with an unprepared or close-hearted spectator, the primary responsibility lies with the creators who must carefully and deliberately prepare an effective performance. Like chefs, the filmmaker must prepare a balanced offering with a narrative that harnesses elements of plot, characterisation and shifts of mood in a coherent and unified whole. They must deploy a host of polished film techniques to create and emphasise the film's emotional impact while offering a necessary critical distance to the viewer. This means that exemplary films deploy the full range of filmmaking techniques, conventions and style to be able to mobilise rasa throughout the narrative. Landmark films like *Mughal-E-Azam*, *Sholay* or *Dilwale Dulhaniya Le Jayenge* also provide a wealth of intertextual meanings and complex technical and narrative structures that simultaneously appeal to a viewer's emotions and intellect. A film that is less successful may only be able to evoke rasa during limited and specific sequences. These may succeed commercially, with particular songs or sequences providing enough motivation to audiences to engage in repeat viewings, but may fail to be memorable in their entirety. Nowhere is this more apparent than for songs or song-and-dance sequences that can be instantly recalled and those that continue to be popular while the film in which they featured has been mostly forgotten. Furthermore, films that fail at the box office despite technical and narrative proficiency, vast budgets and star presence suggest that somehow, despite the filmmakers' best efforts, these either cause an unacceptable rupture of the rasic universe (like *Kaagaz Ke Phool*) or fail to generate rasa due to narrative or structural weaknesses.

This final is most evident in box-office stumbles of films like *Mera Naam Joker* (I am Joker, 1970). Intended as auteur Raj Kapoor's magnum opus, the film was one of the biggest box-office disasters of its time. Despite technical proficiency, lavish cinematography, memorable music and the presence of some of the biggest stars of the era, the film was hampered by a lack of rasic coherence. It begins with three women attending the final performance of a circus clown, Raju (played by the film's producer and director, Raj Kapoor). The film then unfolds in three distinct parts, placing the women in three stages of Raju's life, and follows how he loves and loses each of them. Although it covers not one but three love stories, beginning with Raju's schoolboy infatuation with a teacher, an affair with a glamorous Soviet circus performer, and finally his troubled relationship with an ambitious young actress, the film is unable to marshal the elements of shringar (love) in any meaningful way. Instead, the narrative careens from hasya (humour) to shringar (love) to karuna (sorrow) in an incoherent, inexplicable pattern. By the end of the second segment, karuna turns into self-pity and makes the narrative heavy-handed and self-indulgent. A similar lack of rasic clarity plagues Sanjay Leela Bhansali's lavish *Saawariya* (My Love, 2007), which was co-produced by Sony Pictures and was the first Hindi film to get a major North American release. Despite its extraordinary production design, stunning cinematography and melodious soundtrack, the film failed commercially and was panned critically.

These considerations of box-office and critical success are invariably *ipso facto*, constructed after a film's production, promotion and release. As such they can only hint at the reasons for a film's success or failure. This final element ensures that filmmaking, like all other arts, remains a mysterious exercise where success depends on some unknowable alchemy. However, a survey of the most commercially successful films of the past century suggests there is a possible formula – a blend of narrative, technical and aesthetic elements – that may offer a higher possibility of success for a film. This formula draws on the rasic tradition to produce films that function much like an extravagant feast, one that moves smoothly over multiple and varied courses – or moods – and combines familiar ingredients in endlessly innovative yet balanced ways. The success of the formula depends on an extremely careful blend of cinematic ingredients and an accomplished, delicate directorial touch. This is difficult to achieve but, when successful, it produces commercial and critical gold.

There is no greater master of this formula than Manmohan Desai, one of the most successful producers and directors of the past century and a pioneer of the masala movie. Even within Desai's oeuvre, there is no greater example of this kind of cinema than *Amar Akbar Anthony* (1977) which combines a complex plot line, rapid shifts in mood, catchy songs with comic as well as tragic sequences. In rasic terms, the film deploys and effectively balances all eight classical rasas, ranging from shringar (love) to hasya (humour) to karuna (sorrow) and raudra (wrath), although its dominant rasa is adbhuta (wonder). This final rasa provides the central bindu or point around which coincidences, divine intervention and inexplicable events come together not only to create the story of a family torn asunder by the twists and turns of fate but also to stand for the story of India as a nation, blending marvel at the country's independence but also sorrow at the trauma of Partition and multiple wars.

The primary rasa is established with the frenzied opening sequences where events pile up in rapid succession and are indicated as having occurred in the past. This section of the film quickly switches between an objective camera as Kishanlal (played by Pran) leaves prison after completing a sentence for a crime he did not commit to a subjective one as he arrives to find his family in distress. During his journey from prison to home, the audience realises Kishanlal has left prison on India's Independence Day as streets are decked with the national flag and fireworks are being set off in celebration. Given that the main narrative is set in the 1970s, this opening sequence suggests that the events are set during the first moment of India's freedom. However, Desai does not create a realist historical approximation of 1947 and signals the era with minimal nods such as vintage cars (although not necessarily of the period). Instead, the sequence focusses on evoking an emotional response by highlighting the plight of Kishanlal's family during his enforced absence, summoning up complex memories of the challenges – especially poverty – faced by the newly independent nation. It also signals an unease regarding this initial moment of political change as a furious but powerless Kishanlal confronts Robert (Jeevan) about the latter's broken promises, metaphorically ventriloquising the complaints of the colonised against the coloniser. A further flash-back takes the audience to when Kishanlal accepted blame for Robert's crimes in exchange for promises of support for his family. The two sequences establish the injustice suffered by Kishanlal and his family (a stand-in for the nation). They also prepare the audience for a plot driven by divine interventions on behalf of the powerless but righteous[6] that marks a narrative of adbhuta (wonder) rasa. At the same time, the scenes between Kishanlal and Robert also provide a complex political insight into Desai's team which comprised a number of highly politicised members.[7] Although Robert, as the symbolic coloniser, uses persuasion, the lure of money and charm to persuade Kishanlal, it is finally the latter's poor judgement and naivety that lands him in prison.

As Kishanlal escapes from Robert's wrath to return to his family, he steals one of Robert's cars full of contraband gold, a

---

[6] One of the traditionally favourite moments of adbhuta in Indian narrative is from the epic *Mahabharata* where Draupadi's sari miraculously grows interminably in length when the Kauravas try to pull it off. The Indian audience not only accepts but also expects narratives (performed or otherwise) to deploy adbhuta, especially at moments in the plot that are distressful.

[7] One of the writers for the film, for example, was born at the Andaman jails, the dreaded *kaala pani* (black waters), to parents who had been imprisoned for actions against the colonial state.

clever reference to descriptions of pre-colonial India as the golden bird. On his return, he finds his three sons alone as his wife, Bharati (Nirupa Roy), whose name links her to the nation often termed as Bharat-ma (Mother India), has abandoned them. Bharati's suicide note, left with the second son, establishes that disaster is about to befall the family (and by extension the nation). The fact that the note is left with the second son (who grows up to be Anthony) is not incidental as it later helps identify him. The sequence races on with Kishanlal rushing away in the stolen car with his three sons. Noticing that Robert's men are gaining on him, Kishanlal repeats his earlier mistake of 'abandoning' his sons and leaves them in a park under a statue of Gandhi. Again, Desai privileges the symbolic as there would have been no public statues of Gandhi in 1947.

The brothers are quickly separated as the oldest, Amar, runs after his father and is knocked down by one of the cars chasing Kishanlal. He is then found by a benevolent police officer who raises him. The second son – Anthony – wanders off to find food for the youngest brother and ends up at the doors of a Catholic church. The youngest is found under Gandhi's statue by a pious Muslim offering prayers in the park. While the sequence provides plot information, it also functions symbolically on multiple levels, including a critique of Gandhi whose presence cannot prevent the brothers being separated. The choice of those who raise the three children is also not coincidental: the eldest son who abandoned his younger brothers to chase after his father and must learn to be responsible is raised by a policeman; the compassionate but impulsive second son is entrusted to the Church; the youngest infant (Akbar), who is abandoned by successive members of his family, is adopted by a Muslim, to be brought up without resentment. Given Partition and the lingering Islamophobic discourse, this final choice is most politically loaded: Akbar is not only abandoned by everyone in his family but is also the one incapable of walking away.

Akbar is also the only one to cross paths with a parent after the initial separation. While driving home with the baby found in the park, Akbar's adoptive father finds Bharati who has been blinded by an accident (another incidence of adbhuta). Bharati notices the baby, asks about him, caresses his hair and blesses him, but is unable to recognise him. Not only has Bharati (and, by extension, India) been rendered blind, but she is incapable of recognising her own son's cries. This narrative loop is closed by Bharati regaining her sight (adbhuta, again) later in the film after she is guided by Akbar's voice to a multifaith shrine. It is his face that she sees first, and it is Akbar that she recognises first as her long-lost son.

Such symmetries of plot are pleasurable not only for the eventual reunion of the family but also for the predictable fulfilment of audience expectations. Amar, the oldest brother, is first recognised by his father, providing a neat contrast and mirror to Akbar's meeting with Bharati. Anthony's meeting with the family is delayed the longest, although this provides its own pleasures as he interacts with all members of his family without knowing their true identities: he saves Bharati when she has an accident, befriends and protects Akbar much as he did as a child and clashes with Amar but treats him as an elder brother. Finally Kishanlal recognises Anthony when the latter gifts him a rose that Bharati had given to him (the film plays on the colloquial use of 'baap' – which means father but is used in the film, and in slang, to signify anyone in authority). The key to the film's pleasures are not surprises of plot but rather how this expected eventual reunion is brought about.

Desai not only piles on a dizzying series of events throughout the film but also shifts rapidly between moods to ensure that no single emotion can overwhelm the spectator. The opening sequence switches rapidly from shringar (love, albeit familial rather than romantic) as Kishanlal leaves prison, karuna (sorrow) as he discovers his family living in penury, raudra (wrath) in his encounter with Robert, bibhatsa (disgust) when he discovers his wife's suicide note, bhayanaka (terror) as he tries to outrun Robert's men, karuna (sorrow) as he is forced to abandon his sons, and then back to adbhuta again as each of the children

221

finds new loving homes. Towards the end of the film, the climax is set up with a similar rapid change of rasas, beginning with adbhuta (wonder) with Jenny's (Parveen Babi) realisation that her lover Anthony is her adopted father Kishanlal's lost son, bhayanak (terror) as she and Laxmi (Shabana Azmi) are abducted, and bibhatsa (disgust) as the priest who raised Anthony is murdered in his church. The scene that follows shifts even more rapidly from hasya (humour) as Anthony, unaware that the priest who is kneeling before the altar is dead, shows off his wedding suit, to karuna (sorrow) when he realises that the priest has been murdered. It quickly moves to raudra with Anthony's fury at the murderers and the deity's inability[8] to protect the priest, then to vira (heroism) when he decides to seek vengeance. The sequence returns to adbhuta (wonder) as a locket slips from the priest's hand and provides a lead to Anthony for not only finding the murderers but also the reunion with his long-lost family.

With adbhuta as its dominant rasa, *Amar Akbar Anthony* works primarily on symbolic levels. The film also offers a scale of pleasure to the viewer based on their level of knowledge, interest and criticality. At its most obvious, the film can be enjoyed for its high-powered star cast and the wonderful plot devices that separate and reunite the family or for the varied range of emotional states depicted and evoked by the performances. However, a knowledge of the region's political history is important to the viewing pleasures as the film provides complex commentaries on social and nationalist aspects of the new nation; asserts a postcolonial reversal of power with a possibility of receiving justice for colonial suffering; and offers a metaphoric wish-fulfilment that Partition can be undone and the region reunited like the film's three brothers even as it emphasises that such an event can only be achieved by wondrous means rather than human endeavour.

---

[8] Anthony's rage echoes the scene from *Deewar* (Wall, 1975) and is structured in similar style with shot/reverse shot, this time cutting between Anthony's pleas and complains and the silent icon of Christ on the cross.

Director Ramesh Sippy's *Sholay* provides a similar balancing of the various rasas although vira (heroism) is the dominant one. A single sequence from the film demonstrates how rasa can be mobilised even when the on-screen events are unpleasant, tragic or traumatic. It also demonstrates how a multi-stranded narrative, often relying on minor characters, informs and enhances the primary narrative and dominant rasa. The killing of Thakur's (Sanjeev Kumar) family by the dacoit chief Gabbar (Amjad Khan) serves as the explanation for the former hiring Jai (Amitabh Bachchan) and Veeru (Dharmendra) to hunt down Gabbar. Framed as a flashback, the sequence lasts just under fifteen minutes and can be split into four narrative sections, with the most horrific sections lasting just under two minutes. The first section emphasises the dominant vira (heroism) rasa as Thakur, a police officer, chases and arrests Gabbar. In retaliation, Gabbar threatens retribution against Thakur's family. The scene ends with Thakur leaving for home just before we learn that Gabbar has escaped from prison, establishing a sense of dread (bhayanak).

The second section begins with a shot of a young man shooting birds and cuts to a young child excited about his grandfather's return. This section, set in Thakur's home, is mostly presented in long and medium shots, and cuts to various members of the family who are preparing for his arrival. The dominant rasa remains bhayanak although the sequence leavens it with hasya as the family jokes, laughs and interacts with each other. The sequence establishes these minor characters as objects of karuna (sorrow) despite their minimal role in the film. None of the characters, except for two who leave the home midway through the scene, are seen in the film again. The dialogue is punctuated by soft background music that is ruptured by the occasional sounds of gun-shots which intensify a growing sense of fear.

The actual murders happen in little over two minutes and begin with a close-up of the youngest sister who is hanging clothes on a clothesline. A gun-shot rings out and, in a close-up, the eldest brother looks up towards the brother who has been

223

shooting birds. In a long shot, and in slow motion, the younger man begins to fall off his perch. The camera cuts back to the elder brother who shouts and breaks into a run. Another shot rings out and he freezes. The next cut shows his wife leaving the swing with a scream and beginning to run. Background music provides a sense of frenzy till a third shot rings out. Again, the camera freezes the wife as if in shock. The next cut is very brief, with the sister turning and freezing to the sound of a gun-shot. This entire sequence lasts approximately thirteen seconds. The next cut reverts to the first long shot of the younger brother falling off his perch. All sound cuts out as the body falls in slow motion, and the only sound effect is a muffled thud. The camera switches again to the eldest brother and the freeze ends as his body falls to the ground in slow motion. With the third cut, this time of the wife falling, again in slow motion, the creaking of the swing becomes the primary sound effect. After the next shot of the sister falling to the ground, pulling the clothesline with her, the camera switches to an extreme low-angle shot. In a long shot, a horse appears on the horizon. The camera cuts to a medium shot of the rider. It is Gabbar. An intercut of shots establishes him surveying the house, preparing tobacco and watching as the young child runs out of the house.

The camera then switches to an unusual, multiple perspective, the effect of which is disturbing as it interlaces shot/reverse shot between the child and Gabbar, long shots of other bandits seen from the perspective of the terrified child, and objective shots from the perspective of an unseen observer. As Gabbar makes his way down the hill, the camera switches to a position behind the child, as if the spectator is also trapped in the scene, watching Gabbar approach yet unable to act. However, this perspective is only maintained for two brief cuts, and the camera again changes to shot/reverse shot between Gabbar and the child. As Gabbar approaches, the creaking of the swing is matched by the sound of hoof-beats from a horse. The camera moves to a medium shot of Gabbar aiming his rifle and cuts to the terrified face of the child. What appears to be a gun-shot rings out, but the scene has cut to the close-up of a steam train arriving at a station. The sound of the shot blends into the noise of the steam engine, and the camera moves to a close-up of Thakur arriving home.

The fourth and final section again lasts approximately five minutes and goes from karuna (sorrow) as Thakur realises that his family has been killed, to raudra (wrath) as he grabs a horse to chase after Gabbar, moves to bhayanak (terror) when Gabbar captures Thakur and finally to bibhatsa (disgust) as Gabbar amputates his arms. Like the murder scene, this sequence does not present the violence on screen, with the amputation carried out in a medium shot that only shows Gabbar bringing down two swords. The flashback sequence ends and the rasa returns to vira (heroism) as Jai and Veeru promise to help Thakur achieve his revenge.

A similar spiral movement from the dominant rasa to the subordinate ones and back runs through the entire film. However, the murder sequence is an especially effective example of how to simultaneously heighten the emotional impact of a scene and distance the spectator from on-screen events as it deploys familiar techniques such as freeze-frames and slow motion to emphasise the artificiality of the horrific on-screen narrative. At the same time, other techniques including the sound effect (of the creaking swing) and the camera angle (that positions the spectator as a hidden witness and participant simultaneously) heighten the emotional impact of the scene.

The same characteristics are deployed very differently and thirty years later by Farah Khan's *Om Shanti Om* (2008, hereafter *OSO*), an explicit and elaborate homage to the rasic feast exemplified by the masala movie. The film provides a multi-layered narrative with technology harnessed to create multiple layers of cinematic (un) reality. It also unabashedly mixes familiar filmic elements, references to other films and popular culture as well as popular film stars appearing as themselves.

OSO opens with a ritual invocation that recalls films from the 1950–1970s. The bombastic quote of this invocation is accompanied by the image of a fictional studio logo which ends with a blackout. A voice calls 'Roll, sound, camera, action!' and the screen is filled by a digitally reconstructed song sequence from *Karz* which forms the title of Khan's film. Clips of *Karz*'s star Rishi Kapoor dancing in the original song sequence are placed alongside shots of SRK as Om, a junior artist playing an audience member on the set, as well as a fantasy sequence where he imagines himself in the place of the older star. The sequence locates Khan's film on the sets of *Karz* and thus in the late 1970s. This setting in the past is reinforced by a guest appearance of the earlier film's director, an eerily un-aged Subhash Ghai. An additional twist is added as the sequence ends with Om arguing with another extra on the set. The film again mobilises extra-cinematic knowledge of the habitual Hindi film viewer who would instantly recognise this second extra as *OSO*'s director, Farah Khan herself.

The knowledgeable viewer would also recognise the theme of reincarnation from the earlier film (*Karz*) and thus be prepared for a variation of the same. The opening sequence also sets up the main rasa of *OSO* as adbhuta (wonder) where divine interventions help wish-fulfilment: the murdered junior artist Om is reincarnated as the son (also named Om) of a major film star and thus able to benefit from privileges of wealth and status that he had previously lacked but which help him achieve his ambitions of stardom this time around. The reincarnation also inverts the fandom that marks the film's first half where Om is a junior artist in love with Shanti (played by Deepika Padukone), a successful film star.

However, the *mise-en-scène* depicts not the historical period of the 1970s but rather the era constructed by films of that decade. This directorial choice leaves the spectator in no doubt that the on-screen narrative is not meant to be real but rather a recreation of a filmic reality from the past. At a superficial level, the sequence can be enjoyed as a much-loved song-and-dance spectacle from an old familiar film albeit with a modern twist. However, it deploys an inverse time scale as a device to enhance the unreality of the action unfolding on screen: how does Om know the final edit of a sequence that is still being shot? What

226

exactly is the film's viewer watching? Is this a part of an old favourite film of the past, this time while it's being shot? Or an entirely new narrative that is impossible without updated film techniques and technologies? The sequence simultaneously lays bare the artifice of cinema while emphasising the wonder (adbhuta) of the film apparatus itself that allows the inversions and even the collapse of time itself.

OSO is structured as a tribute to Manmohan Desai and the film not only reproduces the frenetic pace – albeit with fewer characters – of his films, including *Amar Akbar Anthony*, *Dharam Veer*, *Naseeb* and *Coolie*, but also draws on various supernatural elements that emphasise adbhuta as the dominant rasa. However, the film still cycles through a series of subsidiary rasas including shringar (love) with Om's unrequited love for Shanti; hasya with comic sequences in both halves; bhayanaka (fear) when both Om and Shanti are murdered by Shanti's husband and producer Mukesh (played by Arjun Rampal); karuna (sorrow) as Om's mother Bela (Kirron Kher) and friend Pappu (Shreyas Talpade) mourn Om's death; and vira (heroism) as the reincarnated Om brings together loyal people from his previous life with material resources of a wealthy star in the present to bring Mukesh to justice. However, the narrative spins back each time to adbhuta (wonder) as the primary rasa, and never more so than at the finale, which requires the intervention of Shanti's vengeful ghost.

*   *   *

The Covid-19 pandemic that began in early 2020 highlighted the downsides of being far from home. My parents were in India, which had closed its borders even before the first lockdown began in Britain, and suddenly things I had taken for granted for much of my life became impossible. My mother had long insisted that I keep enough money on hand to be able to take the most expensive flight home in case of emergencies. The choice of living in London these past years has in large part been guided by the ease and speed with which I can reach home in an emergency. But with airlines suspending flights and the closing of international borders, no amount of money would get me back. During my waking hours I told myself I would not panic, although sleep, even in fragments, unleashed the same fears of frantically trying to find a way home and failing, of my parents being gravely ill, and sometimes worse.

Sleep became the enemy as I could not control my thoughts, so I began napping, forcing myself to rest before waking up, often less than an hour later. I could no longer focus on reading or make myself watch an entire film. Instead, I relentlessly made playlists and labelled them by the month, sometimes even week. Soon I had playlists for social distancing, for walking fast or slow, for running. There were playlists for parties I would have when the pandemic finally ended, for flirting with strangers who would cross my path, for travelling long hours on trains and buses. And mixed in were lists that I pretended did not exist, of songs about death and loss and mourning.

I booked my flight to India the day after the country eased border restrictions. That same day I agreed to meet a friend at her home to introduce her to Hindi cinema. It was surprisingly warm for a late-summer evening, and we spent much of our time on the balcony sipping wine. I knew I was procrastinating, unsure if I wanted to watch a film, even one of my own. By the time the night settled over the city, the dark chased away by the bright lights along the river, I had run out of excuses. I had chosen *OSO* because I thought it was an exemplary introductory movie and ideal for the novice viewer.

Afterwards, I felt sated, drained, yet oddly relaxed. As I made my way home after the film, choosing to walk through streets that were quieter than I remembered from before times, I paused on the riverbank to soak in the city that is my home. To the south, the London Eye cast a shimmering pink reflection on the dark waters of the Thames. Somehow the sight comforted me, made me smile. As I turned to walk away, I reminded myself of a dialogue from *OSO*: '*Hamari filmon ki tarah, hamari zindagi mein bhi end mein sab theek ho jata hai. Happys endings. Aur agar theek na ho toh woh the end nahin hai doston. Picture abhi baaki hai!'* (Like our films, everything in our lives too turns out all right. Happy endings. And if it doesn't, my friends, then it isn't the end. The movie isn't over yet.)

The Heart is Still Indian[1]

1983 REMAINS IN MY mind for three reasons. India won the cricket World Cup for the very first time. *Coolie* was released and I watched the matinee show on the very first day. It was also the year I returned to India from Islamabad for my 'boards', the terrifying equivalent of British O levels. Although the 'boards' were nearly two years in the future, our teachers had begun chivvying us to create exam schedules and seemed to draw perverse pleasure from pointing out our weakest subjects. My school had set up an extensive preparatory schedule with periodic, and extremely stressful, practice tests that replicated the examinations we would eventually face. My classmates boasted about strict personal study schedules, often created by their parents, that they had to follow: 'three hours of physics every day and another three for other subjects. My physics is so weak.' That came from the student who had ranked first in class every year since kindergarten! 'Can we buddy up on geography,' a friend shopped around, offering chemistry tutorials in exchange. Worst of all, it seemed that movies had been banned for all my classmates!

---

[1] *'Phir bhi dil hai Hindustani...'* from *Phir Bhi Dil Hai Hindustani* (The Heart is Still Indian, 2000). The song echoes the refrain from *Mera Joota Hai Japani...*) (My shoes are from Japan ... (Shree 420, 1955).

My mother had left instruction for me to 'do well', a vague goal but one that went well with her second injunction, 'and be happy.' My grandmother, who I was living with, was surprisingly relaxed, neither creating a study schedule for me nor demanding that I spend every free hour poring over schoolbooks. She also seemed to focus more on the 'be happy' part, so my film consumption was not curtailed. Nor was I banned – unlike most of my classmates – from reading books that weren't part of the syllabus. Instead of plotting rivers on blank templates of world maps or trying to balance chemistry equations, I read every adult book on our shelves that caught my eye. Toni Morrison's *The Bluest Eye* joined Maxim Gorky's *Creatures That Were Once Men* and Yashpal's *Meri, Teri, Uski Baat* (Mine, Your, Their Story).

I soon found myself obsessed with Salman Rushdie's *Midnight's Children*. For months, I would read it cover to cover (leaving out the last few dozen pages after the first couple of times as I had decided they didn't work), put it down for a day, and then pick it up to re-read again. It told a familiar story but also used English in ways I had never seen before, whimsical, hilarious, joyous. On its pages, I could hear my family, my friends and neighbours, even myself, speak as loudly and clearly and in as many shades and tones as we did in our own books, songs and films, in our own homes and streets. Here again was a mystery, this time not of how a story could unfold but of how one language could magically transmute into another. Most importantly, the book did not require me to pretend that what I was reading was real. Instead, the novel itself exposed the flesh and bones that held it together. It was like a great masala movie had been turned into a grown-up, serious book!

While my classmates studied for the big exams, I set myself a schedule. I looked through the books that lined the many shelves in my grandmother's home, starting with my uncle's prized *Phantom* and *Mandrake* comic books, old copies of children's magazines *Paraag* and *Champak*, Soviet fairy stories and children's books by Arkady Gaidar and Nikolai Nosov. To my pile, I added the *Amar Chitra Katha* comics about Indian heroes and deities

231

that were somehow entirely different from British and American ones even when in English. And then the epics, the *Mahabharata* and the *Ramayana*, in their comic-book, abridged and multivolume forms, comparing and contrasting how they all worked. While my classmates worried about chemistry and physics and maths, I worked my way through contemporary poetry collections and novels in Hindi. Finally, as I began topping up my reading with French, German and Italian novels – either in English or Hindi translations – my aunt gently reminded me about the impending exams. 'You can read what you want. You'll be fine in most subjects, but can you please try not to fail maths?'

So, while my classmates studied, I focussed my attentions on my extra-curricular project. As I read through my notes, neatly disguised as a study notebook, I knew what I wanted to do in life: to keep reading more stories, to continue learning what made stories work, and one day, some day, when I had something to say, to tell my own stories. I promised myself that, like my movies and epics, and even Mr Rushdie, my stories would be about everything – love and anger, tears and laughter, fears and dreams – all at the same time!

* * *

The long days of pandemic lockdown had one upside: I spent hours on end watching old favourites online and searching out new – often smaller budget – films that I had missed on Netflix and Amazon. I also discovered a vast treasure trove of recent cinema in Tamil, Telugu and Malayalam. While significant industries within India, films in these languages have often been harder to find abroad, although this varies by region and market.

Although there are many unresolved questions regarding content-streaming services, they have made the dissemination of cinema easier and cheaper not only within India but across the world. Greater access has also helped shape audience tastes within India, so films like *K.G.F. Chapter 1* (2018) and *Chapter 2* (2022), a period film in Kannada, set in a brutally administered gold mine, or *Baahubali: The Beginning* (2015) and *Baahubali 2: The Conclusion*, a fantasy in Telugu about lost princes and stolen kingdoms, get general release in theatres across the country, have enjoyed enormous box-office success across the country and continue to reach audiences via streaming platforms. Although quieter films, like the finely crafted *Kumbalangi Nights* (2019) in Malayalam, about a family living in a fishing village, have not yet posted similar box-office returns beyond their primary linguistic audience base, streaming services have helped create a cult following even amongst non-Malayalam audiences.

Similarly, many small-budget Hindi films that may not be financially sustainable in theatres can now be released directly on streaming platforms, which in turn enables filmmakers to tell localised stories such as *Badhaai Do* (Give Blessings, 2022), about a small-town couple in a marriage of convenience. The film draws on tropes made familiar by blockbusters like *DDLJ* but with a queer twist as the couple must fend off intrusive family members, find true love with different partners and negotiate an archaic legal system. Even a decade ago, films like *Maja Ma* (2022) with an older female star, Madhuri Dixit, as the lead and focussing on a middle-aged housewife whose life is overturned by rumours about her sexuality, or the dark yet comic *Darlings* (2022), about a woman who decides to punish her abusive husband with similar violence, were unlikely to be imagined, made or watched. Global streaming giants like Netflix and Amazon are also financing new content like the successful yet very specific series *Mirzapur* (2018, 2020, 2023), a small-town crime drama set in rural and semi-urban northern India, or films like *Shakuntala Devi* (2020), about the eponymous female mathematician.

However, the same period has seen the political rise and consolidation of Hindu supremacist ideology in the country, with the Bhartiya Janata Party (BJP) winning parliamentary elections in 2014 and 2019. The party insists on an ahistorical idea of culture and has weaponised Islamophobia. Unsurprisingly, the Hindi film industry amongst cinemas of the country, with its historically significant presence of minorities and foundationally inclusive worldview, has been increasingly cast as anti-India and criminal. Much of the intimidation has focussed on Muslim stars as well as Hindu actors and directors perceived as 'too liberal'. Political and religious leaders affiliated to the party have called for, condoned and participated in the violence against film sets and theatres, stars and directors. Organised social media activity accusing the film industry of everything from drug use to child sex abuse and terrorism has been steadily ramped up and gleefully, if fecklessly, amplified by the country's increasingly uncritical legacy media. At the same time, the country's southern films, especially in Telegu, are held up as exemplars of appropriately traditional, i.e. Hindu, filmmaking, bolstered by the same political groups and presented as a more nationalist alternative.

By 2020, there was evidence of the state apparatus being deployed against members of the film industry perceived as not toeing the ruling party's diktat. Soon after actress Deepika Padukone attended a student protest against police brutality, her name was included in a highly publicised investigation into the tragic death by suicide of actor Sushant Singh Rajput, which itself had been weaponised by the far right as a tale of the naive outsider destroyed by a corrupt and corrupting industry.[2] The investigation conducted by the country's major agencies including the Central Bureau of Investigation, the Narcotics Control Bureau, Enforcement Director which focusses specifically on money laundering and violations of foreign exchange laws, dragged on for over two years. No criminal charges were brought against Padukone or

---

[2] While deaths by suicide are not new in Indian film industries, no other has been weaponised for political gain like that of Rajput. The disinformation campaign originating on social media framed the actor's death as a drug-related murder resulting in arrests of his girlfriend and members of her family who were eventually released. The disinformation campaign was amplified by the legacy press for months and formed the basis of the organised Boycott Bollywood campaign in 2020–2022. The activity died down in early 2023, although that is no guarantee that it will be not be revived as India heads to another general election in 2024.

other actors, and internal agency reports suggest there was insuf-
ficient evidence and initial investigations had likely broken
multiple laws. The tipping point came in October 2021 when the
son of Shah Rukh Khan was arrested on what have been revealed
to be trumped-up drug charges and held in prison for over a
month. As the high-profile case collapsed in the full blinding glare
of the press, the organised political, media and state apparatus
targeting of the industry became all too clear.

For decades, Hindi commercial films – under the general label
of Bollywood – have been seen domestically and overseas as the
quintessentially Indian cultural product. Since Independence,
successive governments have considered Hindi films as a powerful
form of the country's soft power and part of its diplomatic arsenal.
So the organised and sustained public vilification and intimidation in recent years has left many filmmakers (and audiences)
baffled and cowed. Between the depredation wrought by the
pandemic, unabated rise of the Hindu far right, incrementally
more graphic and explicit threats of violence against stars and
filmmakers, and loud boycott campaigns, the industry has
floundered. Its demise was loudly and gleefully predicted by its
detractors and, as successive films failed at the box office, it
seemed that the magical story of the Hindi film was coming to
an end.

Then on 25 January 2023, in the lead-up to India's Republic
Day, Bollywood pulled off a miracle straight out of a Manmohan
Desai film. The release of *Pathaan*, starring Shah Rukh Khan,
marked the return of the star in a lead role after four years. As
had become customary, the first publicity clips for the film were
met with loud protests by the Hindu far right which claimed
that an orange bikini worn in the film by the lead actress,
Deepika Padukone, offended religious sensibilities not because
of its scantiness but because it was a sacred colour. BJP minis-
ters in two states indicated that they planned to ban the film's
screenings. Even more grotesque threats of violence against
Khan were issued by religious figures aligned with the party.
Yet, as the date of release neared, there seemed to be the first

indication of a fightback against the calls for boycott. For the first time in India's history, Khan's fans organised group viewings at theatres, often purchasing tickets in bulk for movie shows. They posted online videos of themselves dancing to the film's songs. On social media calls went out to fight the boycott campaign with 'happiness and love', and fans posted clips of dialogues from Khan's earlier movies about the power of love over hate. The film opened mid-week, on a working day, shattered all previous box-office records for a Hindi film and was declared a blockbuster after just two days of screening.

Since its release, the film has been on a winning spree, although it is too early to predict whether its success can be repeated by other upcoming films. *Pathaan*'s ticket sales, however, are only one of the part of the story. The other, perhaps more important, part of the story is composed of the joyful videos posted from inside movie theatres across the country. Viewers gyrated on seats and bopped in aisles, in many cases turning movie theatres into impromptu nightclubs. In the old-fashioned single-screen theatres that had slowly been shutting down across the country, fans climbed up on the stage to dance and celebrate while flash mobs, some organised and others spontaneous, burst into the familiar dance steps in malls where multiplex cinemas are usually based. The celebrations have been a reminder that Hindi cinema is not only about intellectual or aesthetic or cultural pleasure. It's not even about representations and narratives on screen. My movies – call them Indian, or commercial Hindi cinema, or Bollywood – are about a shared experience of connecting and celebrating with family, friends, acquaintances and even strangers. Like *Pathaan*, they are about spontaneous, unexpected, joyful wonder.

*   *   *

At the end of 2022, my family came together at my parents' home. After three long years of seeing each other only via screens, there was so much to share and mourn that everything except each other's tangible, physical, presence fell by the wayside. We did nothing but talk, through endless cups of tea, breakfasts that flowed into lunches, evening drinks that turned into dinners that in turn stretched late into the night. We left each other's company only for the most essential chores and then raced home to maximise family time. The pandemic had left an overwhelming recognition of mortality in its wake and each moment, conversation and hug felt urgent and momentous. Even watching a film on television felt like a distraction from our time together, no longer a shared activity but something that took our focus away from each other.

After a few days, when the urgency had receded a little, music made its way back into our home. A speaker was summoned up, almost as if by magic, one that could be connected via Bluetooth to all our phones, and we took turns playing samba and salsa, classic American rock and rap, South African and Lebanese pop and Spanish rumba – music acquired on our wanderings across the world. My mother remembered a Pashto folk song that had been her favourite during the Soviet–Afghan War, so we all searched online music repositories until we found a scratchy recording. We commandeered the dinner table for Dad, who sang our favourite Hindi film songs as we drummed out a supporting rhythm with our knuckles against the heavy wood. We sang each song for a verse or two, then switched to another, and another because there would never be enough time to cover all our favourites. One afternoon while we argued – happily – over where to plant a new apple tree, my phone accidentally began playing 'Kal ho naa ho . . .' (Tomorrow May Never Come, 2003). I hastily forwarded it to something peppier.

When the holidays came to an end, I was the last to leave. My mother watched me prepare and then suggested we catch the year's first major movie release, 'first day, first show'. Much had changed since the last time I had watched a film – Coolie back in 1983 – on the day of its release. Tickets were acquired within minutes on my phone. The old vast single-screen theatres have almost entirely been replaced by multiplexes and there was a new(ish) one near our home.

As we settled into comfortable, well-upholstered seats for the matinee, I realised that the theatre was full of young people, who gave us sheepish looks, probably expecting censure for skipping classes from the only two women with grey hair in the audience. I slumped back in the reclining seat and prepared myself for disappointment. Not with the film but the experience of watching it. The theatre was too nice, the ticket prices too expensive to attract anyone but the comfortably middle class. And the kids were too nicely dressed, too polite to watch a Hindi film the way I remembered . . . with hoots and whistles, claps and jeers.

However, with the very first shot of *Pathaan*, the entire hall erupted in applause and joyful shouts. When Shah Rukh Khan first appeared on screen, the hoots and whistles became louder than the soundtrack piped in from the high-tech surround-sound system. An exultant cheer of 'Entry!' recognised the dramatic impact of the star's return to the big screen. Amidst the noise, I realised that the surfeit of phone cameras was the only change in how we watched our movies. I marvelled at the speed with which spectators could leap to their feet, turn their back to the screen, snap a selfie and sit back down. The whole operation took less than two seconds and seemed to be magically co-ordinated so each one had a clear shot of the screen. When the final song sequence began, a group of young people ran down to the front and began dancing, perfectly matching the choreographed steps on the screen. The credits began rolling over the song and we all rose, swaying and dancing at our seats and in the aisles as we picked our way to the exit. For the duration of the film, we had all been transported back to a land where religious and political divisions could be overcome, where good won over evil, and love triumphed. And most of all, where hope that this was all possible not only existed but flourished. As the audience filed out into the winter sunshine, still excitedly chatting about the movie, some of that hope seemed to cling to us, as it has for the past century.

While *Pathaan*'s wild success across India can be attributed to a combination of tight plotting, superb action sequences, innovative marketing strategies and star power, especially of Khan, it also marks a return of the 'all-India' film which refuses limits of region, creed, language and more. With a diverse cast of Muslim, Hindu and Christian stars in lead roles and a screenplay that forcefully rejects the Islamophobia pedalled by the Hindu far right, the film explicitly makes the case for the kind of secular, diverse nation that Hindu supremacists deny.

Later that evening, as I packed my suitcase, Dad kept walking in and out of my room. Each time he would stroll around, humming, adjusting curtains and cushions that were already straight, just lingering. As I finally zipped up my suitcase, a memory suddenly rose from thirty years before. It had been winter then too. We had spent our time the same way then, talking and laughing and singing together. I had been packing to leave for university that time and Dad had spent days organising my paperwork. He had wandered in and out of the room for hours and I had assumed that he was checking that I didn't leave anything essential behind. I had been shocked when he told me, 'You don't have to go if you don't want to.' Of course, I did, I assured him, it had been my idea to head to a university so far from home. He had started to walk away and was almost at the door when he spoke again. 'You know you can come home any time?' I had nodded. Like my films, this reprise was slightly different. I had finally grown up enough to understand that Dad's reticence was, still is, because he loves me too much to ask me to stay.

On the flight back to London, I found myself humming a song from a film I have never seen. I have known the song since my childhood. Dad would sing it as we wound through dizzying hairpin bends in the Himalayas, and I waved at the army convoys that went past. I'd sing along with him as we drove through the Khyber Pass, the wide road lined with heavy trucks ferrying American aid and weapons into Afghanistan. Dad had comforted my siblings and me by getting us to sing it louder than the noise of the wind and rain when it rattled our car and we slid across a Florida highway during a hurricane.

And our voices had lifted the song together into the vast Kalahari sky when I had re-joined my family in Namibia after years of wandering elsewhere. *'Chalte chalte mere yeh geet yaad rakhna, kabhi alvida na kehna ...'* (Keep my songs in your memory, and never say goodbye).

Acknowledgements

FIRST AND FOREMOST, this book is for my mother, who encouraged me to dream and continues to support my efforts to turn those dreams into reality. She also insisted that I complete a PhD because 'every writer needs a back-up plan.' As always, Mom, you were right!

All my love to my family: Mom, of course; Dad, who remains perplexed that my work involves watching endless movies; and my siblings, Rashmi and Sid, without whom I could not write, and nor would I want to. And so much love to my extended family who first gave me stories and taught me to share them with the world.

The first avatar of this book was my doctoral thesis at the University of Barcelona. I am grateful to everyone at the Facultat de Filologia for the support, encouragement and enthusiasm. There are not enough words in any of the three languages we share to express my gratitude to Prof. Susan Ballyn, who encouraged me towards actively, perpetually, decolonising work. Most of all, I am grateful to my guruji, Oscar Pujol, who did not balk at my ambition of applying rasashastra to popular cinema. 'You will find your answer in *Dasarupaka*,' remains the most reliable advice I have received.

Huge gratitude to Vidisha, Candida, Fritha and the brilliant folk at Footnote who got this book from the very first moment.

Thank you for the encouragement, support and yummy pink drinks!

Massive love to my agent, Laura Susijn. You are the best agent any writer can ask for!

Finally, this book would not be possible without the grand, magical and, yes, impossible dreams that have powered over a hundred years of movie-making in India. So, thank you, all you dreamers and moviemakers for spinning dreams that sustain our worlds. Oh, and Shah Rukh Khan, if you read this, please visit the Valley of the Kings. You have a fan there who is desperate to meet you!

Further Reading

This book has been in the making for many years, if not my entire lifetime. Many thousands of articles, newspaper reports, radio shows, journal articles, essays and books have formed my thinking over this period. The list here includes not only texts that informed my thinking but many thought-provoking, insightful works that deserve to be read as widely as possible.

Appadurai, Arjun and Arien, Mack (eds), *India's World: The Politics of Creativity in a Globalised Society* (New Delhi: Rupa & Co, 2012).

Anjaria, Ulka, *Understanding Bollywood: The Grammar of Hindi Cinema* (London and New York: Routledge, 2021).

Bahadur, Jaya Wadiyar, *An Aspect of Indian Aesthetics* (Madras: Madras University Press, 1956).

Baskaran, S. Theodore, *In the Eye of the Serpent: An Introduction to Tamil Films* (Madras: East-West Books, 1996).

Barnouw, Erik and Krishnaswamy, S., *Indian Film* (New Delhi: Galaxy Books, 1980).

Baumer, Rachel and Brandon, James R. (eds.), *Sanskrit Drama in Performance* (Honolulu: University of Hawaii Press, 1981).

Bharata, *Natyaśastra. The Natyasastra* trans and ed. Adya Rangacharya (New Delhi: Munshiram Manoharlal Publishers Pvt. Ltd, 1996).

Bharat, M. and Kumar, N. (eds), *Filming the Line of Control: The Indo-Pak Relationship Through the Cinematic Lens* (London and New Delhi: Routledge, Taylor and Francis Group, 2008).

Bhaskar, Ira and Allen, Richard, *Bombay Cinema's Islamicate Histories* (London & New Delhi: Intellect Books and Orient Blackswan, 2002).

Bhat, G.K., *Theatric Aspects of Sanskrit Drama* (Poona: Bhandarkar Oriental Research Institute, 1983).

Bhattacharya, Nandini, *Hindi Cinema: Repeating the Subject* (Abingdon, Oxon: Routledge, 2013).

Bhattacharya, Roshmila, *Matinee Men: A Journey Through Bollywood* (New Delhi: Rupa Publications, 2020).

Bhattacharya Mehta, Rini, *Unruly Cinema: History, Politics and Bollywood* (Champagne, IL: University of Illinois Press, 2020).

Bhattacharya Mehta, Rini and Pandharipande, Rajeshwari V., *Bollywood and Globalization: Indian Popular Cinema, Nation and the Diaspora* (London: Anthem Press, 2011).

Blackburn, Stuart and Dalmia, Vasudha (eds), *India's Literary History: Essays on the Nineteenth Century* (New Delhi: Permanent Black, 2004).

Bose, Derek, *Bollywood Uncensored: What You Don't See On Screen And Why* (New Delhi: Rupa & Co., 2005).

Bose, Mihir, *Bollywood: A History* (New Delhi: Lotus Collection/ Roli Books Pvt. Ltd, 2007).

Chabria, Suresh and Paolo, Cherchi Usai. (eds), *Light of Asia: Indian Silent Cinema 1912–1935* (New Delhi: Wiley Eastern, 1994).

Chakravorty, Sumita S, *National Identity in Popular Indian Cinema 1947–1987* (Austin: University of Texas Press, 1993).

Chari, V.K., *Sanskrit Criticism* (Honolulu: University of Hawaii Press, 1990).

Chatterji, Shoma A., *Subject Cinema, Object Women: A Study of the Portrayal of Women in Indian Cinema* (Kolkata: Parumita, 1998).

Chopra, Anupama, *King of Bollywood: Shah Rukh Khan and the Seductive World of Indian Cinema* (New York: Warner Books, 2007).

Chowdhry, Prem, *Colonial India and the Making of the Empire Cinema: Image, Ideology and Identity* (New Delhi: Vistaar Publications, 2000).

Cooper, Darius, *In Black and White: Hollywood and the Melodrama of Guru Dutt* (Kolkata: Seagull Books, 2005).

Coorlawala, Uttara Asha, 'It Matters for Whom You Dance: Audience Participation in Rasa Theory' in *Audience Participation: Essays on Inclusion in Performance,* Susan Kattwinkel (ed.) (Westport, CT: Praeger Publishers, 2003).

Coorlawala, Uttara Asha, 'Darshan and Abhinaya: An Alternative to the Male Gaze' in *Dance Research Journal*, Vol. 28, No. 1, (Spring, 1996) pp. 19–27.

Das Gupta, Chidananda, *The Painted Face: Studies in India's Popular Cinema* (New Delhi: Roli Books, 1991).

Dasgupta, Chidananda, *Talking About Films* (New Delhi: Orient Longman, 1981).

Dasgupta, Rohit K. and Datta, Sangeeta, *100 Essential Indian Films* (Lanham, MD: Rowman and Littlefield Publishers, 2018).

Dasgupta, Rohit K. and Gokulsing, Moti K. (eds), *Masculinity and Its Challenges in India: Essays on Changing Perceptions* (Jefferson, NC, 2013).

Dehejia, Vidya (ed), *Representing the Body: Gender Issues in Indian Art* (New Delhi: Kali for Women, 1997).

Desai, Jigna, *Beyond Bollywood: The Cultural Politics of South Asian Diasporic Film* (New York: Routledge, 2004).

Devasundaram, Ashvin Immanual (ed), *Indian Indies: A Guide to New Independent Indian Cinema* (London: Routledge, 2022).

Dhananjaya. *Dasarupaka of Dhananjaya.* trans and ed. Sudhakar Malviya, with 'Avaloka' Sanskrit commentary of Dhanika (Varanasi: Chaukhambha Sanskrit Bhavan, 2004).

Dissanayake, Wimal, 'Rethinking Indian Popular Cinema: Towards new frames of understanding' in *Rethinking Third Cinema,* Anthony R. Guneratne & Wimal Dissanayake (eds) (London & New York: Routledge, 2003), pp. 202–225.

Dissanayake, Wimal, *Cinema and Cultural Identity: Reflections on Films from Japan, India and China* (New York: University Press of America, 1988).

Dissanayake, Wimal, and Sahai, Malti, *Sholay, A Cultural Reading* (New Delhi: Wiley Eastern Limited, 1992).

Doraiswamy, Rashmi, 'Hindi Commercial Cinema: Changing Narrative Strategies' in *Frames of Mind: Reflections on Indian Cinema*, Aruna Vasudev ed. (New Delhi: UBS Publishers' Distributors Ltd, 1995), pp. 171–189.

Dudrah, R., *Bollywood Travels: Culture, Diaspora and Border Crossings in Popular Hindi Cinema* (London: Routledge, 2012).

Dudrah, Rajinder and Desai, Jigna (eds), *The Bollywood Reader* (Berkshire and New York: Open University Press, 2008).

Dwyer, Rachel, *Bollywood's India: Hindi Cinema as a Guide to Contemporary India* (London: Reaktion Books, 2014).

Dwyer, Rachel and Patel, Vidia, *Cinema India: The Visual Culture of Hindi Film* (London: Reaktion, 2002).

Dwyer, Rachel and Pinney, Christopher (eds), *Pleasure and the Nation: The Politics and Consumption of Popular Culture in India* (Delhi: Oxford University Press, 2001).

Eck, Diana, *Darsan: Seeing the Divine Image in India* (Chambersburg, PA: Anima Books, 1981).

Gandhy, Behroze and Rosie Thomas, 'Three Indian film stars' in *Stardom: Industry of Desire*, Christine Gledhill (ed.) (London: Routledge, 1991), pp. 107–131.

Ganguly, Suranjan, *Satyajit Ray: In Search of the Modern* (Lanham, Maryland and London: The Scarecrow Press, Inc., 2000).

Ganti, Tejaswini, *Producing Bollywood: Inside the Contemporary Hindi Film Industry* (Durham, NC: Duke University Press, 2012).

Ganti, Tejaswini, *Bollywood: A guidebook to Popular Hindi Cinema* (London: Routledge, 2004).

Garga, B.D., *The Art of Cinema: An Insider's Journey through Fifty Years of Film History* (New Delhi: Penguin/Viking, 2005).

Gargi, Balwant, *Folk Theatre of India* (Seattle: University of Washington Press, 1966).

Gargi, Balwant, *Theatre in India* (New York: Theatre Art Books, 1962).

Geetha, V., Rao, Sirish and Dhakshna, M.P., *The Nine Emotions: Of Indian Cinema Hoardings* (Chennai: Tara Books, 2008).

Gehlawat, Ajay, *Reframing Bollywood: Theories of Popular Hindi Cinema* (New Delhi, Thousand Oaks, CA, London and Singapore: Sage Publications, 2010).

Gehlawat, Ajay and Dudrah, R. (eds), *The Evolution of Song and Dance in Hindi Cinema* (London and New York: Routledge, 2020).

Ghosh, Bishnupriya, *Global Icons: Apertures to the Popular* (Durham: Duke University Press, 2011).

Ghosh, Shohini, 'Queer Pleasures for Queer People: Film, Television and Queer Sexuality in India' in *Queering India: Same-Sex Love and Eroticism in Indian Culture and Society*, ed., Ruth Vanita (New York: Routledge, 2002), pp. 207–221.

Ghosh, Tapan, K., *Bollywood Baddies: Villains, Vamps and Henchmen in Hindi Cinema* (New Delhi: Sage Publications, 2013).

Goenka, Tula, *Not Just Bollywood: Indian Directors Speak* (New Delhi: Om Books International, 2014).

Gokulsing, Moti, K. and Dissanayake, Wimal, *Routledge Handbook of Indian Cinemas* (London: Routledge, 2013).

Gopal, Sujata, *Conjugations: Marriage and Form in New Bollywood Cinema* (Chicago, IL: University of Chicago Press, 2012).

Gopal, Sangita and Moorti, Sujata (eds), *Global Bollywood: Travels of Hindi Song and Dance* (Minneapolis: University of Minnesota Press, 2008).

Gopalan, Lalitha, *The Cinema of India* (London: Wallflower Press, 2010).

Gulzar, Nihalani, Govind, & Chatterjee, Saibal (eds), *Encyclopaedia of Hindi Cinema* (London: Encyclopaedia Britannica Inc. 2003).

Gupt, Somnath, *The Parsi Theatre: Its Origins and Development*, trans. Kathryn Hanse (Kolkata: Seagull Books, 2005).

Gupta, Manjul, *A Study of Abhinavabharati on Bharata's Natyasastra and Avaloka on Dhananya's Dasarupak* (New Delhi: Gyan Publishing House, 1987).

Gupta, Neerja, A. *Abhinavagupta's Comments on Aesthetics in Abhinavabharati and Locana* (Newcastle Upon Tyne: Cambridge Scholars Publishing, 2017).

Haham, Connie, *Enchantment of the Mind: Manmohan Desai's Films* (New Delhi: The Lotus Collection, an imprint of Roli Books Pvt. Ltd, 2006).

Hansen, Kathryn, *Grounds for Play: The Nautanki Theatre in North India* (Berkeley: University of California Press, 1992).

Hasan, Zoya (ed.), *Forging Identities: Gender, Communities and the State* (New Delhi: Kali for Women, 1994).

Hogan, Patrick Colm, *Understanding Indian Movies: Culture, Cognition and Cinematic Imagination* (Austin: University of Texas Press, 2008).

Iyer, U., 'Looking for the Past in Pastiche; Intertextuality in Bollywood Song-and-Dance' in *Movies, Moves and Music: The Sonic World of Dance Films,* M. Fogarty and M. Evans (eds), (London: Equinox, 2016).

Jain, Kajri, *Gods in the Bazaar: The Economies of Indian Calendar Art* (Durham, NC: Duke University Press, 2007).

Jones, Matthew, 'Bollywood, *Rasa,* and Indian Cinema: Misconceptions, Meanings and Millionaire' in *Visual Anthropology,* Vol. 23, Issue 1, 2009, pp. 33–43.

Joshi, Lalit Mohan and Malcolm, Derek, *Bollywood: Popular Indian Cinema* (New Delhi: Dakini Books Ltd, 2002).

Joshi, Sam, 'How to Watch a Hindi Film, The Example of *Kuch Kuch Hota Hai*' in *Education About Asia* 9:1, 2004.

Kaarsholm, Preben (ed.), *City Flicks: Indian Cinema and the Urban Experience* (Kolkata: Seagull Books, 2007).

Kabir, Nasreen Munni, *Bollywood: The Indian Cinema Story* (London: Channel 4 Books, 2001).

Kabir, Nasreen Munni, *Talking Films: Conversations on Hindi Cinema with Javed Akhtar* (New Delhi: Oxford University Press, 1999).

Kakar, Sudhir, *Intimate Relations: Exploring Indian Sexuality* (Chicago: University of Chicago Press, 1989).

Kapur, Anuradha, 'The Representations of Gods and Heroes: Parsi Mythological Drama of the Early Twentieth Century', *Journal of Arts and Ideas*, Vol. 23, No. 4 (1993), pp. 85–107.

Kapur, Geeta, *When was Modernism: Essays of Contemporary Cultural Practice in India* (New Delhi: Tulika, 2000).

——. 'Mythic Material in Indian Cinema' in *Journal of Arts and Ideas*, 14/15 (July-Dec 1987), pp. 79–108.

Karnad, Girish, 'Theatre in India' in *Daedalus* 118.4 (Fall, 1989), pp. 331–352.

Kaul, Gautam, *Cinema and the Indian Freedom Struggle* (New Delhi: Sterling Publishers Pvt Ltd, 1998).

Kaur, Raminder and Sinha, Ajay J. (eds), *Bollyworld: Popular Indian Cinema Through a Transnational Lens* (New Delhi: Sage Publications Ltd, 2005).

Kavoori, Anandam & Punathambekar, Aswin, *Global Bollywood* (New York: New York University Press, 2008).

Kavi, Ashok Row, 'The Changing Image of the Hero in Hindi Films' in *Queer Asian Cinema: Shadows in the Shade,* ed. Grossman, Andrew (New York: Harrington Park Press, 2000), pp. 307–313.

Kazmi, Fareed, *The Politics of India's Conventional Cinema: Imaging a Universe, Subverting a Multiverse* (New Delhi: Sage Publications, 1999).

Kazmi, Nikhat, *The Dream Merchants of Bollywood* (Delhi: UBS Publishers, 1998).

Kesavan, Mukul, 'Urdu, Awadh and the Tawaif: The Islamicate Roots of Hindi Cinema' in *Forging Identities: Gender, Communities and the State*, ed. Zoya Hasan (New Delhi: Kali for Women, 1994) pp. 244–57.

Khanna, Amit, *Words. Sounds. Images: A History of Media and Entertainment in India* (New Delhi: HarperCollins India, 2020).

Kishore, Vikrant and Saxena, Ambrish, *Indian Cinema: Filmic Content, Social Interface and New Technologies* (New Delhi: Kanishka Publishers, 2019).

Kumar, Akshaya, *Provincialising Bollywood: Bhojpuri Cinema in the Comparative Media Crucible* (New Delhi: OUP India, 2021).

Lal, Vinay and Nandi, Ashis (eds), *Fingerprinting Popular Culture: The Mythic and the Iconic in Indian Cinema* (New Delhi: Oxford University Press, 2006).

Lawrence, Michael, *Indian Film Stars: New Critical Perspectives* (London: BFI/Bloomsbury, 2020).

Lenglet, Phillippe & Vasudev, Aruna (eds), *Indian Cinema Superbazaar* (New Delhi: Vikas Publishing House, 1983).

Lutgendorf, Phillip, 'Is there an Indian Way of Film-making?' in *International Journal of Hindu Studies*. Vol. 10, No. 3 (December, 2006), pp. 227–256.

——. 'Jai Santoshi Maa Revisited' in *Representing Religion in World Cinema: Filmmaking, Mythmaking and Culture Making*, ed. S. Brent Plate (New York: Palgrave Macmillan, 2003), pp. 19–42.

Lynch, Owen M. (ed.), *Divine Passions: The Social Construction of Emotion in India* (Berkeley: University of California Press, 1990).

Majumdar, Neepa, *Wanted Cultured Ladies Only: Female Stardom and Cinema in India*, 1930s–1950s (Champaign: University of Illinois Press, 2009).

Majumdar, Rochona, *Art Cinema and India's Forgotten Futures: Film and History in the Postcolony* (New York: Columbia University Press, 2021).

Marfatia, Meher, *Laughter in the House: 20th Century Parsi Theatre* (Mumbai: 49/50 Books, 2011).

Mazumdar, Ranjani, *Bombay Cinema: An Archive of the City* (Minneapolis: University of Minnesota Press, 2007).

Mazumdar, Ranjani & Majumdar, Neepa, *A Companion to Indian Cinema* (Hoboken, NJ: Wiley Blackwell, 2022).

Mankekar, Purnima, *Screening Culture, Viewing Politics: An Ethnography of Television, Womanhood and Nation in Postcolonial India* (Durham: Duke University Press, 1999).

Manto, Sadat Hasan, *Stars from Another Sky: The Bombay Film World of the 1940s* trans. Khalid Hasan (New Delhi: Penguin, 1998).

Masud, Iqbal, *Dream Merchants, Politicians and Partition: Memoirs of an Indian Muslim* (New Delhi: HarperCollins India, 1997).

Mehta, Monika, 'DVD compilations of Hindi film songs: (Re-) shuffling sound, stardom, and cinephilia' in *South Asian Popular Culture*, Vol. 10, No. 3 (2012), pp. 237–248.

Mishra, Vijay, *Bollywood Cinema: Temples of Desire* (London, New York: Routledge, 2002).

Mitra, Ananda, *Television and Popular Culture in India: A Study of the Mahabharata* (New Delhi: Sage Publications, 1993).

Morcom, Anna, *Hindi Film Songs and the Cinema* (Aldershot: Ashgate, 2007).

Nandy, Ashis (ed.), *The Secret Politics of Our Desires: Innocence, Culpability and Indian Popular Cinema* (New Delhi: Oxford University Press, 1998).

Narayan, Birendra, *Hindi Drama and Stage* (Delhi: Bansal and Company, 1981).

Oza, Rupal, *The Making of Neo-Liberal India: Nationalism, Gender and the Paradoxes of Globalization* (New York: Routledge, 2012).

Pande, Anupa, *A Historical and Cultural Study of the Natyaśastra of Bharata* (Jodhpur: Kusumanjali Book World, 1996).

Panjwani, Narendra, *Emotion Pictures: Cinematic Journeys into the Indian Self* (New Delhi: Rainbow Publishers Ltd, 2006).

Paniker, Ayyappa, 'Traditional Indian Theatre and Experimental Western Theatre' in the *Journal of Arts and Ideas*, No. 4 (July-Sept 1983), pp. 5–18.

Patankar, R.B., 'Does the "Rasa" Theory Have Any Modern Relevance?' in *Philosophy East and West*. Vol. 30, No. 3 (July 1980), pp. 293–303.

Pendakur, Manjunath, *Indian Popular Cinema: Industry, Ideology and Consciousness* (Cresskill, NJ: Hampton Press Inc., 2003).

Poduval, Satish, 'The Affable Young Man: Civility, Desire and the Making of a Middle-Class Cinema in the 1970s' in *South Asian Popular* Culture, eds. Priya Joshi and Rajinder Dudrah, April 2012.

Prasad, M. Madhava, 'Darshan(a)' in *BioScope: South Asian Screen Studies*, Vol. 12, Issue 1–2 (2021), pp. 53–56.

Prasad, M. Madhava, *Ideology of the Hindi Film: A Historical Construction* (Delhi: Oxford University Press, 1998).

Punathambekar, Aswin, *From Bombay to Bollywood: The Making of a Global Media Industry* (New York: New York University Press, 2013).

Puri, Rajika, 'The Dance in India' in *Journal of Arts and Ideas*, No. 3 (April-June 1983), pp. 21–32.

Raghavan, V., 'Sanskrit Drama in Performance' in Baumer and Brandon (eds), *Sanskrit Drama in Performance* (Honolulu: University of Hawaii Press, 1981), pp. 9–44.

Raghavan. V., *The Social Play in Sanskrit* (Bangalore: Institute of Indian Culture, 1952).

Raghavendra, M.K., *Philosophical Issues in Indian Cinema: Approximate Terms and Concepts* (New Delhi: Routledge India, 2020).

——. *Beyond Bollywood: The Cinemas of South India* (New Delhi: HarperCollins India, 2016).

——. *Seduced by the Familiar: Narration and Meaning in Popular Indian Cinema* (New Delhi: Oxford University Press India, 2014).

Raj, Ashok, *Hero: Amitabh Bachchan to the Khans and Beyond* (London: Hay House, 2010).

Raja Rao, R., 'Memories Piece the Heart: homoeroticism, Bollywood-style' in *Journal of Homosexuality*, 39 (3–4) (2000), pp. 299–306.

Rajadhyaksha, Ashish and Willemen, Paul, (eds), *Encyclopaedia of Indian Cinema,* 2nd ed. (London: Routledge, 2014).

Rajadhyaksha, Ashish, *Indian Cinema: A Very Short Introduction* (Oxford: Oxford University Press, 2016).

Rajagopal, Arvind, *Politics After Television: Hindu Nationalism and the Reshaping of the Public in India* (Cambridge: Cambridge University Press, 2001).

Rajendran, C. (ed.), *Living Traditions of Natyasastra* (Delhi: New Bharatiya Book Corporation, 2002).

Ramaswamy, Sumathi (ed.), *Beyond Appearances? Visual Practices and Ideologies in India* (New Delhi: Sage Publication, 2003).

Rangacharya, Adya, *The Indian Theatre*, 2nd edn (Delhi: National Book Trust, 1980).

Rangoonwalla, Firoze, *Indian Cinema: Past and Present* (New Delhi: Clarion Books, 1983).

———. *Indian Filmography: Silent and Hindi Films (1897–1969)* (Bombay: J. Udeshi, 1970).

Ray, Satyajit, *Our Films, Their Films* (Bombay: Orient Longman, 1976).

Roychoudhury, Amborish, *In a Cult of Their Own: Bollywood Beyond Box Office* (New Delhi: Rupa Publications, 2018).

Saran, Renu, *History of Indian Cinema* (New Delhi: Diamond Pocket Books, 2013).

Sarkar, Bhaskar, *Mourning the Nation: Indian Cinema in the Wake of Partition* (Durham, NC: Duke University Press, 2009).

Schwartz, Susan L., *Rasa: Performing the Divine in India* (New York: Columbia University Press, 2004).

Schechner, Richard, 'Rasaesthetics' in *TDR (1988-)*, Vol. 45, No. 3 (Autumn 2001), pp. 27–50.

Sen, Meheli, *Haunting Bollywood: Gender, Genre, and the Supernatural in Hindi Commercial Cinema* (Austin: University of Texas Press, 2017).

Sen, Meheli and Basu, Anustup (eds), *Figurations in Indian Film* (London: Palgrave Macmillan, 2013).

Sen, Mrinal, *Montage – Life, Politics, Cinema* (Kolkata: Seagull Books, 2018).

Sen, Mrinal, *Views on Cinema* (Kolkata: Ishan Publications, 1977).

Sidhar Wright, Neelam, *Bollywood and Postmodernism: Popular Indian Cinema in the 21st Century* (Edinburgh: Edinburgh University Press, 2015).

Singh, Sunny, *Amitabh Bachchan* (London: BFI/Palgrave, 2017).

Sinha, Mrinalini, *Colonial Masculinity: The 'Manly Englishman' and the 'Effeminate Bengali' in the Late Nineteenth Century* (Manchester: Manchester University Press, 1995).

Sippy, Sheena and Ramachandran Naman, *Lights, Camera, Masala: Making Movies in Mumbai* (Mumbai: India Book House, 2006).

Sivathamby, K., *The Tamil Film as a Medium of Political Communication* (Madras: New Century Book House, 1981).

Somaaya, Bhawana, *Cinema: Images and Issues* (New Delhi: Rupa & Co., 2004).

Tejaswini Niranjana, P. Sudhir and Vivek Dhareshwar (eds), *Interrogating Modernity: Culture and Colonialism in India* (Kolkata: Seagull Books, 1993).

Tharoor, Shashi, *Inglorious Empire: What the British Did to India* (London: C. Hurst & Co., 2017).

Thomas, Rosie, *Bombay Before Bollywood: Film City Fantasies* (Albany, NY: SUNY Press, 2015).

C. Rajendran (ed.), 'Folk Elements in Classical Theatre' in *Living Traditions of Natyasastra* (New Delhi: New Bharatiya Book Corporation, 2002).

Valicha, K., *The Moving Image: A Study of Indian Cinema* (Bombay: Orient Longman, 1988).

Vanita, Ruth (ed.), *Queering India: Same-Sex Love and Eroticism in Indian Culture and Society* (New York: Routledge, 2002).

Varadpande, M. L., *History of Indian Theatre: Loka Ranga Panorama of Indian Folk Theatre* (New Delhi: Abhinav Publications, 1992).

Varia, Kush, *Bollywood: Gods, Glamour, and Gossip* (New York: A Wallflower Press Book, Columbia University Press, 2012).

Vasudev, Aruna (ed.), *Frames of Mind: Reflections on Indian Cinema* (New Delhi: UBS Publishers' Distributors Ltd, 1995).

Vasudev, Aruna and Lenglet, Phillippe (eds), *Indian Cinema Superbazaar* (New Delhi: Vikas Publishing House, 1983).

Vasudevan, Ravi, *The Melodramatic Public: Film Form and Spectatorship in Indian Cinema* (Delhi: Permanent Black, 2010).

Vasudevan, Ravi (ed.), *Making Meaning in Indian Cinema* (New Delhi: Oxford University Press, 2000).

Vatsyayan, Kapila, *Traditional Indian Theatre: Multiple Streams* (Delhi: National Book Trust, 1980).

Vijayakar, Rajiv, *Main Shayar Toh Nahin: The Book of Hindi Film Lyricists* (New Delhi: HarperCollins India, 2018).

Virdi, Jyotika, *The Cinematic ImagiNation: Indian Popular Cinema as Social History* (New Brunswick: Rutgers University Press, 2003).

Viswamohan, Aysha Iqbal (ed.), *Women Filmmakers in Contemporary Hindi Cinema: Looking Through Their Gaze* (New York and London: Palgrave Macmillan, 2023).

Viswamohan, Aysha Iqbal and Wilkinson, Clare M., *Stardom in Contemporary Hindi Cinema: Celebrity and Fame in Globalized Times* (New York, London, New Delhi: Springer, 2020).

Viswamohan Aysha Iqbal and John, Vimal Mohan (eds), *Behind the Scenes: Contemporary Bollywood Directors and Their Cinema* (New Delhi: Sage Publications, 2017).

Viśvanātha, *Sāhityadarpana*, 1986, trans. and with commentary and translation of Shaligrama Sastri (Delhi: Motilal Banarasidass Publishers Pvt Ltd, 1986).

——. *The Sahityadarpana or Mirror of Composition of Visvanatha*, trans. and ed. J.R. Ballantyne and Pramada Das Mitra (Delhi: Motilal Banarsidass Publishers Pvt Ltd, 1994).

Von Tunzelmann, Alex, *Indian Summer: The Secret History of the End of an Empire* (New York: Henry Holt and Co., 2007).

Wadia, Pheroze S., 'The Aesthetic Naturalism of Abhinavagupta: A Non-Aristotlean Interpretation' in *Philosophy East West*, Vol. 31, No. 1 (January 1981), pp. 71–77.

Wenner, Dorothee, *Fearless Nadia: The True Story of Bollywood's Original Stunt Queen* (New Delhi: Penguin, 2005).

Willemen, Paul and Gandhy, Behroze (eds), *Indian Cinema* (London: British Film Institute, 1980).

Yajnik, Y.K, *The Indian Theatre* (London: George Allen and Unwin, 1933).

Zutshi, Somnath, *What's 'Indian' About Indian Cinema?* (Kolkata: Seagull Books, 2002).

About the author

Sunny Singh is a writer, novelist, academic and a champion for decolonisation and inclusion across all aspects of society.

She is the author of three critically acclaimed novels – *Nani's Book of Suicides*, *With Krishna's Eyes* and *Hotel Arcadia*. Her first book of non-fiction was *Single in the City: The Independent Woman's Handbook*, a first-of-its-kind exploration of single women in contemporary India. Her pioneering study of the Indian superstar Amitabh Bachchan was published in the BFI Bloomsbury Film Stars series. She has contributed to a collection selected by Khushwant Singh, stories in honour of Ruskin Bond; American anthologies, *The Drawbridge*, International PEN, numerous academic journals and newspapers worldwide.

She is the founder of the Jhalak Prize, the Jhalak Children's and YA Prize, and the Jhalak Art Residency.

Sunny lives in London where she is Professor of Creative Writing and Inclusion in the Arts at the London Metropolitan University.